# First Maryland Artillery

## and

# Second Maryland Artillery

*George L. Sherwood*

HERITAGE BOOKS
2007

# HERITAGE BOOKS
*AN IMPRINT OF HERITAGE BOOKS, INC.*

**Books, CDs, and more—Worldwide**

For our listing of thousands of titles see our website at
www.HeritageBooks.com

Published 2007 by
HERITAGE BOOKS, INC.
Publishing Division
65 East Main Street
Westminster, Maryland 21157-5026

Copyright © 2007 George L. Sherwood

All rights reserved. No part of this book may be reproduced or transmitted in any form or by any means, electronic or mechanical, including photocopying, recording or by any information storage and retrieval system without written permission from the author, except for the inclusion of brief quotations in a review.

International Standard Book Number: 978-0-7884-4495-1

# CONTENTS

List of Maps and Illustrations......................................................iv
Acknowledgments .......................................................................v
Introduction ............................................................................. vii

## FIRST MARYLAND ARTILLERY

CHAPTER I  Background........................................................ 1
CHAPTER II  Organization and Training................................ 3
CHAPTER III  Baptism of Fire (1862).................................... 13
CHAPTER IV  The Major Battles (1863)............................... 25
CHAPTER V  In and Out of the Trenches: 1864................... 37
CHAPTER VI  1865 ................................................................ 39
CHAPTER VII  Statistical Summary....................................... 41
NOTES....................................................................................... 45
APPENDIX A:  The Battle of Stephenson's Depot ............... 47
COMPILED SERVICE RECORDS ROSTER ...................... 51
BIBLIOGRAPHY ..................................................................... 87

## SECOND MARYLAND ARTILLERY

CHAPTER I  Background....................................................... 91
CHAPTER II  Organization and Training.............................. 93
CHAPTER III  Into the Breach: 1862..................................... 97
CHAPTER IV  Continuing the Fight: 1863 ......................... 117
CHAPTER V  At It Again: 1864 .......................................... 137
CHAPTER VI  Faithful to the End: 1865 ............................. 157
CHAPTER VII  Statistical Summary..................................... 161
NOTES..................................................................................... 167
COMPILED SERVICE RECORDS ROSTER .................... 171
BIBLIOGRAPHY ................................................................... 201
ABOUT THE AUTHOR......................................................... 203

# LIST OF MAPS AND ILLUSTRATIONS

Richard Snowden Andrews, Captain, First Maryland Artillery ..... 6

Area of Operations ..... 11

Battle of Cedar Run, August 9, 1862 ..... 19

Second Winchester, June 15, 1863 ..... 28

J. Thomas Scharf, Private, First Maryland Artillery ..... 33

William Hunter Griffin, Captain, Second Maryland Artillery ... 128

Battle of Moorefield, August 7, 1864 ..... 150

# Introduction

Both the First and Second Maryland Artillery served with distinction with the Army of Northern Virginia for nearly the entire war. Both units suffered extensive losses (killed, wounded and captured) and both units were, as their names imply, made up mainly of men from Maryland.

The first leader of the First Maryland Artillery, Richard Snowden Andrews, was wounded so severely at the Battle of Cedar Run that no one expected him to live. But he did, with a twelve-inch-square silver plate in his abdomen. The First Maryland Artillery was part of the force that blocked the retreat of Union forces near the end of the Second Battle of Winchester on June 15, 1863. Thirteen of the sixteen men manning the two cannon blocking the Union forces were killed or wounded during the engagement, which was fought at nearly point-blank range.

The Second Maryland, or Baltimore Light, Artillery was often "borrowed" by cavalry units to support their actions. The Second Maryland Artillery took heavy losses in men, horses and equipment in the Battles of Yellow Tavern (May 11, 1864) and Woodstock (October 9, 1864). In both cases the unit was overrun by Union forces. In fact, General J. E. B. Stuart was mortally wounded while trying to rescue the Second Maryland Artillery at Yellow Tavern.

# FIRST MARYLAND ARTILLERY

# Chapter I

## Background

In late 1861, the First Maryland Artillery (Andrews' Battery) was part of General Isaac Trimble's command at Evansport, Virginia. In the Peninsula Campaign, Andrews' Maryland Battery was one of nine batteries in the A. P. Hill's (light) Division, Magruder's Corps. In the Maryland campaign during August and September 1862, the First Maryland Artillery, now called Dement's Maryland Battery, was in the artillery of Ewell's Division (commanded by Brigadier General Jubal Anderson Early) in Stonewall Jackson's Corps. Other batteries in this artillery battalion were Balthis' Battery, Brown's Battery (Chesapeake), O'Aquin's Battery, John R. Johnson's Battery and Latimer's Battery. In the Gettysburg Campaign during June and July 1863, the First Maryland Artillery was in the Artillery of Johnson's Division, with the Alleghany (Virginia) Artillery; the Chesapeake (Maryland) Artillery and the Lee (Virginia) Battery.[1]

The First Maryland Artillery served with distinction with the Army of Northern Virginia for the entire war. It has been said "no battery in the Army saw harder fighting or lost more men." The First Maryland Artillery fought in the Peninsular Campaign (especially the Seven Days Battles), the Maryland Campaign (especially at Harper's Ferry) and in the trenches around Petersburg. The unit sustained heavy casualties in the Seven Days Battles (June 1862), near Cedar Run (August 1862), near Winchester (June 1863) and at Gettysburg (July 1863). Desertion became a problem in mid-1864, as noted in General R. E. Lee's letter to the Secretary of War dated August 14, 1864. "...ten men from Dement's (Maryland) battery deserted...." In addition, thirty-eight men were discharged by writ of habeas corpus in the fall of 1864.[2]

There are seven extant rosters for the First Maryland Artillery, covering the periods from:

> September to October 1861, dated October 31, 1861, when located near Dumfries, Virginia;
> November to December 1861, dated December 31, 1861, when near Evansport, Virginia;
> January and February 1862, station not recorded;
> July to August 1864, dated August 31, 1864, when located near Petersburg, Virginia;
> September to October 1864, dated October 31, 1864, when located near Petersburg, Virginia;
> November to December 1864, dated December 31, 1864, when at Drewry's Bluff, Virginia; and
> January to February 1865, dated February 28, 1865, still located at Drewry's Bluff, Virginia.[3]

These rosters, along with clothing receipts and other sources, have been used to compile the unit's roster.

In January 1863, the First Maryland Artillery was in Andrews' Battalion, Second Corps, under Major R. Snowden Andrews, along with Carpenter's Virginia Battery, Caskie's Virginia Battery and Raine's Virginia Battery. In March 1863, the First Maryland Artillery was in Andrews' Battalion, Second Corps, under Lieutenant Colonel R. S. Andrews, along with Brown's Maryland Battery, Carpenter's Virginia Battery and Raine's Virginia Battery.

On September 30 and October 31, 1863, the First Maryland Artillery was in Lieutenant Colonel Andrews' Battalion, Second Army Corps, along with the Chesapeake Maryland Artillery, the Alleghany Artillery and the Lee Battery. On March 19, 1864, this battalion had the same composition, was commanded by Lieutenant Colonel Carter Braxton and was called Braxton's Battalion. On August 31, 1864, Braxton's Battalion was similar and the Stafford Virginia Artillery had replaced the Chesapeake Artillery.

# Chapter II

## Organization and Training

The First Maryland Artillery was formed in June and July 1861. It was recruited from Maryland men brought into Virginia from Maryland in early 1861. Others were stranded in Virginia after the war began. On August 5, 1861, the unit had one hundred officers and men, two servants and forty-two horses. By August 18, 1861, there were sixty-one horses. On March 7, 1862, there were seventy-six horses and on April 14, 1862, there were 107 horses.[4]

The First Maryland Artillery was made up of several distinct groups. The first commander of the unit, Richard Snowden Andrews of Baltimore, arrived in Richmond with eighteen recruits from Maryland and opened a recruiting office there in July 1861. The second commander of the battery, William Fendlay Dement, had previously crossed over to Virginia with twenty-five men in May 1861. These men previously served in a Charles County, Maryland, cavalry militia company. Andrews' cousin, Charles Snowden Contee, First Lieutenant of the First Maryland Artillery, opened a recruiting office in Fredericksburg and enlisted twenty-four men there on June 27, 1861. Walter Hanson Jenifer had recruited men for a cavalry unit. Many of his men apparently ended up joining the First Maryland Artillery.[5]

Training took place at Brooks' Station and at Evansport. On October 31, 1861, the First Maryland Artillery was near Dumfries in Prince William County, Virginia. Private A. James Albert, Jr. in his unpublished reminiscence had the following memory of the period.

> Our company was composed principally of sons of gentlemen planters, from the Southern Counties of Maryland and the great mass of the Confederate army were just such a class of men. In my mess were a young Dr. of Maryland, two civil Engineers, a graduate

## Acknowledgments

This book would not exist without the inspiration and support of my good friend and mentor Jeff Weaver of Saltville, Virginia. What little I know about researching Civil War history, I learned from him. This book also benefited greatly from resources and volunteers in the Maryland Room of the C. Burr Artz Library in Frederick, Maryland, and the Civil War materials available at the Maryland Historical Society in Baltimore, Maryland. The National Archives was the source of the microfilmed records of the individual soldiers in the two artillery units.

I also thank my wife Ruby and son Jeff for their support and assistance in transcribing information from the individual soldiers' records. In addition, I thank Roxanne Carlson of Crofton, Maryland, for preparing the manuscript for publication.

of Harvard, Frank Ransom and myself, our profession being to have as good a time as possible and two others. Our first camp in Richmond was the only time during the war, except about a month that winter while we were building our log huts, that we had tents for shelter. It was hard to get used to camp life. Eight fellows to go to sleep in a small tent, four on each side, with feet touching, arranged spoon fashion, so that when one turned over all on that side had to turn the same way. We also had to learn to cook our own meals. At first we had an abundance of rations, frying pans and skillets. It was not until the second year of the war that food commenced to get scarce. The change to our inexperienced mode of cooking made many sick, and all of us fell off so much that in about six weeks, our clothes were hanging on us like bags. I remember my first experience in making soda biscuits. We had moved camp near Fredericksburg. I heard, that by putting soda in the flour it would make nice light rolls, so I got one of our fellows, who was going into town, to get me ¼ lb of soda. I made up a nice large pile of dough and mixed in with it ½ of my soda. The biscuits were made and placed in the skillets and coals piled on top. In a short time yellow steam commenced puffing out from under the lid, and the biscuits got so light that they lifted the lid off the skillet. There were eight very disappointed fellows looking on. I don't know which looked the most yellow, they or the biscuits.[6]

The First Maryland Artillery was first commanded by Captain R. Snowden Andrews and was also known as the Maryland Flying Artillery. R. Snowden Andrews had accepted a commission as Major of Cavalry on June 14, 1861. However, he resigned his commission as Major of Cavalry on July 31, 1861, and accepted appointment as Captain of Artillery.[7]

The initial officers of the battery were:
Captain R. Snowden Andrews
First Lieutenant William F. Dement

Organization and Training 5

Second Lieutenant Charles S. Contee
Third Lieutenant Frederick Y. Dabney

The following individuals served as non-commissioned officers of the First Maryland Artillery:[8]
DeWilton Snowden, First Sergeant
Gratial C. Thompson, Second Sergeant, later 2nd Lieutenant
J. Harris Stonestreet, Third Sergeant, later 2nd Lieutenant
J. Harris Forbes, Fourth Sergeant
John Gale, Fifth Sergeant, later 1st Lieutenant
F. W. Bollinger, Corporal, later Sergeant Major
P. A. L. Contee, Corporal, later Quartermaster Sergeant
John G. Harris, Corporal, later Sergeant
George H. Hilliary, Corporal
William J. Hill, Corporal, later 2nd Lieutenant
Theodore Jenkins, Corporal
E. C. Moncure, Acting Corporal
John F. Ransom, Corporal
George T. Scott, Corporal

The following privates were later promoted:[9]
Thomas Brooke, to Quartermaster Sergeant
William P. Compton, to Corporal and Sergeant
Charles H. Harris, to Corporal
Robert S. Bryan, to Corporal
Robert B. Chew, to Sergeant
John W. Fillius, to Corporal
Frederick K. Freayer, to Sergeant
George Griswold Coombe, to Corporal
John Gilpin, to Corporal
John Edwin Glascock, to Sergeant and later Sergeant Major
John W. Gunby, to Corporal and Sergeant
J. W. F. Hatton, to Corporal
II. J. Langsdale, to Sergeant
William H. May, to Corporal and later Sergeant
Ephraim McLaughlin, to Master Mate (C.S. Navy)
John M. Shuster, to Corporal and later Sergeant
Samuel Thompson, to Corporal

Richard Snowden Andrews, Captain, First Maryland Artillery
*(Illustration by Jeff Sherwood)*

## Organization and Training 7

In addition, Private Nicholas Snowden Hill, discharged on August 13, 1861, became Chief Commissary (Major) for the District of Arkansas.

The following individuals had special duties and skills:[10]
Enoch R. Barry, Teamster
Michael Blummenaur, Farrier and Smith
Robert Bowles, Ordnance Sergeant
Thomas Brooke, Quartermaster Sergeant
William Broughton, Harness Maker
Samuel E. Byrne, Teamster
James Crowley, Teamster
Frederick Hunter, Assistant Surgeon
Edward Magruder, Bugler
William E. Phipps, Bugler
Charles Riddle, Teamster
DeWilton Snowden, Assistant Surgeon
Samuel Somers, Machinist
Thomas Sunderland, Teamster

In addition to all these previously-named individuals, the following had medical training or degrees:[11]
James Shields Beale, M.D.
George Griswold Coombe, D.D.S.
John T. Diggs, M.D.
Philip Barton Duvall, M.D. (KIA on May 14, 1863)
Samuel Fulton Duvall, M.D.
J.W.F. Hatton, M.D. (wounded in action twice)
Washington M. Hilliary, M.D. (KIA on June 26, 1862)
Frederick Hunter, M.D. (Assistant Surgeon)
DeWilton Snowden (Assistant Surgeon, Dumfries)

The following individuals served as hospital stewards or were detailed, after being seriously wounded or very sick:[12]
William Brown, (Tax Collector's Office, Richmond)
S. D. Dunlop, (Clerk, QM Department)
William H. Harper (Hospital Steward)
George Taylor Jenkins, Jr. (Clerk, Engineer Ofice)
C. Page Mackenheimer (Hospital Steward)

Samuel McClintock (Clerk, Adjutant and Inspector General's Office)
Benjamin Welsh Owens (Provost Marshall's Office, Gordonsville, Virginia)
George W. Perrie (Hospital Steward)
Junius Slemaker (Manchester Wood Mill)
Joseph E. Stinchcomb (C.S. Arsenal, Richmond)
Albert Tolson (Courier)

| Name | Court-Martial Date | No. |
| --- | --- | --- |
| George H. Hilliary | 12/26/63 | G.O. No. 109-6 |
| George H. Marriott | 3/7/64 | G.O. No. 17-10 |
| William L. Sherburne | 3/7/64 | G.O. No. 17-10 |
| J. Harris Stonestreet | 12/26/63 | G.O. No. 109-5 |

The first Maryland Artillery was originally equipped with four Parrotts and four Napoleons. The four Parrotts were discarded and two of the four Napoleons were replaced with captured artillery, after two of the Seven Days Battles. The unit retained these four Napoleons until nearly the end of the war.

The Napoleons were smoothbores, with a bore of 4.62 inches, a barrel length of 66 inches, a muzzle velocity of 1,440 feet per second and a weight, without carriage, of about 1,200 pounds. The Napoleons required 2.5 pounds of powder per round as opposed to the pound charge required for the 10-pounder Parrotts or the 3-inch rifles.[13]

The Napoleons were sometimes called light 12-pounders. Their major disadvantage was their range, only about 1,600 yards. The 10-pounder Parrotts and the 3-inch rifles had ranges more than 200 yards further. Thus, the Napoleons were often used against troops, while being fired upon by enemy artillery, with its longer ranges.

The Napoleons were pulled by a team of four horses and typically served by a crew of seven to ten men, distributed as follows:

    In-charge            Sergeant
    Gunner                 Corporal
    Ammunition Chest   1-3 Privates

Ramrod          1 Private
Loader          1 Private
Aimer           1 Private
Firer           1 Private

One or more teamsters would be present with the horses, or, in the rear with the horses. On occasion, guns were served with smaller crews, with some loss in speed. Sometimes officers pitched in and relieved members of their exhausted crews.

The ideally outfitted light artillery battery had the following list of equipment for each gun:

| Sponges & rammers | 2 | Sponge covers | 2 |
|---|---|---|---|
| Worm & staff | ½ | Handspikes | 2 |
| Sponge bucket | 1 | Prolonge | 1 |
| Vent cover | 1 | Tar bucket | 1 |
| Water bucket | 2 | Gunner's haversacks | 2 |
| Tube pouch | 2 | Vent pouch | 1 |
| Gunner's pincers | 1 | Tow hook | 1 |
| Thumb stalls | 2 | Priming wire | 1 |
| Lanyards | 2 | Gunner's gimlet | 1 |
| Fuse cutter | 1 | Tarpaulin | 1 |

These items were scarce in the Confederacy and any battery with a full stock of these items could consider itself lucky.

Almost every battery found itself equipped with a variety of armaments during the course of its history. Some of the terms may be unfamiliar to modern readers, therefore the following chart on the types of artillery is provided for reference:

| Piece | Bore Diameter (in.) | Range (yds.) | Weight (lbs.) |
|---|---|---|---|
| 3-inch ordnance rifle | 3.00 | 1830 | 967 |
| 6-pounder (bronze field gun) | 3.67 | 1523 | 884 |
| 12-pounder mountain howitzer | 4.62 | 900 | 220 |
| 12-pounder Napoleon | 4.62 | 1680 | 1227 |
| 10-pounder Parrott | 2.9 or 3.0 | 1850 | 890 |
| 20-pounder Parrott | 3.67 | 2100 | 1750 |
| 24-pounder (bronze field gun) | 5.82 | 1322 | 1318 |

According to Private A. James Albert, Jr.:

> Our battery remained near Richmond until after the battle of Manassas and then moved up towards Fredericksburg and Quantico Creek on the Potomac. The latter part of November I had a camp fever and was two weeks in the old hut that was so dilapidated that I could see the stars shining through the roof at night. Thanks to my friend George Lemon, who was on General Trimble's staff, he was able to get an ambulance and took me down to Fredericksburg.[14]

Organization and Training 11

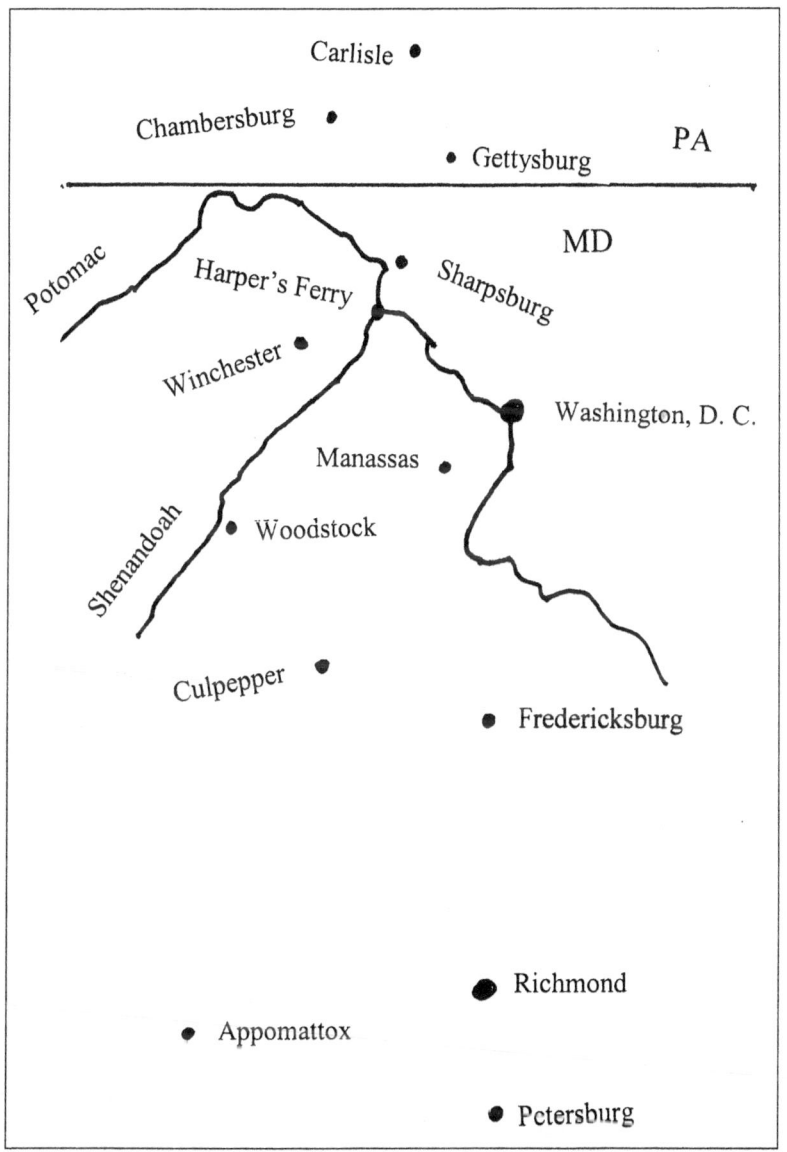

Area of Operations

## Chapter III

## Baptism of Fire (1862)

On January 14, 1862, the First Maryland Artillery was in the Aquia District in Brigadier-General French's Brigade:[15]

| | |
|---|---|
| 2nd Arkansas | Maryland Flying Artillery |
| 35th Georgia | Braxton's Artillery |
| 22nd North Carolina | |
| 2nd Tennessee | Carolina Light Dragoons |
| 47th Virginia | Stafford Rangers |

In January, February and March the artillerists continued training and were supplied with clothing (e.g. one hundred pairs of shoes; sizes 6, 7 and 8 on March 21, 1862) and additional horses. James Albert wrote after the war:

> When I returned to my company the first winter of the war seemed very cold to me. One night I was on picket duty on a hill overlooking the Potomac, during a severe snow storm and my feet got frozen. I suffered torture until the time came in the early Spring, about March 10th, when we had to fall back and it was left to me to decide, whether I should walk to the rear or remain in the little log hut we had built for ourselves, and be taken prisoner. As my feet were so swollen that I could not get on my shoes, I decided to remain. When however I saw the guns and my companions start off, I changed my mind. I got to my feet into an old cast off pair of shoes of Bill Brown's, whose feet were much larger than mine, and made the first days march of about three miles, with my company...

> It took our Company of six guns from daybreak to night to make the first three miles. The roads were so cut up that most of the guns and wagons had to be halted along in the fields. The teams many times had to be doubled and as many men as could get hold of their guns and caissons would be lifting and pushing, often up to their knees in mud. I am sure that day I saw a dozen horses and mules lying dead, drowned in the mud holes in the roads. That night our guns were packed in a field, and the next morning we found nearly all of them had sunk down to the axles in the soil. They had to be dug and prized up; fence rails and branches of trees put under the wheels, and the horses feet.[16]

In the battles before Richmond, June 26 to July 2, 1862, the First Maryland Artillery suffered its first battle losses: one killed in action and eight wounded. Brigadier General William D. Pender's report on these battles (Mechanicsville, Gaines' Mill and Frazier's Farm) stated "...Andrews' battery behaved on all occasions with conspicuous coolness and bravery..." and "the section of Andrews' Maryland Battery was under Lieutenant William F. Dement, who also did fine service."[17]

Private A. James Albert, Jr. had a lot to say about this campaign. He wrote:

> At this time we were attached to Pettigrew's North Carolina Brigade. Shortly after early in April, we started on our march to Yorktown to reinforce Gen. Magruder. About May 30th we fell back to Richmond. May 31, at the battle of Seven Pines or Fair Oaks, was the only time I ever saw President Davis. Our battery was in a field expecting to be ordered into position. The balls flying over us and the rattle of the musketry so excited me to see something of the fight, that I slipped off through the woods to the front. When I reached the opening I saw Mr. Davis quite near me, sitting like a statue on his horse all by himself. On the other side of the field were our infantry, evidently

trying to force their way across a stream or some other obstructions and the musket balls were singing and nipping the leaves off the trees making quite a little shower on our President. That night we spent in a field in the most thunderous thunderstorm I ever saw and the next day fell back closer to Richmond. We had several right severe artillery fights across the swamp during the next few weeks. An incident in one of them so often comes back in my mind. There was a man middle age, a carpenter by trade, named Bradley in our battery. He was one side of the gun exactly opposite me. A shrapnel shell burst just over the front of the gun. Bradley threw his hands up to his neck and said in a most pathetic tone as he fell to the ground "Old Bradley's house has fallen," and he was dead. Then June 26th came the Seven Days fight. The first stampede I ever saw was on our first night's march to join Gen. Jackson. It was 1 or 2 o'clock in the morning. One of our Lieutenants who was tired sitting on his horse, let me ride him, and I went forward to the head of the Company where were Capt. Andrews and the staff of a Cavalry regiment that was marching along side our battery on the road. It was so dark that we could not see much more than 100 feet in front of us. We heard a singular rumbling of voices far ahead of us, growing nearer and we saw the infantry which crowded the road in front of us, gradually disappearing, until the last of them had rushed off into the woods on one side of the road. As those near us disappeared we caught the words "The Yankees are coming!" The Col. and Capt. Andrews and all of us that were on horseback, immediately galloped forward to see what was the matter. When we got up to the head of the infantry regiment, we found an ambulance with a big white horse tied behind it that had had the blind staggers and had fallen back on the first files of the regiment behind him, they back on the next behind them and so on like a row of bricks, until some fellow, who did not know what was the matter said "Yankees are coming" which also went down the line, and all followed the example of the ones who thought the woods would be the safest place during a cavalry charge by the enemy. It was amusing, the shouts of laughter and the fun among the infantry as we rode back hollowing "No Yankees are coming." We had more or less fighting every day during the seven days. One day a musket ball struck my left arm but only made a slight wound, another day were in a field just back of the infantry line when a splendid horse whose rider had probably been killed came running to the rear and I was able to catch him. I thought I was in great good luck and decided I would convert my position from foot to mounted artillery and would have no more hard marching to do. I at once mounted, but, although I had been raised, since I was ten years old on horseback, I had never sat up so high with bullets whistling around my head, so I determined I would get down again and lead him. Just as my feet touched the ground a shell exploded in front of me. A piece of it struck a very large Bowie Knife I bought just before leaving home, for camp use, and which was on my belt in front. The knife was broken to pieces and I was reported killed. I was however only very much bruised and had my breath knocked out of me, and much to the surprise of my companions I joined them in about half an hour in time to help in repulsing a charge of infantry and by a countercharge of our infantry, capturing their lines and about 24 pieces of artillery. I then saw what the artists so often portray on the battlefield. There were the pieces of Artillery in line and behind them the limbers with nearly all the horses killed or wounded and in some places piled on top of each other. Many of the Artillery men were lying dead or wounded. The whole field in front of them was sprinkled with the dead of both sides, and when we reached their infantry line, in rear of the guns, where they received our last charge, there were hundreds lying dead and wounded in a regular line of battle. It was here our battery exchanged with the enemy our 6 lb howitzers for their 12 lb Napoleon guns. The night at Malvern Hill ended the fight. We were certainly a used up set. Captain Andrews who was shot through the leg several days before, but would not give up, had to be lifted off his horse and carried back to a hospital.[18]

Captain Andrews received his first wound in the leg in the Battle of Mechanicsville, early in the Seven Days fighting. According to tradition, he did not leave the field and was later promoted to major for gallantry.

After the Battle of Malvern Hill, William Dement was promoted to Captain, replacing R. Snowden Andrews, who was severely wounded.

After the Seven Days' Battles the battery was ordered to Gordonsville. Here Lieutenant Dabney, who had been a civil engineer, was detached and sent to Port Hudson. This necessitated the election of two lieutenants, for the vacancy occasioned by the promotion of Lieutenant Dement had not been filled. William I. Hill was made Second Lieutenant. It proved a happy selection, for there were no more gallant and efficient officers in the artillery service of the Confederacy.[19]

This revised set of officers, given below, served together from mid-1862 until nearly the end of the war.

> Captain William F. Dement
> First Lieutenant Charles S. Contee
> First Lieutenant John Gale (from March 1863)
> Second Lieutenant William I. Hill
> Third Lieutenant J. H. Stonestreet

Charles S. Contee was badly wounded at Winchester on June 15, 1863 and extensively hospitalized August 25, 1863, until January 18, 1864. He left the unit on June 26, 1864, when he was appointed enrolling officer for Wythe County by Governor Letcher (sic). At the surrender at Appomattox Captain Dement commanded Smith's battalion of light artillery serving as infantry, containing the First Maryland Artillery. The battery was commanded by First Lieutenant John Gale.

In the Battle of Cedar Run (Mountain) and associated battles (August 1862), the battery had more casualties: one killed in action and six wounded. The following excerpts from Major A. R. Courtney's report of August 15, 1862 on the August 9 battle gives a good idea of the action:

> Captain Dement's (First Maryland) battery and Captain Brown's Chesapeake Artillery, also from Maryland...opened fire on a large body of cavalry.... Captain Dement with two of his Napoleon guns and Captain Brown, with his 3-inch rifle posted about 600 yards from the enemy's extreme right battery.... The other section of Captain Dement's battery (two Napoleons) posted on a ridge behind Mrs. Crittenden's house—about 800 yards from the battery on their extreme left...fired until sundown...exhausted [their] ammunition.... The officers and men of Captain Dement's (First Maryland) battery—the only one which had been in action before—showed more coolness and deliberation.[20]

Major Courtney was chief of artillery, third division at this time.

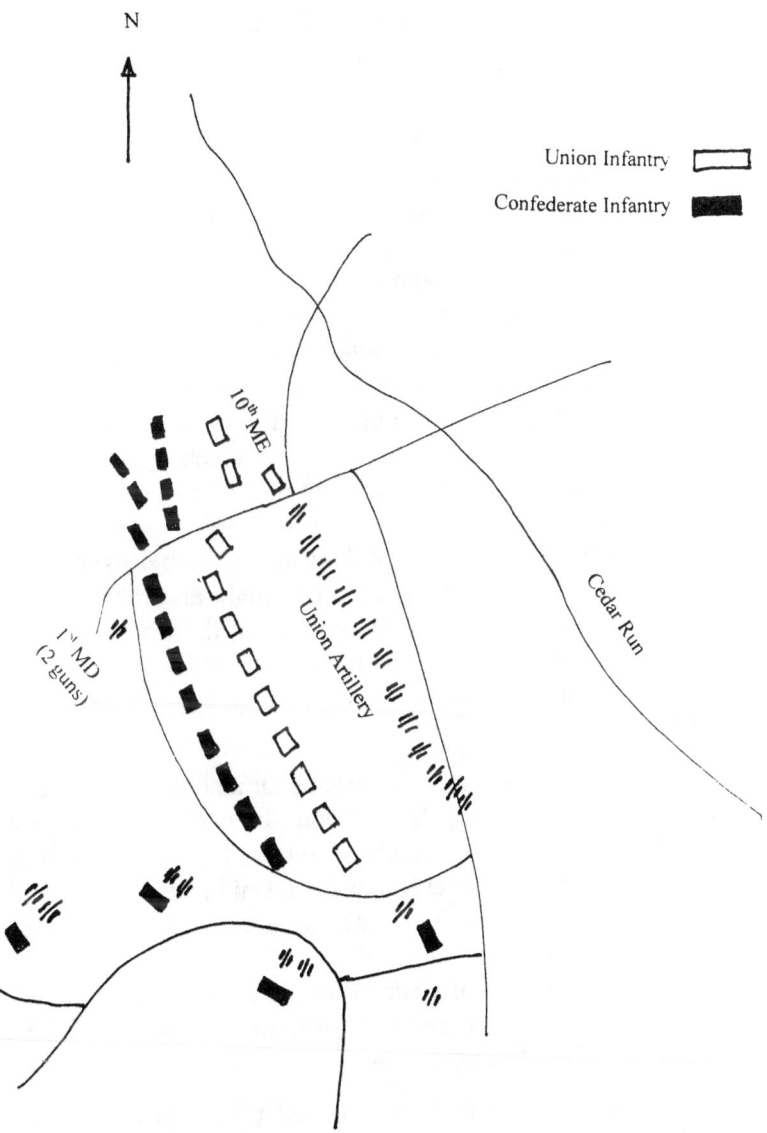

Battle of Cedar Run, August 9, 1862

The First Maryland Artillery was very effective at Cedar Run. As can be seen on the map, the Tenth Maine Infantry was one of the Union regiments in the direct line of fire for the First Maryland Artillery. A letter from Abial Hall Edwards, a private in the Tenth Maine, described the action.

> ...About noon the Rebel Batteries commenced firing which was replied to by our own Batteries they kept this up until about ½ past four in the afternoon then the Rebel Infantry came up and our Brigade had orders to advance and fire at them.... Our Brigade went into action with just 1,630 men and the[re] was only 811 men come out uninjured being just ½ lacking four killed and wounded. The 10th Maine went into action with 480 men and had 176 killed and wounded. 24 out of the number killed on the field my company went into the fight with near 20 men out of it th[ere] was 16 wounded 1 killed and 1 missing. General Pope says that was the hardest battle of the war. The Rebels held possession of the Battle ground that night and robbed our dead and even robbed the Pockets of the wounded taking of the shoes from both our dead and wounded also stripping our dead officers of everything they had on.[21]

Captain (now Major) Andrews was again among the wounded. He was wounded so severely that surgeons did not treat him at first, since they believed he was surely going to die. Later, when he didn't die right away (shrapnel had nearly taken his guts out) he was treated: "a silver plate twelve inches square [was] added to his abdomen."[22] Amazingly, he survived.

Just before the Battle of Cedar Run, A. James Albert, Jr. was detailed as Ordnance Sergeant on Major George H. Bier's staff. He also described Major Andrews' injury:

> Our next moved was August 9, Cedar Run, in which fight Capt. Andrews was struck by a shell and his side torn open so that his entrails were lying out in the dust. The surgeon said there was no use to move him, but as the Capt. insisted they got some water and washed the

entrails as clean as possible, put them back inside of him, and carried him to a farmhouse where a mother and her daughter took him in, and he soon came back to the Army as a Major.[23]

After the Battle of Cedar Run, the First Maryland Artillery continued on with Stonewall Jackson. The following paragraphs, from W. W. Goldsborough's *The Maryland Line in the Confederate Army,* tell what happened next.

After the battle of Cedar Run Jackson took up his line of march in the direction of Warrenton Springs, where his command arrived in the afternoon of the next day, when Early's Brigade and the First Maryland and Chesapeake batteries were thrown across the river. The night a terrific rainstorm came up, and next morning Early found himself cut off, as the rain had so swollen the Rappahannock that it was not fordable.

This was an unlooked-for catastrophe; but that grand old hero was equal to the emergency. Placing his infantry and artillery in position, and spreading them out as much as possible to deceive the enemy as to his force. Early calmly awaited the attack which he knew must speedily come, for he was in the presence of the greater part of the Pope's army.

And he had not long to wait, for presently the enemy advanced his infantry in force, and his artillery opened, but so destructive was the fire of the two Maryland batteries that he was speedily driven back. Again and again he essayed, but cautiously, for he fortunately believed Lee's whole army was in his front.

But Jackson across the river was fully alive to the dangers that beset this little band, and set to work with the might and main to build a bridge across the river higher up. All day long this unequal struggle continued, when at nightfall, the bridge being completed, the grand old soldier [Early] marched his command across it and re-joined Jackson....

After leaving Manassas, Jackson moved around to Centreville, and thence to the old battle-field of Manassas. On the 28th of August Pope made his attack on Jackson, and Dement's battery fired the first shot by order of General A. P. Hill in person. In the desperate struggle that ensured, the battery was fought with utmost desperation. The conduct of Lieutenant Hill in command of a section of the battery was particularly noticeable. As the enemy pressed on in overwhelming numbers he would limber his pieces to the rear for a hundred yards, halt, and renew the fight. This he did several times, until at length the enemy was driven back with heavy loss.[24]

Then it was on to Maryland. The First Maryland Artillery crossed the Potomac into Maryland on September 5, 1862, at White's Ford. The unit spent about five days in the vicinity of Frederick and then headed toward Harper's Ferry.

The battery, now commanded by Captain Dement, played a major role in the Confederate success at Harper's Ferry, just prior to the battle of Sharpsburg (Antietam). The First Maryland Battery and the Chesapeake Artillery were two of seven artillery batteries in Ewell's Division, Jackson's Corps. At this time, Dement's Battery consisted of four Napoleons and Brown's Battery had two 10-pounder Parrotts and one 3-inch rifle.

In short the batteries of Brown and Dement were carried across the Shenandoah to the shelf below the heights on the east side of the river (Loudoun Heights). In this location, they commanded Harper's Ferry and Bolivar Heights. The end was in sight for the Federal forces at Harper's Ferry when "...guns of Captains Brown and Dement opened from the rear..." on September 15, 1862.[25] These two batteries clearly made a major contribution to the Confederate victory at Harper's Ferry.

However, the major contribution made at Harper's Ferry meant that the First Maryland Artillery was not able to contribute at the Battle of Sharpsburg. According to the reports of Colonel Stapleton Crutchfield, Chief of Artillery Operations, the batteries were initially left behind at Harper's Ferry. "The batteries of Captains Brown, Dement and Latimer had been left at Harper's Ferry, as disabled, on account of the condition of their horses. I therefore had horses turned over to them, filled them up with ammunition, ...and started them for the battlefield."[26] The First Maryland Artillery never reached Sharpsburg. Worse, several men straggled and were captured.

Sergeant A. James Albert, however, reached Sharpsburg in time. He wrote:

> Some of our men on the front line were entirely out of Ammunition and by order of Gen. Jackson, I was detailed to take 2 wagon loads to them. The wagons were driven by colored men, and I must say I never saw two braver, more obedient follows. As we went the hill through the woods to the front the musket balls were flying thick and the artillery shells cutting off the limbs of the trees in every direction. They obeyed my commands without a sign of wavering. At the foot of the hill I found a safe shelter for the wagons and then hunted up Gen. Jackson. It was late in the afternoon and he ordered me to wait further orders, so I had the pleasure of a long talk with Major Kyd Douglas who was on Gen. Jackson's staff and was a friend of my sister Jeannie's and used to visit my father's house. After the fight was over we rode off the field together with the General. A short time before we left, Gen. A. P. Hill rode up and had quite a talk with Gen. Jackson. They both seemed much pleased with the result of the day and it ended by Gen. Hill's inviting Gen. Jackson to take supper with him that evening which Gen. Jackson seem to think was a very good joke. That night and the next day all our troops crossed over the river. I was determined with one wagon to secure some ammunition left in a field and our skirmishers helped me to load up under a brisk fire, as the enemy was advancing. Just as I reached the Virginia side of the river the U.S. Artillery opened fire on us from the Md. side.[27]

The men of the First Maryland Artillery finished the year with minor participation in the Battle of Fredericksburg on December 13, 1862. The only losses were "4 horses disabled...." Apparently, they were in reserve for that battle, and thus were not engaged at any time. "On the next day, [December 14] Captain Dement and his battery were placed in position on the hill on the right occupied by the batteries the day before but did not become engaged."[28]

## Chapter IV

## The Major Battles (1863)

In 1863, the First Maryland Artillery, now called Dement's Maryland Battery, was heavily engaged in four major battles:

Fredericksburg, May 3, 1863
Winchester, June 13-15, 1863
Gettysburg, July 1-3, 1863
Mine Run, November 27-28, 1863

A. James Albert rejoined the First Maryland Artillery in early 1863. Times were getting tough and he described them:

> I sent in an application to Col. Allen [who replaced Major Bier as Stonewall Jackson's Chief of Ordnance] to allow me to go back to my battery, which he granted and I joined it a little farther down the river and spent the rest of the winter in a log hut with those who were left of my old mess. Provisions had commenced getting very scarce. We had nothing issued to us but flour and bacon, about 1/6 lb. of bacon and a pint of flour per day. Most of us got the scurvy, and our throats were so swollen that we could only swallow our bacon raw. When spring came and the wild garlic commenced sprouting, the fields for miles over were covered with men gathering it and we thought it the finest vegetable we ever ate. Those who could drink it made their coffee from parched wheat and we had no sugar.[29]

The First Maryland Artillery had been in winter quarters at Bowling Green, Virginia, until about May 1, when it was ordered to Fredericksburg. The unit was still in Andrews' battalion and participated in the Second Battle of Fredericksburg on May 3, 1863.

The twenty pieces of Andrews' Battalion were partly hidden near the Telegraph Road and did considerable damage when they opened upon the Federals at close range. The First Maryland Artillery lost two men killed and three men captured.

A. James Albert, Jr. was there and described the losses:

> Gen. Ewell with about 9000 men including our battery was left at Fredericksburg to oppose Sedgwick who crossed the river on the 29th and until May 4th we had continual fighting. At this time one of the Penningtons who had just crossed the river and joined our battery was killed. The Lieutenant of my section John Gale, was shot through the legs and when the surgeon told him one of them must be taken off he pulled out his pistol and said he would kill any one who attempted to do it. He did not die from his wound but was unable to return to field service.[30]

Another member of the unit, Jonathan T. Scharf, described the action:

> The next morning [May 3], the enemy opened from their batteries on the right to draw our attention, and we were all sitting down amusing ourselves when Raines Battery on our right opened on the enemy and fired some few shots, but the enemy did not return it. All at once their batteries came in view and unlimbered and took position in our front. General Early and Major Latimer gave us orders not to fire on their artillery, or return theirs but to fire on nothing but infantry as we had to hold our position, for all the infantry had gone to Chancellorsville. The enemy now opened upon us with their artillery and at the same time their infantry filed out from a woods before us, within three hundred yards. The word "Fire" now rang out from the different gunners and the dogs of war belched out their flame of fire and the shells went bursting in the air above the enemy. We fought them long and gallantly until we drove the infantry back. They tried to charge but could not do so. They formed and filed first to the right and

then to the left and advanced in column, but to no purpose for we gave them grape and canister every step they took and at last they broke and fled in great disorder. At last we were relieved by two batteries and went to the rear. When we got out of range, our old Captain, now Lt. Col. Andrews, rode up to us and said that the General had been noticing our behavior from a prominent point and he had sent his compliments to every man in the battery for their gallant and noble conduct on the field. We came out of the fight with three killed and seven wounded. I was amongst the last number, this now my third time wounded. I was struck in the knee by a piece of shell which burst at about five feet from me. A noble fellow, W. Robey was killed by half a shell which entered on the top of his right shoulder and came out the left side. He was in the act of loading his gun. He was about six feet tall and well proportioned. Another J. Pollett, while carrying shot, was stuck in the back by a piece of shell and came out through the heart killing him instantly. The other, P. Duvall, was truck in the side in three places. Of the wounded, Lt. Gale had his leg smashed, Tolson was wounded in the breast by a minnie ball that came out at the elbow.

This has been my last battle with that noble old company and I was sent to the hospital at Richmond where I was laid up for seven weeks.[31]

The First Maryland Artillery did its most heroic work, and suffered its greatest casualties, in the Battle or Winchester, June 13, 14 and 15, 1863. The battery had three killed in action, fourteen wounded in action and twenty-five cited for gallantry in action. "On the thirteenth Dement's First Maryland Battery which was not engaged, but exposed to the fire, lost one man killed."[32] On the fourteenth Dement's Battery, with Stonewall, Nicholls and three regiments of Steuart's brigades, was sent to a point on the Martinsburg Pike, about two and one-half miles from Winchester. Its mission was to block an enemy retreat expected during the night.

In addition to the unit's losses, its former commander, now Lieutenant Colonel and Artillery Battalion Commander R. S. Andrews, was wounded again, in the arm this time. The unit also had sixteen horses killed or disabled.

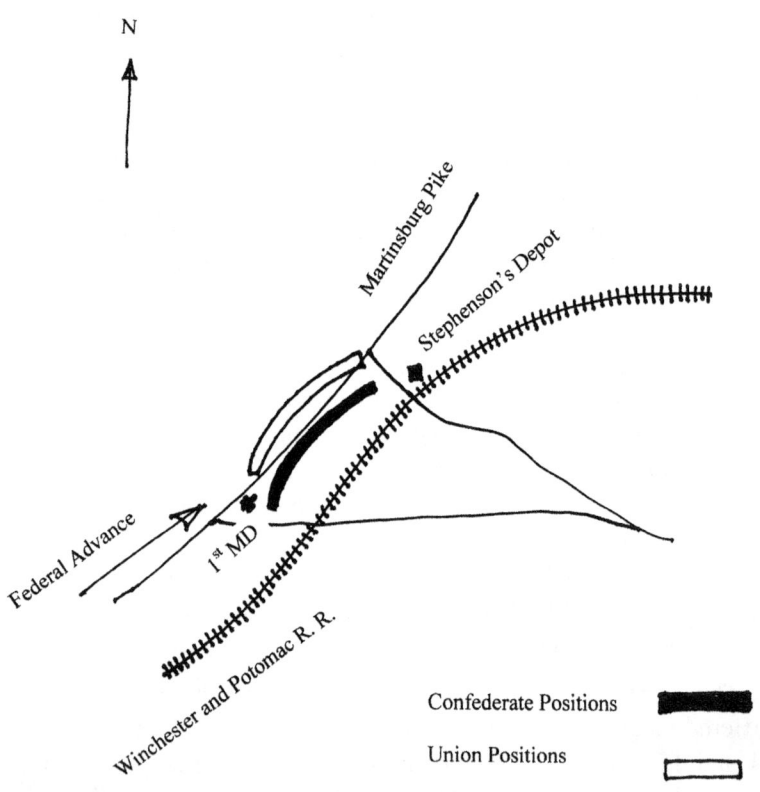

Second Winchester, June 15, 1863

That section of the Battery commanded by Lieutenant Charles S. Contee did its heroic work on the fifteenth. The following citation is from Lieutenant General Ewell's report on the Gettysburg campaign.

> Lt. C. S. Contee's section of Dement's battery was placed in short musket-range of the enemy on June 15, and maintained its position till 13 of the 16 men in the two detachments were killed or wounded, when Lieut. John A. Morgan of the First North Carolina Regiment, and Lieut. R. H. McKim, aide-de-camp to Brig. Gen. G. H. Steuart, volunteered and helped to work the guns till the surrender of the enemy. The following are the names of the gallant men belonging to this section: First gun—Sergt. John G. Harris; Corpls. William P. Compton, Samuel Thompson; Privates Robert Chew, William Koester, Charles Pease, A. James Albert, Jr., William T. Wooten, John R. Yates, Jr., H. J. Langsdale, and John R. Buchanan. Second gun—Sergt. John E. Glascocke, Corpls. William H. May, Charles Harris; Privates Thomas Moore, William Gorman, G. Frayer, William W. Wilson, Samuel Thomas, R. T. Richardson, William Sherburne, James Owens, William Dallam, and Joseph Mockabee.[33]

The First Maryland Artillery was part of the force blocking General Milroy's retreat from Winchester. In addition to inflicting considerable damage to the enemy forces, the unit clearly greatly aided the capture of several thousand Federal troops.

A. James Albert, Jr. was a gun crewmember and described the action in detail, quoted below and included in Appendix A.

> On June 10, 1863, we started with Ewell's Corps for the Shenandoah Valley. On the 14th Milroy was defeated at Winchester. Before daylight on the 15th Gen. Johnson's division with our battery cut off his retreat at Stephenson's Depot. Our first knowledge of having cut them off was a volley of musketry from their infantry, at close quarters in the dark. Some of our infantry were marching in the road with our battery.

We pushed forward at once and got possession of the railroad cut, running parallel with the Winchester and Martinsburg turnpike, along which Milroy's forces were retreating. There was a bridge over the cut connecting the road between the turnpike and Jordan's springs. There was only an opening for two of our guns. The one I was with was ordered in position on the bridge and the other in the opening to our left. Our skirmishers had advanced, but as it grew light they were quickly driven back by a charge of their infantry, and our two guns had to stand the full force of a succession of charges of their infantry and drove them back with double charges of canister until they surrendered. At the two guns we lost eighteen men killed and wounded. It was B. Welsh Stevens the only one left at the gun. My friend Wm. Brown told me that after the battle he went down the road in front of our gun, and counted over 50 of their poor fellows lying just in front of the gun, most of them torn to pieces by our short range shot. May God forgive us. The fight at this point was about as hot as anything during the war. In the early dawn their line of battle, which had formed on the turnpike, advanced, and got within fifty yards of us before our skirmishers fell back and we were able to fire on them. The whistling of their bullets was tremendous and what made me realize even more their number, was the rattle those made that struck the wooden uncovered bridge on which we were standing, making a sound very much like a watchman's alarm rattle. During an interval between their efforts to cut their way through our lines on this road we saw Gen. Millroy who, with some of his staff, rode at full run across the field on our left front. We fired a shrapnel shot at him. He escaped, but nearly all of his men and a line of wagons and cannon reaching almost up to Winchester were captured. Our Col. Snowden Andrews was again wounded during one of the last charges. After nearly all our men were wounded

## The Major Battles (1863)     31

Randolph McKim on Gen. Steuart's staff and two infantry officers helped. An incident happened during this fight that showed what a finely disciplined set of privates we had in our army and the sad ending has kept me from ever forgetting it. Wm. Wooten a fine tall handsome boy, a private at my gun, had been very disrespectful to one of his officers some few days before this battle, and had been put under arrest. The day before this morning, when the fight began at Winchester, he sent a message to Capt. Dement asking to be released until the fight was over and <u>he would then go back under arrest</u>, as he wished it distinctly understood that he was unwilling to make any apology. His release was granted. Our Lieutenant Contee stood by the gun exclaiming "Give it to them boys, give it to them!" until Bill Wooten got tired of hearing it and said, "Charlie Contee, if you don't shut your mouth I will pick you up and throw you off the bridge." The dispute was shortly settled by Contee's being wounded a short time after. When I was wounded and leaving the bridge, I saw Wooten lying down, as if asleep. I touched him and said, "what is the matter Willie?" And I found he was dead and poor Willie did not go back under arrest. The bullet that struck my left arm tore out about an inch of the bone and the blood commenced running from my sleeve in a little stream. I had been firing the gun and as soon as I turned over my lanyard and the primers to Owens I started off the bridge. I always had a horror of being hit in the back, and I decided to walk off the bridge backwards. After getting down on the road I was only able to walk a short distance, as I got so dizzy from the loss of blood and I had to sit down on the side of the road. I think, just in time to save me, Sergeant Bowling came by and jumped off his horse to help me. I gave him my handkerchief, which he tied with his giant strength so tight around my arm that the blood stopped. Later Bill Brown helped me to walk to a house nearby, the lawn of which was covered with wounded fellows and on one side I found about a dozen of my company. In the afternoon we were taken to Jordan Springs, which was turned into a hospital. I always thought and said, I would rather have my head shot off than an arm or leg, so, when Dr. Hunter told me my arm must be amputated, I refused positively to allow it. He then sent Dr. McGuire to see me, who, after an examination told me there was only one chance in ten for my life if it remained on and not one in ten of my dying if it was taken off, so I decided I would rather live. It was quite a severe operation as I was conscious most of the time, it being impossible for our people to get enough chloroform. I was at Jordan's until after the Battle of Gettysburg.[34]

J. Thomas Scharf, Private, First Maryland Artillery
*(from* History of Maryland *by J. Thomas Scharf,
New York: Arno Press, Inc., 1879)*

Private A. James Albert, Jr. was also hospitalized at Richmond. He later "crossed the lines" and spent some time recovering at home in Baltimore. In late 1863 he returned to the staff of Colonel Allen, where he served until after the Battle of Monocracy (July 9, 1864). The starvation and fatigue of this last campaign so weakened him that he was discharged. Finding Richmond "full of one-armed and one-legged broke down fellows" he returned to Baltimore. He then sailed to Paris to join his mother there and did not return until the war was over.

The First Maryland Artillery was one of four batteries in the Artillery of Major General Edward Johnson's Division, Second Army Corps (Ewell's) for the Gettysburg Campaign. The other batteries were the Alleghany (Virginia) Artillery, the Chesapeake (Maryland) Artillery under Captain William D. Brown, and the Lee (Virginia) Battery. The losses at Gettysburg for the First Maryland Artillery were not as severe as those at Winchester two weeks earlier. At Gettysburg, the First Maryland Artillery had one man killed in action and four wounded in action. The battery also lost nine horses and one caisson. Records of the Battle of Gettysburg indicate that the unit fired a total of 237 rounds from its four light 12-pounders.[35]

The last battle for the First Maryland Artillery in 1863 was at Mine Run on November 27, 1863. Although the unit was in action only for a little while, it had one man killed in action and one wounded. The following excerpt from the report of Major Carter M. Braxton, recently appointed artillery battalion commander, gives a good idea of the action:

> A section of Napoleons from the First Maryland Battery commanded by Lieutenant Hill, was ordered to report to Col. J. T. Brown, and was placed in position on the left of General Stafford's brigade by him. This section was engaged but a short time when the enemy pressed our left wing back, necessitating the withdrawal of these guns under a heavy flank fire from infantry.[36]

Major General Edward Johnson's February 4, 1864, report on the battle provides additional information:

A second of Dement's battery, placed in front of our center, though under a galling fire of musketry, played with telling effect upon the ranks of the enemy.... The officers and men of these commands (composing part of Andrews' battalion) exhibited on this as every previous occasion when they have served under me in action, a courage and efficiency of the highest order.[37]

Jonathan Scharf summarized the battles of 1863 after Fredericksburg:

My company has done some hard service since I have left them. They suffered more at Winchester than any company that was there. They lost five killed and eighteen wounded, and twenty-two horses. General Stuart and staff got off their horses and assisted in carrying ammunition. All of this loss was only with two guns. At Gettysburg, they lost another killed [Sam Thompson] the one who had his mustache shot off. The caisson blew up and tore him to pieces. At Mine Run, the noble Corporal Scott was killed—the finest gunner in service. He was shot in the head. Of all the men that left Richmond with the Company when she went into service only fifteen now remain by the guns.[38]

J. T. Scharf never returned to the unit. Instead, he applied for a Midshipman's appointment in the Confederate Navy, received it and appropriate training and later served as Master Mate of the gun deck, C. S. Steamer *Chicora*, at Charleston, South Carolina.

## Chapter V

## In and Out of the Trenches: 1864

The First Maryland Artillery apparently spent January, February and part of March 1864 at Frederick's Hall. It was basically winter quarters again, a chance to recover from the battles and hardships of 1863 and prepare for those of 1864. Some members of the unit, such as W. H. Bowen, W. Brown and J. E. Stinchcomb were still in the various hospitals. Other members probably enjoyed furloughs, but records for this period do not exist. First Lieutenant Charles Snowden Contee was discharged from the Farmville Hospital on January 18, 1864. He had been in that hospital for treatment of his wounds since October 3, 1863. His recovery was not complete and on June 26, 1864, he was appointed enrolling officer for Wythe County, Virginia by Governor "Extra Billy" Smith.

In early 1864, the major problem for the First Maryland Artillery was related to several courts-martial. First, Captain Dement, who was a member of a court-martial session, was captured, along with all the other members of the group of eight officers who were not aware of an impending enemy attack, and thus they were captured while they were in session. Second, on March 7, 1864, two members of the unit were court-martialed.

Also in March, the First Maryland Artillery was transferred to the Maryland Line. The Maryland Line was assigned to Breckinridge's Division during April 1864 and was at Cold Harbor in late May 1864. The unit participated in skirmishing along the Totopotomoy River on May 31 and June 1. On June 2 the First Maryland Artillery, under Captain Dement, provided covering canister fire from in front of Breckinridge's line at Cold Harbor while the infantry line of battle was being formed and breastworks were being prepared. By all accounts, this was very successfully done.

The First Maryland Artillery had four men wounded in action at Cold Harbor. Welsh Owens was wounded on June 2, Charles Holmead was wounded in both thighs and Alexander Young was wounded in the left shoulder on June 3, and Samuel Thomas was wounded in the face on June 4.

On June 22, 1864, the First Maryland Artillery, under command of Lieutenant John Gale, supported Mahone's attack on the Federal Forces at Weldon Railroad. This unit was part of Lieutenant Colonel McIntosh's battalion. The battalion provided direct covering fire for the infantry, which successfully over-ran part of the Federal line and captured many prisoners and four artillery pieces. George A. Dougherty, Dr. J. W. F. Hatton and John W. Fillius were all wounded during the battle. Dougherty was so severely wounded that he was never able to return to the unit. John Fillius was hospitalized through September 1864 but he returned and surrendered as a corporal at Appomattox Court House on April 9, 1865. Dr. Hatton was hospitalized from June 25 to July 24 and again from August 30 to September 30, 1864. He was discharged by writ of habeas corpus shortly after he rejoined the unit.

Brigadier General Pendleton's after action report, dated February 28, 1865, recalled the June 22, 1864 events. He wrote, "At the proper time Dement's battery moved rapidly forward, took position near the enemy's works and opened...."[39]

The First Maryland Artillery suffered its heaviest losses of the war in the trenches around Petersburg in the late summer and early fall of 1864. Not only did eighteen men desert from the trenches during August, but no less than thirty-eight men were discharged by writs of habeas corpus issued by Judge Hallyburton. By late 1864, Dement's Battery at Drewry's Bluff, Virginia was down to about sixty men. These losses were only partially offset by six new enlistments during late 1864. These late joiners were J. Bailey, W. Ballard, F. G. Gardiner, C. Goldsborough, M. Wilson, and William Wilson.

## Chapter VI

## 1865

In late December 1864 or early January 1865, the First Maryland Artillery was sent to Drury's Bluff, leaving their Napoleons behind. According to tradition, they never fired a shot from the heavy guns at Drury's Bluff. Their last battle occurred at Sailor's Creek on April 6, 1865. Harry Pennington was killed there, the last man of the unit to die in battle.

The men of the First Maryland Artillery ended the war as infantry, becoming part of Smith's Battalion. This was a battalion of light artillery, acting as infantry, assigned to Ewell. It consisted of thirteen officers and 252 men and was commanded by Captain W. F. Dement. Forty-one officers and men of the First Maryland Artillery surrendered at Appomattox Court House on April 9, 1865. The war was now over for them.

Seventeen men surrendered or were paroled later elsewhere, four men were released from Northern prisoner of war camps later and at least one man was still in the hospital after the war ended.

## Chapter VII

## Statistical Summary

During the war, at least 247 men served in the First Maryland Artillery. Recruiting continued throughout the war and the unit's strength did not drop much below one hundred men until late 1864. The following tables provide some selected strength information. Additional details are provided in this section.

| Date | Strength (Officers and men) |
|---|---|
| August 5, 1861 | 172 |
| March 1862 | 140 |
| August 31, 1864 | 95 |
| December 1864 | 50 |
| February 2, 1865 | 55 |
| April 9, 1865 | 41 |

Significant battery losses are as follows:

| Statistics | Number | Percent of 1st Maryland Artillery |
|---|---|---|
| KIA | 13 | 5% |
| WIA | 48 | 19% |
| POW | 30 | 12% |
| Deserted | 18 | 7% |
| Transferred | 7 | 3% |
| Detailed | 14 | 6% |
| Discharged as unfit or provided substitute | 18 | 7% |
| Discharged by writ of habeas corpus | 38 | 15% |
| Died of disease | 7 | 3% |

In addition to the above, at least eighty-four members (34%) of the battery were hospitalized for treatment for wounds or illness during the war. Additionally, at least eighty men (33%) also served with the Hampton Legion Light Artillery, a South Carolina unit, during 1862.

## Enlistment Statistics

| | | |
|---|---|---|
| Total Enlisted | 244 | |
| From Maryland | 112 | 46% |
| From Other States | 13 | 5% |
| Unknown | 119 | 49% |

Residence by County:

| | | |
|---|---|---|
| Anne Arundel | 13 | 5% |
| Baltimore | 29 | 12% |
| Charles | 19 | 8% |
| Frederick | 10 | 4% |
| Prince George's | 22 | 9% |
| Calvert | 2 | |
| Caroline | 1 | |
| Carroll | 1 | |
| Cecil | 2 | |
| Dorchester | 2 | |
| Howard | 2 | |
| Montgomery | 3 | 1% |
| Somerset | 9 | 3.6% |
| St. Mary's | 3 | 1% |
| Talbott | 1 | |
| Washington | 1 | |
| Wicomico | 2 | |
| Worcester | 1 | |

## Statistical Summary

| Enlistment by Year | | | | | |
|---|---|---|---|---|---|
| Year | 1861 | 1862 | 1863 | 1864 | Unknown |
| Number | 139 | 38 | 15 | 12 | 43 |
| Percent | 56% | 15% | 6% | 5% | 17% |

| Enlistment by Location | | |
|---|---|---|
| Richmond, Virginia | 92 | 37% |
| Fredericksburg, Virginia | 35 | 14% |
| Brooks Station | 19 | 8% |
| Evansport | 15 | 6% |
| Bunker Hill | 16 | 6.5% |
| Petersburg, Virginia | 4 | 2% |
| Frederick, Maryland | 3 | 1% |
| Rappahannock, Virginia | 3 | 1% |
| Dranesville, Virginia | 3 | 1% |
| Other | 21 | 8% |
| Unknown | 37 | 15% |

| Battle Losses (Men) First Maryland Artillery | | | | | |
|---|---|---|---|---|---|
| Battle | Date | KIA | WIA | POW | Total |
| Seven Days | 6/26-7/2/62 | 1 | 8 | 1 | 10 |
| Cedar Run & Manassas | 8/9-29/62 | 2 | 6 | 0 | 8 |
| Sharpsburg Retreat | 10/62 | - | - | 2 | 2 |
| Hamilton Crossing | 5/3/63 | 2 | 6 | 3 | 11 |
| Winchester | 6/13-15/63 | 3 | 14 | 2 | 19 |
| Gettysburg Campaign | 7/1-30/63 | 1 | 4 | 16 | 21 |
| Warrenton | 10/20/63 | - | 1 | 2 | 3 |
| Mine Run | 11/27-28/63 | 1 | 1 | - | 2 |
| Cold Harbor | 6/1-4/64 | - | 3 | - | 3 |
| Weldon Railroad | 6/22/64 | - | 3 | - | 3 |
| Sailor's Creek | 4/6/65 | 1 | - | - | 1 |
| Other/Unspecified | | 2 | 2 | 4 | 8 |
| Total | | 13 | 48 | 30 | 91 |

## First Maryland Artillery

### Battle Losses (Horses)

| Battle | Date | Killed/disabled |
|---|---|---|
| Fredericksburg | 12/13/62 | 4* |
| Winchester | 6/13-15/63 | 16 |
| Gettysburg | 7/1-3/63 | 9 |
| Cold Harbor | 6/1-4/64 | 4** |
| Weldon Railroad | 6/22/64 | 8 |
| Total | | 41 |

### Deserted from Petersburg during August 1864

Charles H. Bartles
James Crowley
Philip F. Edelin
John G. Gainer
Charles Halstead
Sherrod B. Hannon
Joseph Hatton
George H. Hilliary
Richard Henry Lee
George H. Marriott
Thomas G. Morgan
Charles Pease
Albert W. Perrie
Charles Riddle
John M. Rye
Albert Tolson
John Wade
A. M. Wilson

### Discharged by Writ of Habeas Corpus (Fall of 1864)

Augustus J. Albert
George W. Basford
Enoch R. Barry
John H. Briscoe
William R. Brown
John Campbell
William P. Compton
P. A. L. Contee
George G. Coombe
James A. Dorsell
Henry M. Forbes
Joseph T. Franklin
John B. Garden
Frank Gunby
John C. Handy
John G. Harris
J. W. F. Hatton
William G. Higgins
Daniel Lloyd
William H. May
Charles L. McNeal
Francis McWilliams
Edward Middleton
Francis F. Nelson
George W. Perrie
William E. Phipps
Richard Richardson
Harry Sergeant
William Shinburne
John Shuster
Thomas Sunderland
L. M. Sunderland
Samuel Thomas
John Tucker
James N. Weems
Thomas Williams
John R. Yates

\* Two of these belonged to Lt. C. S. Contee, who claimed a loss of $800 for their deaths.
\*\* Four horses were left behind as unfit on the way to Cold Harbor.

# NOTES

[1] *Official Records of the Union and Confederate Armies* (OR), Vol. V, Series I, 851; OR, Vol. XI, 488; OR, Vol. XII, 550.

[2] *Marylanders in the Confederacy*, Family Line Publications, Silver Springs, Maryland, 1986, 33. (Hereafter cited as *Marylanders*); OR, Vol. XLII, 1175.

[3] Record Group 109, Microcopy 321, Rolls 9-10, National Archives, Washington, DC. (Hereafter cited as CSR.)

[4] CSR, First Maryland Artillery.

[5] *Marylanders*, 28, 32-33.

[6] Albert, A. James, Jr., unpublished manuscript, used by permission of the Maryland Historical Society, Baltimore, Maryland, 6. (Hereafter cited as Albert.)

[7] CSR, First Maryland Artillery.

[8] CSR, First Maryland Artillery.

[9] CSR, First Maryland Artillery.

[10] CSR, First Maryland Artillery.

[11] CSR, First Maryland Artillery.

[12] CSR, First Maryland Artillery.

[13] Thomas, Dean S. *Cannons*. Thomas Publications, Gettysburg, PA, 1985, p. 43

[14] Albert, 6-7.

[15] OR, Vol. V, 1031.

[16] Albert, 8-9.

[17] OR, Vol. XI, 900, 902.

[18] Albert, 9-12.

[19] Goldsborough, W. W. *The Maryland Line in the Confederate Army*, 261. (Hereafter cited as Goldsborough.)

[20] OR, Vol. XII, 237-238.
[21] Edwards, Abial Hall. *Dear Friend Anna*, 26.
[22] *Marylanders*, 36.
[23] Albert, 12.
[24] Goldsborough, 261-2.
[25] OR, Vol. XIX, 955.
[26] OR, Vol. XIX, 963.
[27] Albert, 12-13.
[28] OR, Vol. XXI, 666, 669.
[29] Albert, 14.
[30] Albert, 14.
[31] Scharf, Jonathan Thomas, personal memoirs, 68-69.
[32] OR, Vol. XXV, 542.
[33] OR, Vol. XXV, 451.
[34] Albert, 15-17.
[35] OR, Vol. XXVII, 458.
[36] OR, Vol. XXIX, 424.
[37] OR, Vol. XXIX, 847.
[38] Scharf, 70.
[39] OR, Vol. XL, 758.

# Appendix A

## *The Battle of Stephenson's Depot*

(Unpublished memoir by A. James Albert, Jr.
Used by permission of the Maryland Historical Society,
Baltimore, Maryland.)

On June 10, 1863 after our fighting with Sedgwick at Fredericksburg, Gen. Ewell's corps including our artillery company, in command of Capt. Dement, was ordered to the Shenandoah Valley. On the 14th of June Milroy was defeated at Winchester, and retreated down the valley towards Harper's Ferry. Before daylight on the 15th, our first knowledge of their approach was a volley of musketry fire from their infantry. We pushed forward at once and got possession of the railroad cut, running parallel with the Winchester & Martinsburg Turnpike, along which Milroy's forces were retreating. There was a bridge over the cut connecting the road between the turnpike and Jordan's Springs. There was only an opening for two of our guns. The one I was with was ordered in position on the bridge and the other in an opening to our left. Our skirmishers had advanced but as it grew light they were quickly driven back by a charge of Milroy's infantry and out two guns had to stand the full force of a succession of charges of their infantry and we drove them back with double charges of canister until they surrendered. At the two guns we lost eighteen men killed and wounded. The following list is all of whom I can give the names:

 Lieutenant C. S. Contee – wounded leg, severe
 Sergeant J. E. Glasscock – thigh, severe
 Private Robert Chew – arm, severe
 Private Thomas Moore – killed, abdomen
 Private William Wootten – killed
 Private A. James Albert – arm amputated

Private Chas. Pease – hand, slight
Private Fred Frayer – hand, slight
Private James W. Owens – hand, slight
Private Louis Koester – both legs – killed
Private Joseph Macabee – face, killed
Private W. H. Gorman – leg, amputated
Private John Yates – leg, severe

Our former Captain, at this time, Lt. Col. R. Snowden Andrews was wounded, arm, severe. When I was wounded and left the gun, there was only one man left at the gun on the bridge, B. Welsh Owens, and it was just then that R. H. McKim and Morgan came to his aid and helped to fire the gun, until the union troops surrendered.

The fight at this point was about as hot as anything during the war. At early dawn, their line of Battle which had formed on the turnpike found out that they could not get through the rocks and woods on their left or over the deep railroad cut on the right, and the only way would be to charge up the road crossing the Railroad. By the time our skirmishers had fallen back to our rear, so that we could open fire, they were within fifty yards of our guns. The whistling of their bullets was tremendous and the rattle of those that struck the wooden bridge, sounded very much like a watchmans alarm rattle. We returned their fire with canister, as they charged up the road in a solid body. They would fall back and then charge again, until at last they saw our infantry advancing, when they surrendered. During an interval between their efforts to cut their way through our road, we saw Gen. Millroy with some of his staff, ride at full run across the field on our left front. We fired a shrapnel shot at him. He escaped, but nearly all his men, and a line of wagons and cannon reaching almost up to Winchester were captured. After the fighting was over, my friend Wm. Brown told me he walked up the road in front of our gun and counted 50 of their poor fellows lying within 150 feet of our gun, most of them torn to pieces and beyond that distance, there were many hundreds more. My father who knew Gen. R. E. Lee before the war and after the war used to meet him in summer at the Virginia summer resorts. The first time he met him after the war, he said – "Gen. Lee, I am so sorry my son lost his arm at Stephensons." Gen. Lee replied, "Mr. Albert you

## The Battle of Stephenson's Depot

ought to be proud about it, as he lost it in the Thermopylae of the war."

On June 15, 1863, Lieut. Col. R. Snowden Andrews commanding the First Maryland Artillery, placed two guns of Dement's Battery, under Lieut. C. S. Contee, beside a bridge at Stephenson's Depot, near Winchester, within short musket range of Gen'l Milroy's army. Unsupported by infantry these two guns maintained their position until almost all their men were killed or wounded and the enemy surrendered, Gen'l. Milroy and a few mounted officers alone escaping.

Lieut. Randolph H. McKim of Gen. G. H. Stewart's staff and Lieut. John H. Morgan or the 1st N.C. Reg't. voluntarily assisted the one remaining man at No. 1 gun, B. Welch Owens until the end. Gen'l. Edward Johnson thanked Col. Andrews and Lieut. Contee, both severely wounded, for winning the battle for him. Gen'l. Lee referred to this incident as the Thermopylae of his campaign, and ordered the name of every man to be recorded at the Department in Richmond.

| No. 1 Gun | | No. 2 Gun | |
|---|---|---|---|
| Sgt. | John G. Harris | Sgt. | John E. Glasscock |
| Corp. | William P. Compton | Corp. | William H. May |
| | Samuel Thompson | | Charles Harris |
| Pvts. | Robert Chew | Pvts. | Thomas More |
| | William Koester | | William Gorman |
| | Charles Pease | | F. Frayer |
| | A. James Albert, Jr. | | William W. Wilson |
| | William T. Wooten | | Samuel Thomas |
| | John R. Yates, Jr. | | R. T. Richardson |
| | H. J. Langsdale | | William Sherburne |
| | J. R. Buchanan | | William Dallam |
| | B. Welch Owens | | Joseph Mockabee |

On June 10, 1863, after the fighting at Fredericksburg our battery started with Ewell's corps for the Shenandoah Valley. On the 14th Milroy was defeated at Winchester. Before daylight on the 15th as we advanced towards Stephenson's Depot on the road from Jordan's Springs we received a volley of musketry from their Infantry who were trying to escape from the Winchester & Martinsburg turnpike by taking the road we were on. We pushed forward at once and got possession of the railroad our running parallel with the Winchester & Martinsburg road. There was a bridge over the R.R. cut on which my gun was placed and there was only space for one more gun which was to our left on the west side of the cut. As we only had two guns in the fight against Milroy's corps which had five or seven thousand men. As soon as we got in position they commenced charging up the road which was the only way they could advance. We used canister in firing our guns, which swept them down by the hundreds, but they continued charging until our infantry came to our rescue and as soon as they saw them advancing they surrendered. My friend Wm. Brown who was with one of the guns that was not in the fight, told me that when he went down the road in front of my gun and counted 50 poor fellows lying within 150 feet of the gun.

# Compiled Service Records

## Introduction to the
## Compiled Service Records of the First Maryland Artillery

The compiled service records for the soldiers who served in the First Maryland Artillery have been primarily taken from Record Group 109, Microcopy 321, Rolls 9 and 10, located at the National Archives, Washington, D.C. The roster has been supplemented from other official and unofficial sources, including but not limited to family histories, county histories, cemetery records, *The Confederate Veteran,* county records and several incomplete postwar rosters.

Since the muster rolls for the First Maryland Artillery, as well as most other Confederate regiments are not complete, supplemental sources seem to be crucial in determining a complete listing of the battery's soldiers. Consultation with postwar rosters was indispensable to the effort. These rosters are obviously not entirely accurate, but add valuable data to the roster. Spellings found in these various sources are not consistent. Every effort has been made to include everyone who should be listed, and to avoid duplications; however, this effort may not have been entirely successful.

Discrepancies are found in even the official compiled service records. These problems arise from several contemporary organizational problems. Communications were not always efficient. It is entirely possible that a soldier was listed as being AWOL when, in fact, he had been captured, was wounded in the hospital, was sick, or was on detached service somewhere away from the main body of the regiment.

Highlights of each soldier's career are presented to include date and place of enlistment, periods of sickness, wounds, death, capture, incarceration, and physical description. Prewar and postwar residences when known, birth and death dates, and place of burial have also been included. Unless otherwise stated, assume that a soldier was present through the last date given.

## Abbreviations used in the CR

| | |
|---|---|
| AWOL | Absent without leave |
| B. | Born |
| C.S. | Confederate States |
| C.S.S. | Confederate States Ship |
| Capt. | Captain |
| Co. | County or Company (in context) |
| Col. | Colonel |
| Comp. | Complexion |
| Corp. | Corporal |
| D. | Died |
| DFR | Dropped from the Roll |
| disch. | Discharged |
| Enl. | Enlisted |
| GA. | Georgia |
| Gen. | General |
| Hosp. | Hospitalized |
| KIA | Killed in Action |
| Lt. | Lieutenant |
| Md. | Maryland |
| MLCSH | Maryland Line Confederate Soldiers' Home |
| NFR | No further record |
| POW | Captured/Prisoner of War |
| Pres. | Present |
| Pvt. | Private |
| PWR | Post War Roster of Record |
| Q | Quartermaster |
| Res. | Resident of |
| rlsd | release |
| S.C | South Carolina |
| Sgt. | Sergeant |
| Va. | Virginia |
| WIA | Wounded in Action |

# COMPILED SERVICE RECORDS ROSTER

## First Maryland Artillery

**ADCOCK, ROBERT**: Pvt. Enl. on ?. Taken POW on 7/3/63 at Gettysburg, Pa.. Sent to Point Lookout, Md. on 11/1/63, then NFR.

**ALBERT, AUGUSTUS JAMES, Jr.**: Pvt. Enl. 7/6/61 at Richmond, Va. Pres. on 10/31/61 and 2/62 rolls, absent sick in Fredericksburg per 12/31/61 roll; on detail duty as Ordnance Sgt. From 1/1/63 to 4/15/63. WIA at Winchester 6/15/63. In Chimborazo hosp. from 7/29/63 to 8/3/63; with Major Allan, 2nd Corps, from 9/23/63 per S.O. 89; Discharged by writ of habeas corpus in Confederate States District Court, Judge Hallyburton; cited for gallantry at Winchester by Lt. Gen. R. S. Ewell in his report on the Gettysburg Campaign, Official Records, Vol. XXVII, Part II, p. 451. Res. of Baltimore. Also performed duty with Section B, Artillery Battalion, Hampton Legion.

**ALDRIDGE, JOHN H.**: Pvt. Enl. on 7/28/61 at Richmond, Va. Pres. on 10/31/61 and 12/31/61 rolls; on leave in Richmond per 2/62 roll; in Gen. Hosp #21 in Richmond, Va. on 3/30/62. Discharged on 9/11/62, then age 30, hazel eyes, dark hair. Res. of Baltimore, Md.

**ANDERSON, JOSEPH**: Pvt. Enl. on ?. Taken POW on 10/2/63 at Harper's Ferry. Sent to Point Lookout, Md. on 1/23/64, where held until exchange on 2/10/65. Res. Of Cumberland, Md. Also served in Co. A, 1st Maryland Cav.

**ANDREWS, RICHARD SNOWDEN**: Capt./Major/Lt. Col. Accepted commission as Major of Cavalry on 6/14/61. Resigned commission as major and accepted commission as Capt. of artillery on 7/31/61. Commanded 1st Maryland Artillery 7/31/61 to late 6/62. WIA in the leg at Mechanicsville, Va. on 6/26/62. WIA at Cedar Run (Mountain), abdomen, 8/9/62. WIA at Winchester, Va. in the arm on 6/14/63. Attached to the Ordnance Bureau 10/62 until 4/63. Artillery battalion commander from 4/63 to 6/14/63. Sent to Europe to procure cannon 2/64. Commanded artillery battalion again in late 1864. Worked in railroad construction in Mexico 1865-7. Returned to his native Baltimore in 1867. Appointed Brigadier General of Artillery, Maryland National Guard by Governor Carroll in 1877. Held this post for three administrations. Died in 1903 at age 73. Many receipts for pay and many requisitions, especially for forage, are on file. Taken POW at some point, probably Cedar Run, exchanged for Major George F. Smith, 61st Pa. on September 21, 1862 at Aiken's Landing, Va.

**BAILEY, JOSEPH (JAMES) B.:** Pvt. Enl. on 11/23/64 at Richmond, Va. Paid $50 bounty. Pres. on 12/31/64 and 2/28/65 muster rolls. Paroled at Appomattox C.H. on 4/9/65. Res. of Northumberland Co., Va. Light hair, light comp., grey eyes, 5'8". In Sickel U.S. Army General Hosp. at Alexandria, Va. with acute diarrhea 5/6-24/65.

**BALLARD, WILLIAM W.:** Pvt. Enl. on 10/18/64 at Petersburg, Va. Pres. on 10/31/64, 12/31/64 and 2/28/65 rolls. Paroled at Appomattox C.H. on 4/9/65. Res. of Cambridge, Dorchester Co., Md.

**BARRY, ENOCH R.:** Pvt. Enl. on 12/7/61 at Evansport as a substitute for E. K. McLaughlin. Pres. on 12/31/61, 2/62 and 8/31/64 muster rolls. Served on extra duty as teamster. Discharged by writ of habeas corpus issued by Judge Hallyburton.

**BARRY, McC. Y. (McCLINTOCK):** Pvt. Enl. on 3/21/63 at Bowling Green, Va. Detailed to Signal Corps by S.O. 44, dated 2/23/64. Paid $96.20 on 3/28/64.

**BASFORD, GEORGE W.:** Pvt. Enl. on 9/8/61 at Brooks Station. Pres on 10/31/61, 12/31/61, 2/62 and 8/31/64 muster rolls. Discharged by writ of habeas corpus issued by Judge Hallyburton.

**BEALE, JAMES SHIELDS:** Pvt. Enl. on 9/28/62 at Bunker Hill, Va. Pres. on 8/31/64, 10/31/64, 12/31/64 and 2/28/65 muster rolls. Transported to Washington, D.C. on 6/13/65.

**BLUMMENAUR (BLUMENAUR), MICHAEL:** Pvt./Farrier/Smith. Enl. on 10/23/62 at Bunker Hills, Va. Pres on 8/31/64, 10/31/64, 12/31/64 and 2/28/65 muster rolls. Paroled at Appomattox C. H. on 4/9/65. Res. of Frederick, Md. MLCSH.

Compiled Service Records Roster 55

**BOARMAN, RICHARD T.**: Pvt. Enl. on 6/27/61 at Fredericksburg, Va. Pres. on 10/31/61, 12/31/61 and 2/62 muster rolls. Paid $98 on 7/16/62. Discharged for poor health. Applied for position as clerk, Secretary of the Treasury. Letters recommending him sent by Hill and Andrews, then Lt. Col., on 12/17/63. Native of Charles Co., Md. MLCSH.

**BOLLING (BOLLINGER), W. FRANK**: Corporal/Sgt. Major. Enl. on 6/27/61 at Fredericksburg, Va. Pres. on 10/31/61, 12/31/61 and 2/62 muster rolls. Paid $84 on 7/6/64. In Robertson Hosp., Richmond, Va. on 8/19/64. AWOL on 8/31/64 muster roll.

**BOSWELL, RICHARD T.**: Pvt. Enl. on 7/15/61 at Richmond, Va. Pres. At 10/31/61, 12/31/61 and 2/62 muster rolls. Taken POW at Westminster, Md. on 7/5/63, sent to Ft. Delaware on 7/7/63, then to Point Lookout, Md. on 10/26/63. Exchanged on 12/24/63. Res. of Homonky, Charles Co., Md.

**BOTELOR, WALTER P.**: Pvt. Enl. on 7/19/61 at Richmond, Va. Absent on 10/31/61, 12/31/61 and 2/62 muster rolls. Was in Dumfries, Stafford Co., Va. and Richmond, Va. jails, resp.

**BOWEN, W. H.**: Pvt. Enl. on 9/8/61 at Brooks Station. Pres. on 10/31/61, 12/31/61 and 2/62 muster rolls. WIA and taken POW at Gettysburg, Pa. 7/1-4/63. Admitted to DeCamp Gen. Hosp., David's Island, New York Harbor. Paroled on 10/22/63. Admitted to Chimborazo Hosp. #4, Richmond on 1/30/64 with gunshot wound in foot. Died of pneumonia on 3/29/64. Res. of Anne Arundel Co., Md.

**BOWIE, HENRY CONTEE**: Pvt. Enl. on 7/23/61 at Richmond, Va. Pres. on 10/31/61, 12/31/61 and 2/62 muster rolls. Absent sick in Richmond on 8/31/64 muster roll. Died on 10/28/64 at Robertson Hosp. of diarrhea and an abscess of the lungs. Res. of Upper Marlborough, Prince George's Co., Md.

**BOWIE, THOMAS DANIEL**: Pvt. Enl. on 6/30/61 at Fredericksburg, Va. Pres. on 10/31/61 roll. Detached to Gen. French's headquarters per 12/31/61 muster roll. Transferred to the Engineers. Paid $30 on 7/24/62. Paid $22.50 on 9/24/62. Paid $17.60 on 8/31/62, paid $23.25 on 9/15/62, paid $12.40 on 6/23/62, paid $19.20 on 7/19/62. Res. of Montgomery Co., Md.

**BOWLAND, S. G.**: Pvt. Enl. on 8/26/62 at Dranesville. Pres. on 8/31/64, 10/31/64, 12/31/64 and 2/28/65 muster rolls. Surrendered at Appomattox C.H. on 4/9/65. Res. of Somerset Co., Md.

**BOWLES, ROBERT**: Ord. Sgt. Enl. on ?. Pres. on 2/28/65 muster roll, then NFR. May have also served in Co. C, Davis' Maryland Cav.

**BOWLING, ALEXANDER**: Pvt. Enl. on ?. Taken POW on 5/5/6_, then NFR. May have also served in the 1st Maryland Cav.

**BOWLING, WILLIAM FRANCIS**: Sgt. PWR only. Res. of Charles Co., Md.

**BRADFORD, THOMAS G.**: Pvt. Enl. on 7/6/61 at Rappahannock, Va. by Col. Zarona. Pres. on 10/31/61, 12/31/61 and 2/62 muster roll. MWIA. Died of wounds on 6/13/62 in Gen. Hosp. #21, Richmond, Va. Res. of Baltimore, Md.

**BRISCO, JOHN HANSON**: Pvt. Enl. on 8/10/61 at Richmond, Va. Pres. on 10/31/61, 12/31/61, 2/62 and 8/31/64 muster rolls. Discharged by writ of habeas corpus issued by Judge Hallyburton. Also served with Hampton Legion Light Artillery as evidenced by clothing receipts. Res. of Baltimore, Md.

**BRISCOE, WASHINGTON**: Pvt. Enl. on 11/1/63 at Richmond, Va. Discharged for disability on 5/20/64.

**BROMLEY, GEORGE W.**: Pvt. Enl. on 7/28/61 at Richmond. Pres. on 10/31/61, 12/31/61 and 2/62 muster rolls. Also served with Hampton Legion Light Artillery.

**BROOKE (BROOKS), THOMAS**: Pvt./Sgt. Enl. on 11/28/61 at Evansport. Absent on recruiting service on 2/62 muster roll. In private quarters with measles on 6/11/62. In Robertson Hosp. Richmond, Va. 1-2/63, 3-4/63 and 56-6/63. Pres. on 8/31/64 roll as Pvt. Pres. on 10/31/64, 12/31/64 and 2/28/65 rolls as Quartermaster Sgt. Surrendered at Appomattox C.H., Va. on 4/9/65. Res. of Bladensburg, Prince George's Co., Md.

**BROUGHTON WILLIAM THOMAS**: Pvt. Enl. on 10/31/62 at Richmond, Va. Paid $50 reenlistment bounty. Pres. on extra duty as harness maker on 8/31/64. Pres. on 10/31/64, 12/31/64 and 2/28/65 rolls. Surrendered at Appomattox C.H., Va. on 4/9/65. Res. of Somerset Co., Md.

**BROWN, WILLIAM R. (B.?):** Pvt./Sgt. Enl. on 7/6/61 at Richmond, Va. Pres on 10/31/61, 12/31/61 and 2/62 muster rolls. WIA in thigh and artery at Mine Run on 11/27/63. Furloughed for 60 days on 2/5/64. Paid $34 on 6/4/64 and on 7/12/64. Pres. as Sgt. on 8/31/64 muster roll, detached to Tax Collector's Office, Richmond, Va. Discharged by writ of habeas corpus issued by Judge Hallyburton per 10/31/64 muster roll. Res. of 317 Madison St., Baltimore, Md.

**BRYAN, ROBERT S.:** Pvt./Corp. Enl. on 6/1/63 at Richmond, Va. Pres. on 8/31/64 roll as Pvt. Pres. on 10/31/64, 12/31/64 and 2/28/65 rolls as Corp. Res. of Prince George's Co., Md.

**BUCHANAN, JOHN ROWAN:** Pvt. Enl. on 9/26/62 at Bunker Hill, Va. Cited for gallantry at Winchester. Taken POW at Falling Waters (Williamsport), Md. on 7/14/63. Confined at the Old Capital Prison, then transferred to Point Lookout, Md. where held until exchanged on 3/3/64. Furloughed for 30 days on 9/2/64 for diarrhea. Paid $38 on 9/5/64. Furlough issued for 60 days on 10/26/64. Detailed to Signal Corps. on 10/21/64. Listed on clothing receipts. Res. of Baltimore, Md. and Montgomery White Sulphur Springs, Va.

**BUCHANAN, WILLIAM JEFFERSON:** Pvt. Enl. on 7/1/61 at Richmond. Pres. on 10/31/61, 12/31/61 and 2/62 muster rolls. Paid $17.60 and discharged on 12/18/62. Admitted to the Infirmary of St. Francis de Sales, Richmond, Va. for tuberculosis. Applied for position as Lieutenant of Artillery, CSA, on 7/5/62. Applied for 1st Lt. in Signal Corps on 10/17/62. Applied for clerkship in the C. S. Treasury Dept. on 12/30/62. Applied for QM (Captain) on 6/24/63. Several letters are on file endorsing his applications. He apparently became a Lieutenant in the QM Corps. His cousin was C. S. Navy Admiral Buchanan of the C.S.S. *Virginia*. His father was U.S. Minister to Austria and/or Denmark, bur resigned and was in exile in Paris. Pvt. Buchanan volunteered from Europe with his four brothers. He was 28 years old, with dark hair and dark blue eyes, 6' in late 1862. He was a graduate of the College of New Jersey and Res. of Baltimore.

**BURTLES, CHARLES H.**: Pvt. Enl. on 10/12/62 at Bunker hill, Va. Deserted at Petersburg, Va. per 10/31/64 muster roll.

**BUSK, JEROME**: Pvt., Enl. on 8/17/61 at Brooks Station. Pres. on 10/31/61, 12/31/61 and 2/62 muster rolls, then NFR.

**BYRNES, SAMUEL E.**: Pvt. Enl. on 8/17/61 at Brooks Station, Va. Pres. on 10/31/61, 12/31/61, 2/62, 8/31/64, 10/31/64 and 12/31/64 muster rolls. Listed on clothing receipts. Discharged by Order of Secretary of War per 2/28/65 roll. Also served in Hampton Legion Light Artillery. May have also served in the 1st Texas Infantry. Res. of 103 Druid Hill Ave., Baltimore, Md.

**CAMPBELL, JOHN**: Pvt. Enl. on 8/30/61 at Brooks Station. Pres. on 10/31/61, 12/31/61, 2/62 and 8/31/64. Taken POW while in Jordan Springs, Va. Hosp. on 7/26/63. Paroled on 8/2/63. In Gen. Hosp. #9 on 9/7/63. Furloughed on 9/14/63. Discharged by writ of habeas corpus issued by Judge Hallyburton per 10/31/64. Also served in the Hampton Legion Light Artillery.

**CAPERTON, JAMES MOSHER**: Pvt. Enl. on 8/2/62 at Monroe City. Pres. on 8/31/64 and 2/28/65 rolls. Absent on furlough, sick on 10/31/64 and 12/31/64 rolls. May have also served in the 13th Va. Light Art. Res. of Georgetown, D.C. MLCSH.

**CAWOOD, E. MATTHEW**: Pvt. Enl. on 11/27/61 at Evansport. Pres on 12/31/61 roll. Absent detailed to Major Morey, QM, per 2/62 roll. Died of typhoid fever in hosp. on 6/13/62. Res. of Homonky, Charles Co., Md.

**CHEW, ROBERT B.**: Pvt./Sgt. Enl on 9/1/62 at Frederick, Md. Absent on furlough of indulgence on 8/31/64 roll. Pres. as Sgt. on 10/31/64, 12/31/64 and 2/28/65 rolls. Cited for gallantry at Winchester. Mentioned on hosp. registers and clothing receipts. Surrendered at Appomattox C.H. on 4/9/65. Res. of Friendship, Calvert Co., Md.

**CHILES, W.L.**: Pvt. Enl. on 7/8/61 at Fredericksburg, Va. Pres. on 10/31/61, 12/31/61 and 2/62 rolls. Also served in Hampton Legion Light Artillery. Res. of Anne Arundel Co., Md.

Compiled Service Records Roster 59

**CLARK, T.**: Pvt. Enl. on ?. Taken POW at Westminster, Md. on 7/5/63. Discharged from Ft. Delaware on 87/12/63, then NFR.

**CLAYTON, WILLIAM G.**: Pvt. Enl. on 5/1/62 at Richmond, Va. Absent sick in hosp. per 8/31/64 roll. Pres. on 10/31/64, 12/31/64 and 2/28/65 muster rolls.

**CLEARY, ROBERT E.**: Pvt. Enl. on 5/16/63 at Guineas, Va. Pres. on 8/31/64, 10/31/64, 12/31/64 and 2/28/65 rolls. Surrendered at Appomattox C.H., Va. on 4/9/65.

**COALE, WILLIAM AUGUSTUS**: Pvt. Enl. on 7/27/61 at Richmond, Va. Pres. on 10/31/61, 12/31/61 and 2/62 rolls. In Gen. hosp. #21, 7/17-9/30/62. Paid $61.20 on 10/28/62. In Chimborazo Hosp. #5 at Richmond with acute diarrhea on 4/29-5/17/63. Paid $97 on 9/13/63. Discharged for disability on 9/26/63, then 5/6", hazel eyes, dark hair. Res. of Anne Arundel Co., Md. MLCSH. Also served in Hampton Legion Light Artillery.

**COMBE, GEORGE GRISWOLD, D.D.S.**: Pvt./Corp. Enl. on 6/28/61 at Fredericksburg, Va. Pres. on 10/31/61, 12/31/61, 2/62 and 8/31/64 muster rolls. In Chimborazo Hosp. #9, Richmond, Va. 4/30-5/17/63. Discharged by writ of habeas corpus issued by Judge Hallyburton per 10/31/64 muster roll. Also served in Hampton Legion light Artillery. Res. of Baltimore, Md. MLCSH.

**COMPTON, WILLIAM PENN** : Pvt./Sgt. Enl. on 7/8/61 at Fredericksburg, Va. Pres. on 10/31/61, 12/31/61, 2/62 and 8/31/64 rolls as Sgt. Cited for gallantry at Winchester. Paid $34 on 3/14/64. Discharged by writ of habeas corpus issued by Judge Hallyburton per 10/31/64 roll. Also served in Hampton Legion Light Artillery. Res. of Port Tobacco, Charles Co., Md. MLCSH.

**CONLEY, MICHAEL E.**: Pvt. Enl. on 9/5/62 at Drury's Bluff. Transferred from Capt. Epps's Co., Johnson Artillery, then NFR.

**CONNER, WILLIAM**: Pvt. Enl. on 7/25/63 at Madison C.H. Pres. on 8/31/64, 10/31/64, 12/31/64 and 2/28/65 rolls. Surrendered at Appomattox C.H. on 4/9/65. Then 5'4", hazel eyes, dark hair. Res. of Frederick Co., Md.

**CONNOLLY, EDWARD**: Pvt. Enl. on ?. Took the oath of allegiance at Point Lookout, Md. on 6/21/65, then 5' 81/2", blue eyes, dark brown hair. Also served with the Maryland American Rifles. Res. of Baltimore.

**CONTEE, CHARLES SNOWDEN**: 2nd Lt./1st Lt. Enl. on ?. Paid $249 on 8/17/61. Pres. on 10/31/61 and 2/62 rolls. Sick in hosp. on 9/22/62. WIA in left leg on 6/15/63 at Winchester. In Charlottesville hosp. 8/25-9/9/63. In hosp. at Farmville, Va. 10/3/63 to 1/18/64. Requested $800 for two horses belonging to him killed at Fredericksburg on 5/2/63. Paid $60 for travel to Abingdon to Richmond and return on 9/1/64. on receipts for pay, stores, forage, stationary, requisitions and quarters. Served as enrolling officer for Wythe Co., Va., sworn into service by Mayor Mayo of Richmond after 6/26/64 appointment by Governor Letcher (sic). Cousin of Richard Snowdon Andrews. Res. of Pleasant Prospect Plantation, Prince George's Co., Md.

**CONTEE, PHILIP ASHTON LEE (P.A.L.)**: Corp./Q.M. Sgt. Enl. on 6/27/61 at Fredericksburg, Va. Pres. on 10/31/61, 12/31/61, 2/62 and 8/31/64 rolls as Q.M. Sgt. In Charlottesville, Va. Hosp. on 8/11-13/62. Discharged by writ of habeas corpus per 10/31/64 muster roll. Also served in Hampton legion Light Artillery. Res. of Charlotte Hall, Charles Co., Md.

**COPE, J.**: Pvt. Enl. on ?. In Lynchburg, Va. Hosp. on 12/17/62 with dysentery, then NFR.

**COVINGTON, JESSE H.**: Pvt. Enl. on 7/23/61 at Richmond, Va. Pres. on 10/31/61, 12/31/61 and 2/62 muster rolls. Also served in Hampton Legion Light Artillery. Res. of Howard Co., Md.

**CRAVEN, B. L.**: Pvt. Enl. on 8/16/61 at Richmond, Va. Pres. on 10/31/61, 12/31/61 and 2/62 muster rolls.

**CROWLEY, JAMES**: Pvt. Enl. on 9/8/61 at Brooks Station. Pres. on 10/31/61, 12/31/61, 2/62 and 8/31/64 rolls. Deserted at Petersburg, Va. in 8/64 per 10/31/64 roll. on clothing receipt dated 11/1/64. Also served in Hampton Legion Light Artillery. Res. of Prince George's Co., Md.

**DABNEY, FREDERICK Y**: 2nd Lt. Enl. on ?. Paid $249 on 10/16/61 for 2 mos. 23 days service. Pres. on 10/31/61, 12/31/61 and 2/62 rolls. Paid $360 on 5/26/62. Transferred to Engineer Corps at Port Hudson, Louisiana. Res. of Mississippi.

**DAFFIN, FRANCIS D.**: Pvt. Enl. on 8/16/161 at Richmond, Va. Absent in confinement in Dumfries Jail, Stafford Co., Va. and Richmond, Va. per 10/31/61, 12/31/61 and 2/62 rolls. Also served in Zarvona's Maryland Zouaves. Res. of Baltimore, Md.

**DALLAM, WILLIAM**: Pvt. Enl. on ?. Cited for gallantry at Winchester, then NFR.

**DAMAR, JOHN STALFORD**: Pvt. Enl. on 7/13/61 at Richmond, Va. Absent in confinement in Dumfries Jail, Stafford Co., Va. and Richmond, Va. per 10/31/61, 12/31/61 and 2/62 rolls. Res. of Frederick Co., Md. MLCSH.

**DASHIELL (DASHIELD), BENJAMIN**: Pvt. Enl. on ?. Taken POW at Williamsport, Md. on 7/3/63. Sent to Fort Delaware and held there until exchanged on 2/27/65. In Gen. Hosp #9 at Richmond, Va. 3/29-9/65. Also served in Hampton Legion Light Artillery.

**DAVIS, JOHN T.**: Pvt. Enl. on 7/16/61 at Richmond, Va. Pres. on 10/31/61. Discharged on 12/7/61 upon providing J. Heatton as a substitute.

**DEAN, WILLIAM H.**: Pvt., Enl. on 8/17/61 at Brooks Station. Pres. on 10/31/61, 12/31/61 and 2/62 rolls. Also served in Hampton Legion Light Artillery.

**DEMENT, WILLIAM FENDLAY**: 1st Lt./Capt. Sworn in as 1st Lt. by Mayor Mayo of Richmond on 7/13/61. Paid $300 on 1/15/62. Promoted to Capt. on 7/19/62. Sick at Charlestown on 10/22/62. Absent sick at Fredericksburg, Va. per 10/31/61 roll. Pres. on rolls for 8/31/64, 10/31/64, 12/31/64 and 2/28/65. File contains many requisitions and receipts for forage. Recommended for promotion to Major by Lt. Col. Andrews on 12/10/64. Surrendered at Appomattox C.H. on 4/9/65, then commanding Smith's Artillery Battalion, serving as infantry. Res. of Duffield, Charles Co., Md.

**DIGGS, JOHN T., M.D.**: Pvt. Enl. on 9/1/62 at Frederick, Md. Pres. on 8/31/64, 10/31/64, 12/31/64 rolls. AWOL on 2/28/65 roll. Res. of LaPlata, Charles Co., Md.

**DISMUS, A. J.**: Pvt. Enl. on ?. Surrendered at Winchester, Va. on 5/6/65.

**DORSELL, JAMES A.**: Pvt. Enl. on 10/20/62 at Bunker Hill, Va. AWOL on 8/31/64 roll. Discharged by writ of habeas corpus issued by Judge Hallyburton per 10/31/64 muster roll.

**DORSETT, J. HAWKINS**: Pvt. Enl. on 9/1/62 at Harper's Ferry. Pres. on 8/31/64, 10/31/64, 12/31/64 and 2/28/65. Paroled on 4/16/65. Res. of Prince George's Co., Md.

**DORSEY, DANIEL B.**: Pvt. Enl. on 7/23/61 at Richmond, Va. Pres. on 10/31/61, 12/31/61 and 2/62 rolls. Also served in Hampton Legion Light Artillery.

**DORSEY, EVAN L.**: Pvt. Enl. on 11/24/61 at Evansport. Pres. on 12/31/61 and 2/62 rolls. In Gen. Hosp. #21, Richmond on 6/3/62. Requested transfer to Maryland Line on 6/10/62. Request disapproved by Capt. Andrews. Res. of Frederick Co., Md.

**DOUGHERTY, GEORGE A.**: Pvt. Enl. on 8/22/62 at Dranesville, Va. Paid $24 on 3/14/64 and $43.13 on 8/31/64. On clothing receipts. Severely WIA on 6/22/64. Appeared before Medical Examining Boards on 8/4/64 and 9/16/64. Absent on sick furloughs on last four rosters. Res. of Somerset, Orange Co., Va.

**DRYDEN, ROBERT J.**: Pvt. Enl. on 10/31/62 at Richmond, Va. $50 reenlistment bounty paid. Pres. on 8/31/64, 10/31/654, 12/31/64 and 2/28/65 muster rolls. Surrendered at Appomattox C.H. on 4/9/65. Res. of Somerset Co., Md.

**DUNLAP, S. O.**: Pvt. Enl. on 7/23/61 at Richmond. Pres. on 10/31/61, 12/31/61 and 2/62 rolls. WIA in left arm on 6/15/63. Detailed as a clerk in QM Department 8/25/63. Paroled as prisoner of war on 6/19/63. Also served in Hampton Legion Light Artillery.

**DUTTON, JAMES T.**: Pvt. Enl. on ?. $50 reenlistment bounty paid. Died of typhoid fever on 9/24/62 at Charlottesville, Va. Gen. Hosp. Left $20. Res. of Charles Co., Md.

**DUVALL, PHILIP BARTON (M.D.)**: Pvt. Enl. on 6/30/61 at Fredericksburg, Va. Pres. on 10/31/61, 12/31/61 and 2/62 rolls. KIA

5/14/63 at Hamilton Crossing, Va. Also served in the Hampton Legion Light Artillery. Res. of Crownsville, Anne Arundel Co., Md.

**DUVALL, SAMUEL FULTON (M.D.)**: Pvt. Enl. on 7/21/61 at Richmond, Va. Pres. on 10/31/61, 12/31/61 and 2/62. Taken POW at Williamsport on 7/5/63. Sent to Fort Delaware. Exchanged at Point Lookout, Md. on 12/22/63. Pres. at Camp Lee, Va. on 2/21/65. Paroled on 4/22/65. Also served in Hampton Legion Light Artillery. Res. of Anne Arundel Co., Md.

**EDELIN, PHILIP F.**: Pvt. Enl. on 7/23/61 at Richmond, Va. Pres. on 10/31/61, 12/31/61 and 2/62 rolls. AWOL on 8/31/64 roll. Deserted 8/64 at Petersburg per 10/31/64 muster roll. Also shown as taken POW on 8/27/64. Exchanged on 3/17/65. Also served in Hampton Legion Light Artillery. Res. of St. Mary's Co., Md.

**EDGE, JOSEPH G.**: Pvt. Enl. on 5/3/62 at Forsythe, Georgia. Pres. on 12/31/64 and 2/28/65 rolls. Transferred from Sumpter Artillery Battalion (Rhett's 1st S.C. Heavy Artillery). Surrendered at Appomattox C.H. on 4/9/65.

**FIELDS, EDWARD W.**: Pvt. Enl. on 7/6/61 at Rappahannock by Col. Zarona. Pres. on 10/31/61, 12/31/61 and 2/62 rolls. Paid $122 at 10/28/62 and $24 on 10/31/62. Discharged 1/15/63, then age 32, 5'81/2", dark hair and eyes. In Gen. Hosp #9, at Richmond in 10/64. Also served in Hampton Legion Light Artillery.

**FILLUS, JOHN W.**: Pvt./Corp. Enl. on ?. WIA on 6/22/64 in left hand, then age 20. In hosp. 6-9/64. Paid $48 on 7/22/64. Pres. on 10/31/64, 12/31/64 and 2/28/65 rolls. Surrendered as corp. at Appomattox C.H. on 4/9/65.

**FORBES, JOSEPH HARRIS**: 4th Sgt., Enl. on 6/27/61 at Fredericksburg. Pres. on 10/31/61, 12/31/61 and 2/62 rolls. on sick furlough on 10/22/62 as 3rd Sgt. Res. of Aquaser, Prince George's Co., Md.

**FORBUS, HENRY MARSHALL**: Pvt. Enl. on 6/27/61 at Fredericksburg. Pres. on 10/31/61, 12/31/61, 2/62 and 8/31/64. Discharged by writ of habeas corpus per 10/31/64 roll. Also served in the Hampton Legion Light Artillery. Res. of Aquaser, Prince George's Co., Md.

**FORD, JAMES E.**: Pvt. Enl. on 7/23/61 at Richmond. Pres. on 10/31/61, 12/31/61 and 2/62 rolls.

**FOREBARGER, JAMES H.**: Pvt. Enl. on ?. Taken POW at Hagerstown, Md. on 7/12/63. Sent to Elmira, N.Y. Exchanged on 10/29/64 at Point Lookout, Md. May have also served in Co. D, Maryland Regiment or Co. C, 2nd Maryland Cavalry.

**FRANKLIN, JOSEPH T.**: Pvt. Enl. on 10/18/61 at Evansport. Pres. on all rolls through 10/31/64. Discharged by writ of habeas corpus issued by Judge Hallyburton per 12/31/64 roll. Also served in Hampton Legion Light Artillery. Apparently re-enlisted on 1/28/65 at Drewry's Bluff. Pres. on 2/28/65. Surrendered at Appomattox C.H. on 4/9/65. Res. of West River, Anne Arundel Co., Md.

**FREAYER, FREDERICK K. (J.)**: Pvt./Sgt., Enl. on 9/15/62 at Williamsport. Cited for gallantry at Winchester. In Charlottesville, Va. Hosp. on 10/5/63. Pres. on 8/31/64 and 10/31/64 muster rolls. Absent on furlough on 2/28/65 roll. Surrendered at Appomattox C.H. on 4/9/65. Res. of Baltimore, Md.

**FRICK, JAMES**: Pvt. Enl. on ?. Surrendered at Appomattox C.H. on 4/9/65. Res. of Baltimore, Md.

**GAINER, JOHN H.**: Pvt. Enl. on 6/24/62 at Richmond, Va. Paid $26.40 on 9/18/62. Listed as MIA at 2nd Manassas on 8/29/62. On clothing receipt 6/29/64. Pres. on 8/31/64 roll. Deserted at Petersburg, Va. on 10/31/64 muster roll. Took oath at Washington, D.C. on 11/10/64. Res. of Leonardtown, St. Mary's Co., Md.

**GAINES, WILLIAM W.**: Pvt. Enl. on 3/7/62 at Evansport. Paid $82, including $50 re-enlistment bounty, on 3/7/62. Discharged on 6/7/62. Res. of Louisiana.

**GALE, FRANK**: Pvt. Enl. on 7/16/61 at Richmond. Pres. on 10/31/61, 12/31/61 and 2/62 rolls. KIA at 2nd Manassas on 8/29/62. Also served in the Hampton Legion Light Artillery.

**GALE, GEORGE G.**: Pvt. Enl. on 7/16/61 at Richmond. Pres. on 10/31/61, 12/31/61 and 2/62 rolls. Also served in the Hampton Legion Light Artillery.

## Compiled Service Records Roster 65

**GALE, JOHN**: Sgt./1st Lt. Enl. on 7/16/61 at Richmond. Pres. on 10/31/61, 12/31/61 and 2/62 as 5th Sgt. Paid $68 on 7/19/62. WIA at 2nd Manassas on 8/29/62. Paid $99, including $50 re-enlistment bounty on 9/9/62. In Gen. Hosp. #9, Richmond, Va. 9/1-22/62 with typhoid fever, then given 60-day furlough. Paid $200 as 1st Lt. on 4/30/63. Severely WIA in the leg at Hamilton Crossing on 5/3/63. Paid $100 on 6/30/63. In Gen. Hosp. #4, Richmond 9/4-10/263. Paid $100 on 10/31/63. Pres. on 8/31/64 through 2/28/65 rolls as 1st Lt. Surrendered at Appomattox C.H. on 4/9/65 as commander of the 1st Maryland Artillery. Resident of Somerset Co., Md.

**GARDEN, JOHN B.**: Pvt. Enl. on 6/27/61 at Fredericksburg, Va. Absent sick in Fredericksburg, Va. on 10/31/61 and 12/31/61 rolls. In Gen. Hosp. #21, Richmond on 5/2/62. Pres. on 2/62 and 8/31/64 rolls. Discharged by writ of habeas corpus issued by Judge Hallyburton per 10/31/64 roll. Res. of Silversburg, Washington Co., Md.

**GARDINER, F.A.**: Pvt. Enl. on 10/1/64 at Richmond. Pres. through 2/28/65. In Gen Hosp. No. 9, Richmond on 3/14-15/65. Also listed on clothing receipts.

**GARDNER, J. B. W.**: Pvt. Enl. on 7/61. Pres. on 10/31/61, 12/31/61 and 2/62 rolls. In Episcopal Church Hosp. at Williamsburg and Gen. Hosp. #9 Richmond from 4-8/62 with typhoid fever. Paid $48 on 7/18/62. Discharged in 11/63. Applied for position as Clerk in Second Auditor's office on 11/6/63.

**GARDNER, S. J. (T.)**: Pvt. Enl. on ?. Paroled on 4/16/65. Previously served in Holbrook's Independent Maryland Light Artillery. Res. of Charles Co., Md.

**GERMAN, MICHAEL P.**: Pvt. Enl. on 7/6/61 at Rappahannock by Col. Zarona. Pres. on 10/31/61, 12/31/61 and 2/62 rolls. Taken POW at Williamsport, Md. on 7/5/63, sent to Fort Delaware. Transferred to Elmira, N.Y. on 7/22/64, where held until paroled on 5/13/65. Dark hair, blue eyes, 5' 7 1/4". Also served in Hampton Legion Light Artillery. Res. of 168 Howard Street, Baltimore, Md.

**GILPIN, JOHN**: Pvt./Corp. Enl. on 10/9/62 at Bunker Hill. Pres. on all rolls through 2/28/65. Surrendered at Appomattox C.H., Va. on 4/9/65. Res. of Elkton, Cecil Co., Md.

**GLASCOCK, JOHN EDWIN**: Pvt./Sgt./Sgt. Major Enl. on 7/1/61 at Fredericksburg, Va. Pres. as pvt. on 10/31/61 and 12/31/61 rolls. Absent sick on 2/62 roll. Cited for gallantry at Winchester, Va. WIA at Winchester, Va. Sgt. of one of the guns. Applied for a position as Lt. in the Regular Army on 10/31/63, Lt. Col. Andrews endorsed the request. Pres. as Sgt. on 8/31/64 roll. Pres. as Sgt. Major on 10/31/64, 12/31/64 and 2/28/65 rolls. Taken POW at High Bridge, Va. on 4/6/65. Paroled. Black hair, blue eyes, 5'10 ½". Res. of Stafford, Va.

**GLASS, RICHARD C.**: Pvt. Enl. on 7/26/61 at Richmond, Va. Pres. on 10/31/61, 12/31/61 and 2/62 rolls. Paid $98 on 7/17/62. In Gen. Hosp. #9 on 7/62 and Gen. Hosp. #1 in 11/63. Died 11/5/63 of dysentery.

**GOLDSBORO, CHARLES**: Pvt. Enl. on 12/1/64 at Petersburg, Va. Pres. on 12/31/64 and 2/28/65 rolls. Surrendered at Appomattox C.H. on 4/9/65.

**GORMAN, WILLIAM H.**: Pvt. Enl. on 9/1/62 at ____. Cited for gallantry at Winchester, Va. WIA in the thigh at Winchester on 6/15/63. Taken POW at Jordan Springs, Va. on 8/2/63. Leg amputated above the knee. Absent sick at Staunton, Va. Hosp. on all rolls from 8/31/64 to 2/28/65. Paid for service until retired on 10/29/64. Res. of Baltimore, Md.

**GOUGH, JAMES H.**: Pvt. Enl. on 9/30/63 at Richmond, Va. by Capt Brown. Pres. on all rolls through 2/28/65. Paid $48 on 6/18/64. On clothing receipts. Surrendered at Appomattox C.H. on 4/9/65. Res. of Charles Co., Md.

**GUMBY, FRANCIS MARION**: Pvt. Enl. on 7/22/61 at Fredericksburg, Va. In Gen. Hosp. #9 Richmond on 7/64. Pres. on 8/31/64 roll. Discharged by writ of habeas corpus issued by Judge Hallyburton per 10/31/64 roll. Also served in the 10th Va. Inf. Res. of Salisbury, Wicomico Co., Md.

**GUMBY, JOHN W.**: Pvt./Sgt. Enl. on 2/11/62 at Evansport. Pres. as Pvt. on 2/62 roll. Pres. as corp. on 8/31/64 roll. Pres. as sgt. on 10/31/64, 12/31/64 and 2/28/65 rolls. Listed on clothing receipts. Also served in Hampton Legion Light Artillery. Res. of Salisbury, Wicomico Co., Md.

**HALSTEAD, CHARLES**: Pvt. Enl. on 9/5/61 at Evansport. Deserted at Petersburg, Va. on 7/6/64 per 8/31/64 roll.

**HANDY, JOHN C.L**: Pvt. Enl. on 7/23/61 at Richmond, Va. Pres. on 10/31/61, 12/31/61 and 2/62 rolls. In Field Hosp. 3rd Corps Artillery, per 8/31/64 roll. Discharged by writ of habeas corpus issued by Judge Hallyburton on 10/31/64 roll. Also served in Hampton Legion Light Artillery.

**HANNON, LEMUEL M.**: Pvt. Enl. on 7/15/61 at Richmond, Va. on special duty per 10/31/61 roll. Discharged on 11/27/61 on providing E. A. Cawood as substitute. Res. of Homonky, Charles Co., Md.

**HANNON, SHERROD B.**: Pvt. Enl. on 7/15/61 at Richmond, Va. Pres. on all rolls until deserted at Petersburg, Va. in 8/64 per 10/31/64 roll. In Chimborazo Hosp. #5 in 7/64. Res. of Homonky, Charles Co., Md.

**HARPER, WILLIAM H.**: Pvt. Enl. on 3/15/62 at Fredericksburg, Va. Appointed hosp. steward at Atlanta on 3/9/64 per 8/31/64 roll. (S.O. 57) Also served in Hampton Legion Light Artillery. Res. of Upper Marlborough, Prince George's Co., Md.

**HARRIS, CHARLES H.**: Pvt./Corp. Enl. on 7/26/61 at Richmond, Va. Pres. on all muster rolls, except 10/31/64 when sick in Richmond. On clothing receipts. Paid $110 on 12/21/64. Cited for gallantry at Winchester. Also served in the Hampton Legion Light Artillery.

**HARRIS, JOHN F.**: Pvt. Enl. on 12/17/64 at Richmond. Pres. on 12/31/64 and 2/28/65 rolls.

**HARRIS, JOHN G.**: Corp./Sgt. Enl. on 6/27/61 at Fredericksburg, Va. Pres. as corp. on rolls through 2/62. Cited for gallantry at Winchester. On clothing receipts. Paid $51 on 4/22/64 and $48 on 7/22/64. Pres. as sgt. on 8/31/64 roll. Discharged by writ of habeas corpus issued by Judge Hallyburton on 10/31/64 muster roll. Described as having dark hair, grey eyes, 6'1". Also served in Hampton Legion Light Artillery. Res. of Charles Co., Md.

**HARRIS, JOSEPH**: Pvt. Enl. on 9/30./63.at Richmond by Capt. Brown. Absent on sick furlough on 8/31/64. Pres. All rolls through 2/28/65. In hosp. 7-8/64. Res. of Charles Co., Md.

**HATTON, J. W. F. (M.D.)**: Pvt./Corp. Enl. 8/29/61 at Brooks Station. Pres. on 10/31/61, 12/31/61 and 2/62 rolls. WIA on 6/16/62. Paid $98 on 7/18/62. WIA on 6/22/64 in the upper right thigh. Furloughed for 40 days after released from Chimborazo Hosp. #2 on 6/25/64 to 7/24/64. Again in hosp. from 8/30-9/30/64, age 23, occupation student. Discharged by writ of habeas corpus issued by Judge Hallyburton per 10/31/64 roll. Also served in Hampton Legion Light Artillery.

**HATTON, JOSEPH**: Pvt. Enl. 12/7/61 at Evansport. Pres. on 12/31/62 and 2/62 rolls. In Gen. Hosp. #21 in 7/62. AWOL on 8/31/64 roll. Deserted at Petersburg, Va. in 8/64 per 10/31/64 roll. He was a substitute for John T. Davis. Took oath and was released at Harper's Ferry on 9/13/64.

**HATTON, R. H. S.**: Pvt. Enl. 6/27/61 at Fredericksburg. Pres. on rolls through 2/62, then NFR.

**HAWKINS, J. (JOSEPH) S.**: Pvt. Enl. e/1/62 at Americus, GA by Col Cutts. Pres. n 12/31/64 and 2/28/65 rolls. Transferred from Co. A, Sumpter Artillery Battalion (Rhett's 1st S.C. Heavy Artillery) by S.O.242. Surrendered at Appomattox C.H. on 4/9/65.

**HIGGINS, WILLIAM G**: Pvt. Enl. on 9/8/61 at Brooks Station. Pres. on all rolls through 8/31/64. Discharged by writ of habeas corpus issued by Judge Hallyburton per 10/31/64 roll. Also served in the Hampton Legion Light Artillery. Res. of Millersville, Anne Arundel Co., Md.

**HILL, AUGUSTINE (AUGUSTUS)**: Pvt. Enl. on 7/9/61 at Richmond. Paid $15.50 and discharged for disability on 8/6/61.

**HILL, NICHOLAS**: Pvt. Enl. 7/9/61 at Richmond. Paid $31.60 and discharged on 8/13/61. Later served as Chief Commissary, District of Arkansas (Major). Res. of Prince George's Co., Md.

**HILL, WILLIAM J. (I.?)**: Corp./2nd Lt. Enl. on 6/27/61 at Fredericksburg. Pres. on 10/31/61 and 12/31/61 rolls as Corp. Absent detailed to recruiting service per 2/62 roll. Elected 2nd Lt.

on 7/25/62. Pres. on 8/31/64, 12/31/64 and 2/28/65 rolls as 2nd Lt. Absent sick on 10/31/64 roll. Assigned to Maryland Line by order of General Lee in 4/64. In Gen. Hosp. #4 on 11/16/64. Paid $90 on 11/17/64 and again on 12/2/64. Surrendered at Appomattox C. H. on 4/9/65. Also served in Hampton Legion Light Artillery. Res. of Bladensburg, Prince George's Co., Md.

**HILLIARY (HILLEARY), GEORGE H.**: Corp. Enl. on 3/7/62 at Evansport. Court-martialed 12/26/63 (G.O. # 109-6). AWOL per 8/31/64 roll. Deserted at Petersburg during 8/64 per 10/31/64 roll. Also served in Hampton Legion Light Artillery.

**HILLIARY (HILLEARY), WASHINGTON M. (M.D.)**: Pvt. Enl. on 11/28/61 at Evansport. Pres. on 12/31/61 and 2/62 rolls. KIA on 6/26/62. Also served in Hampton Legion Light Artillery.

**HINES (HINDES), J. (JAMES) W.**: Pvt. Enl. at Macon, GA on ?. Transferred from Capt. Epps Company (Johnson Artillery). In Chimborazo Hosp. #2 from 9/23-10/12/64 with gonorrhea. Paid $97.20 on 9/26/62. Pres. on 12/31/64 and 2/28/65 rolls. Surrendered at Appomattox C.H. on 4/9/65.

**HINRICKS (HINNICKS), J. E. C. (T.E.C.)**: Pvt. Enl. on 12/1/61 at Fredericksburg, Va. Discharged on 3/13/63. Paid $317.75. Described as having dark hair, grey eyes, 5'9", occupation student. Res. of Prince George's Co., Md.

**HOLMEAD, CHARLES H.**: Pvt. Enl. 7/5/62 at Richmond, Va. WIA in both thighs at Cold Harbor on 6/3/64. Given 60 day furlough on 7/3/64. Absent in hosp. per 8/31/64 roll. In hosp. on 9/2/64, 10/14/64 and 11/25/64 when surrendered at Appomattox C.H. on 4/9/65. Also served in Co. F, 1st Va. Inf.

**HOPKINS, HENRY**: Pvt. Enl. on ?. In Harrisonburg, Va. hosp. on 3/22/63 with diarrhea, then NFR.

**HOWARD, WASHINGTON**: Pvt. Enl. on 7/15/61 at Richmond, Va. Pres. on 10/31/61, 12/31/61 and 2/62 rolls. Taken POW at Front Royal, Va. on 7/23/63, sent to Old Capitol Prison and held there until released on oath on 9/23/63, then 5'8", black hair, hazel eyes. Also served in Hampton Legion Light Artillery. Res. of Charles Co., Md.

**HOWELL, GUSTAVUS**: Pvt. Enl. on 6/27/61 at Fredericksburg, Va. Pres. on 10/31/61, 12/31/61 and 2/62 rolls. In Episcopal Church Hosp. at Williamsburg, Va. from 4/26/62 to 6/28/62 and in General Hosp. #21 in Richmond, Va. Paid $129 on 7/15/62. Given disability discharge on 7/16/62, then age 25, blue eyes, dark hair, 5'11". Also served in Hampton Legion Light Artillery. Res. of Frederick and Charles Co., Md.

**HUNTER, FREDERICK (M.D.)**: Pvt./Asst. Surgeon. Enl. on 8/7/61 at Richmond, Va. Pres. on 10/31/61 and 12/31/61. Absent on leave in Richmond, Va. on 2/62 roll. Sick at Charlottesville, Va. on 9/22/62. Also served in Pettigrew's Light Artillery.

**HURRY, JOHN C.**: Pvt. Enl. on 10/6/62 at Bunker Hill. Pres. on 8/31/64. Deserted while on furlough on 10/31/64 roll. Also listed on clothing receipts.

**JENKINS, GEORGE TAYLOR, JR.**: Pvt. Transferred from Fort Marion S.C. Artillery. Paid $24 on 3/9/64. Paid $60 on 8/3/64. Detailed to serve as a clerk in Engineer's office after 60 days in hosp. Deserted from Gen. Hosp. #9 on 9/8/64. on clothing receipts. on hosp. rolls with dysentery and debility. Also served in Holbrook's Maryland Light Artillery. Took oath of allegiance on 5/1/65 at Staunton, Va., then age 26, 5'6", brown hair, hazel eyes. Res. of Baltimore, Md.

**JENKINS, JOHN (B. OR E.?)**: Pvt. Enl. on 7/21/64 at Richmond, Va. Pres. on 8/31/64, 10/31/64, 12/31/64 and 2/28/65 rolls. on clothing receipts. Surrendered at Appomattox C.H., Va. on 4/9/65. Also served in Co. I, 1st Maryland Infantry. Res. of Prince George's Co., Md.

**JENKINS, LOUIS WILLIAM**: Pvt. Enl. on 6/27/61 at Fredericksburg, Va. Pres. on 10/31/61, 12/31/61 and 2/62 rolls. AWOL on 8/31/64 roll. Discharged by writ of habeas corpus issued by Judge Hallyburton per 10/31/64 roll. Also served in Hampton Legion Light Artillery. Res. of Baltimore.

**JENKINS, THEODORE ROBERT J**: Corp. Enl. on 7/19/61 at Richmond, Va. Pres. on 10/31/61. 12/31/61 and 2/62 rolls. Also served in Hampton Legion Light Artillery. Transferred from Co. B., 21st Va. Inf. by S.O. No. 225. Res. of Laurel, Prince George's, Md.

Compiled Service Records Roster 71

**JENKINS, WILLIAM KENNEDY**: Pvt. Enl. on 7/1/62 at Richmond, Va. WIA in back on 8/29/62 at 2nd Manassas. WIA in left leg at Warrenton on 10/20/63. Taken POW on 11/7/63, sent to Old Capitol Prison Hosp. Transferred to Point Lookout, Md., where exchanged on 3/4/64. Fractured leg on 5/31/64. Absent sick in Richmond per 8/31/64 and 10/31/64 rolls. Paid $125.13 on 11/1/64. Discharged by Examining Board as unfit for service per 12/31/64 roll. Res. of 204 North Charles St., Baltimore, Md.

**JONES, SAMUEL W.**: Pvt. Enl. on ?. Taken POW on 7/5/63 at Williamsport, Md. Sent to Fort Delaware where held until discharged on 9/16/63, then NFR. May have also served in 3rd Maryland Light Artillery. Res. of Annapolis, Anne Arundel Co., Md.

**KOESTER, LEWIS H.**: Pvt. Enl. on 10/21/62 at Bunker Hill. Pres. on 8/31/64, 10/31/64, 21/31/64 and 2/28/65 rolls. Surrendered at Appomattox C.H. on 4/9/65. Res. of Johnsonville, Frederick Co., Md.

**KOONS, ABRAHAM**: Pvt., Enl. on 7/16/61 at Richmond, Va. Pres. on 10/31/61, 12/31/61 and 2/62 rolls. Also served in Hampton Legion Light Artillery. Res. of Westminster, Carroll Co., Md. MLCSH.

**LANGSDALE, HENRY J.**: Pvt./Sgt. Enl. on 8/26/62 at Dranesville, Va. Cited for gallantry at Winchester, Va. Absent on furlough of indulgence per 8/31/64 roll. Pres. on 10/31/64, 12/31/64 and 2/28/65 rolls as Sgt. Surrendered at Appomattox C.R. on 4/9/65 as QM Sgt. Res. of Quantico, Stafford Co., Va. or Somerset Co., Md.

**LEE, J.C.**: Pvt. Enl. on 6/27/61 at Richmond, Va. Pres. on 10/31/61, 12/31/61 and 2/62 rolls. Paid $48 on 7/18/62, then NFR. Also sent to serve in Hampton Legion Light Artillery, but was sent back sick.

**LEE, RICHARD HENRY**: Pvt. Enl. on 7/17/61 at Richmond, Va. Pres. on 10/31/61, 12/31/61 and 2/62 rolls. Taken POW on 9/62 at Frederick Md. and paroled. In Gen. Hosp. #26 on 2/25/63 and on clothing receipt. Paid $188.38 on 4/24/63, paid $24 on 5/6/63, $36 on 4/22/64. AWOL per 8/31/64 roll. Deserted at Petersburg, Va.

during 8/64 per 10/31/64 roll. Taken POW at Hagerstown, Md. on 8/5/64, sent to Fort Delaware, where held until released on oath. Described as age 25, 5'7", blue eyes, brown hair. Also served in Hampton Legion Light Artillery. Res. of Baltimore Co., Md.

**LITCHFIELD, C.W., Jr.**: Pvt. Enl. on ?. Took oath on 5/9/65, described as 5'10", dark hair, hazel eyes. Res. of Northumberland Co., Va.

**LLOYD, DANIEL, Jr.**: Pvt. Enl. on 7/26/61 at Richmond, Va. Pres. on 10/31/61, 12/31/61, 2/62 and 8/31/64 rolls. Discharged by writ of habeas corpus issued by Judge Hallyburton per 10/31/64 roll. Res. of Cambridge, Dorchester Co., Md. Also shown as a resident of Talbot Co., Md.

**LOVELY, JOHN EMMANUEL (MANUEL)**: Pvt. Enl. on 5/30/62 at Richmond, Va. Taken POW at Winchester, Va. on 12/2/62. Paroled on 12/4/62. Paid $100. May have also served in Co. A, 1st Maryland Infantry. Res. of Frederick Co., Md.

**MACKENHEIMER, C. PAGE**: Pvt. Enl. on 7/9/61 at Fredericksburg, Va. Absent sick on 10/31/61 roll. Pres. on 12/31/61 and 2/62 roll. Paid $98, including $50 reenlistment bounty on 7/18/62. Became a hosp. steward.

**MAGRUDER, EDWARD W.**: Bugler Enl. on 7/23/61 at Richmond, Va. Pres. on 10/31/61, 12/31/61 and 2/62 rolls. Also served in Hampton Legion Light Artillery. Transferred to Capt. William I. Rasin's Company, Cavalry, Maryland Line on 3/19/63. Res. of Upper Marlboro, Prince George's Co., Md.

**MANN, CHARLES S.**: Pvt. Enl. on 8/15/61 at Richmond, Va. Pres. through 2/62, then NFR.

**MARRIOTT, GEORGE H.**: Pvt. Enl. on 6/27/61 at Fredericksburg, Va. Pres. on 10/31/61, 12/31/61 and 2/62 rolls. Court-martialed on 3/7/64 (G.O. No. 17-10). AWOL on 8/31/64 roll. Deserted from Petersburg during 8/64 per 10/31/64 roll. Also served in Hampton legion Light Artillery. Res. of Savage, Howard Co., Md.

**MAY, WILLIAM H.**: Pvt./Corp./Sgt. Enl. on 9/16/61 at Brooks Station. Pres. on 10/31/61, 12/31/61 and 2/62 rolls as pvt. Cited for

Compiled Service Records Roster 73

gallantry at Winchester as a corp. Pres. on 8/31/64 as sgt. Discharged by writ of habeas corpus issued by Judge Hallyburton per 10/31/64 roll. Also served in Hampton Legion Light Artillery.

**McCLINTOCK, SAMUEL**: Pvt. Enl. on 8/15/61 at Richmond, Va. Pres. on 10/31/61, 12/31/61 and 2/62 rolls. In Chimborazo Hosp. #1 5/28-6/10/62. In Liberty Hosp. 11-12/62 and in Samaritan Hosp. 3-6/63. Paid $121.02 on 8/6/63, after being discharged for disability on 7/25/63. Paid $84 on 5/5/64. Paid $25.56 on 5/26/64. Paid $24 on 6/1/64 and $186 on 6/9/64 for extra duty as clerk at Adjutant and Inspector General's Office during 5/1-31/64.

**McCORMICK, V. N. (H.?)**: Pvt. Enl. on 9/10/62 at Charlottesville, Va. Pres. on 8/31/64, 10/31/64, 12/31/64 and 2/28/65 rolls. Surrendered at Appomattox C.H. on 4/9/65. May have also served in Co. A, 1st Va. Cavalry. Res. of Prince George's Co., Md.

**McGLONE, BARNEY (BERNARD) F.**: Pvt. Enl. on 6/27/61 at Richmond, Va. Pres. on 10/31/61, 12/31/61 and 2/62 rolls. Severely WIA in arms on 8/29/62 at 2nd Manassas. Taken POW and paroled on 11/14/62. Paid $118.52, including $50 bounty on 12/2/62. In Petersburg Hosp. 11/18/62. Deserted from hosp. 12/62 per 10/31/64 roll. Paid $24 on 1/5/63. AWOL on 8/31/64 roll. Also served in Hampton Legion Light Artillery. May have also served in Zarvona's Maryland Zouaves. Res. of Timonium, Baltimore Co., Md.

**McKINNEY, MICHAEL**: Pvt. Enl. on ?., Taken POW as a rebel deserter on 7/2/63. Set to Fort Mifflin, Pa.. Took oath and was released on 11/17/63. Described as having auburn hair, gray eyes, 5'6 ½". Res. of Ky.

**McLAUGHLIN, E. K. EPHRAIM)**: Pvt. Enl. on 8/14/61 at Richmond, Va. Pres. on 10/31/61. Discharged on 12/7/61 upon providing E. R. Berry as a substitute per 12/31/61 roll. Later served as acting Master Mate on C.S.S. *Virginia* "The Merrimack."

**McNAIR, H.**: Sgt. Enl. on ?. Paroled on 4/22/65. Res. of Princess Ann Co., Md.

**McNEAL (McNEIL), CHARLES L.**: Pvt. Enl. on 7/24/61 at Richmond, Va. Pres. on 10/31/61, 12/31/61, 2/62 and 8/31/64 rolls.

Slightly WIA in arm on 8/29/62 at 2nd Manassas and slightly WIA in leg on 5/3/63 at Hamilton Cross, Va. In Howard's Grove and Robertson Hosps., Richmond 5-6/63. Discharged by writ of habeas corpus issued by Judge Hallyburton per 10/31/64 roll. Also served in Hampton Legion Light Artillery.

**McWILLIAMS, J. FRANCIS**: Pvt. Enl. on 6/27/61 at Fredericksburg, Va. Pres. on 10/31/61, 12/31/61, 2/62 and 8/31/64 rolls. Discharged by writ of habeas corpus issued by Judge Hallyburton per 10/31/64 roll. Also served in Hampton Legion Light Artillery.

**MIDDLETON, EDWARD (M.?)**: Pvt. Enl. on 7/27/61 at Richmond, Va. Pres. on 10/31/61, 12/31/61, 2/62 and 8/31/64 rolls. Paid $49 on 9/9/62. Discharged by writ of habeas corpus issued by Judge Hallyburton per 10/31/64 roll. Also served in Hampton Legion Light Artillery.

**MILLER, H. D.**: Pvt. Enl. on 10/9/62 at Bunker Hill, Va. Pres. on 8/31/64, 10/31/64, 12/31/64 and 2/28/65 rolls. Surrendered at Appomattox C.H. on 4/9/65. Res. of Elkton, Cecil Co., Md.

**MITCHELL, JOHN**: Pvt. Enl. on 8/25/63 at Richmond, Va. Pres. on 8/31/64 and 2/28/65 rolls. Absent sick on 10/31/64 and 12/31/64 rolls. Absent in Chimborazo Hosp. #2 from 12/18/64 to 2/11/65 with an ulcer in the groin. Surrendered at Appomattox C.H. on 4/9/65. Res. of Somerset Co., Md.

**MOCKABEE, JOSEPH**: Pvt. Enl. on 9/8/61 at Brooks Station. Pres. on 10/31/61, 12/31/61 and 2/62 rolls. Cited for gallantry at Winchester. Also served in Hampton Legion Light Artillery.

**MONCURE, CHARLES H.**: Pvt. Enl. on 7/1/61 at Fredericksburg, Va. Pres. on 10/31/61, 12/31/61 and 2/62 rolls, then NFR.

**MONCURE, E.C.**: Acting Corp. Enl. on 7/1/61 at Fredericksburg, Va. Absent sick on 10/31/61, 12/31/61 and 2/62 rolls, then NFR.

**MOORE, THOMAS**: Pvt. Enl. on ?. cited for gallantry at Winchester, then NFR.

**MORGAN, THOMAS G.**: Pvt. Enl. on 6/27/61 at Richmond, Va. Pres. on 10/31/61, 12/31/61 and 2/62 rolls. Paid $48 on 7/18/62 and $9 on 9/12/62. In various hosp. fall/winter 1862. AWOL on 8/31/64 roll. Taken POW on 9/27/64 at Baltimore. Sent to Fort Delaware. Released on oath on 5/11/65. Described as 5'4", black hair, hazel eyes. Also served in Hampton Legion Light Artillery. Res. of Leonardstown, St. Mary's Co., Md.

**MUDD, EDWARD M.**: Pvt. Enl. on 5/4/64 at Richmond,Va. Absent sick on 8/31/64 roll. In Robertson Hosp. from 8/10/64 to 9/16/64 with complications from typhoid fever. Pres. on 10/31/64, 12/31/64 and 2/28/65 rolls. Surrendered at Appomattox C.H., Va. on 4/9/65. Res. of Bainbridge, Ga., or Nottingham, Prince George's Co., Md.

**MUSGROVE, THOMAS H**: Pvt. Enl. on 10/9/62 at Bunker Hill, Va. Pres. on 8/31/64 and 10/31/64 rolls. AWOL on 12/31/64 and 2/28/65 rolls.

**NEALE, CHARLES A.**: Pvt. Enl. on 6/27/61 at Richmond, Va. Pres. on 10/31/61, 12/31/61 and 2/62 rolls. In hosp. 10/62. Paid $122.10, including $50 re-enlistment bounty on 10/20/62. Also served in Hampton Legion Light Artillery.

**NELSON, CALEB W.**: Pvt. Enl. on 10/28/64 at Richmond, Va. Pres. on 10/31/64, 12/31/64 and 2/28/65 rolls. Surrendered at Appomattox C.H., Va. on 4/9/65.

**NELSON, FRANCIS FLETCHER**: Pvt. Enl. on 7/23/61 at Richmond, Va. Pres. on 10/31/61, 12/31/61, 2/62 and 8/31/64 rolls. In Chimborazo Hosp. #5 on 5/1/63 to 11/20/63 with gunshot wound in left thigh. Discharged by writ of habeas corpus issued by Judge Hallyburton per 10/31/64 roll. Also served in Hampton Legion Light Artillery. Res. of Snow Hill, Worchester Co., Md. MLCSH.

**OWENS, BENJAMIN W. (WELSH)**: Pvt. Enl. on 6/1/63 at Richmond, Va. Cited for gallantry at Winchester. WIA at Cold Harbor, Va. on 6/2/64. AWOL on 8/31/64 roll. Detailed to provost Marshal's Office, Gordonsville, Va. through 2/28/65 roll. Paroled on 4/20/65. Took oath on 5/9/65. Described as 6', brown hair and hazel eyes. Res. of Anne Arundel Co., Md. MLCSH.

**OWENS, JAMES WILLIAM:** Pvt./Corp. Enl. on 10/26/62 at Bunker Hill. Cited for gallantry at Winchester. In Jordan Springs Hosp. 6/63. Pres. on 8/31/64 roll as pvt., as corp. on 10/31/64, 12/31/64 and 2/28/65 rolls. Surrendered at Appomattox C.H. on 4/9/65. Res. of Bristol, Anne Arundel Co., Md. MLCSH.

**PATTERSON, WILLIAM W.:** Pvt. Enl. on 6/27/61 at Fredericksburg, Va. Pres. on 10/31/61 roll. Deserted 12/7/61 per 12/31/61 roll.

**PEARSON, WALTER H.:** Pvt. Enl. on 6/27/61 at Fredericksburg, Va. Pres. on 10/31/61, 12/31/61 and 2/62 rolls. Deserted while on furlough in 1863 per 10/31/64 roll. Taken POW, sent to Fort McHenry, Md. on 6/11/63 as a suspected spy. Sent to Fort Delaware, then NFR.

**PEASE CHARLES:** Pvt. Enl. on 8/15/61 at Richmond, Va. Pres. on 10/31/61, 12/31/61 and 2/62 rolls. Cited for gallantry at Winchester. Deserted at Petersburg, Va. in 8/64 per 10/31/64 roll.

**PENNINGTON, HENRY C.:** Pvt. Enl. 4/30/63 at Hamilton's Crossing, Va. Given 30-day furlough on 8/23/64 for chronic diarrhea alternating with dysentery. Absent on sick furlough on 8/31/64 roll. Pres. on 10/31/64, 12/31/64 and 2/28/65 rolls. KIA at Sailor's Creek, Va. on 4/6/65. Res. of Baltimore, Md.

**PERRIE, ALBERT W:** Pvt. Enl. on 8/28/61 at Brooks Station, Va. Pres. on 10/31/61, 12/31/61, 2/62 and 8/31/64 rolls. In Chimborazo Hosp. #5 and #9 10-11/63. Deserted in 8/64 at Petersburg, Va. per 10/31/64 roll. Also served in Hampton Legion Light Artillery. Res. of Horse Head, Prince George's Co., Md.

**PERRIE, GEORGE W.:** Pvt. Enl. on 8/28/61 at Brooks Station. Pres. on 10/31/61, 12/31/61 and 2/62 rolls. Paid $100.90 on 9/27/62. Absent in Richmond Hosp. on 8/31/64. Acting Hosp. Steward, Camp Winder, Gen. Hosp., Richmond on 10/4/64. Appointed Steward on 10/29/64. Discharged by writ of habeas corpus issued by Judge Hallyburton per 10/31/64 roll. on hosp. rolls of 10/31/64 and 12/31/64. Given 30 day furlough on 1/17/65.

**PHIPPS, WILLIAM E.:** Pvt./Bugler. Enl. on 10/18/61 at Evansport. Pres. on 10/31/61, 12/31/661, 2/62, 8/31/64 and 10/31/64 rolls. Discharged by writ of habeas corpus in Richmond per 12/31/64 roll. Took oath of allegiance on 7/27/65. Res. of Tracey Landing, Anne Arundel Co., Md.

**PIERCE, RICHARD**: Pvt. Enl. on ?. Took oath at Point Lookout, Md. on 6/16/65. Black hair, blue eyes, 5'9 5/8". Res. of Baltimore, Md.

**POLLITE (POLLITTE), NEHEMIAH**: Pvt. Enl. on 8/13/61 at Richmond, Va. Pres. on rolls through 2/62. KIA on 5/3/63 at 2nd Battle of Fredericksburg. Res. of Princess Anne, Somerset Co., Md.

**PRICE, ADRIAN D.**: Corp.?. Enl. on ?. Taken POW on 7/5/62 at Harrison Landing, Va. Age 24, 5'7", black hair, grey eyes. Sent to Fort Delaware on 7/15/62. on Steamer Katskill 8/5/62, exchanged same date. Died in Gen. Hosp #6 on 10/20/62 of gastritis. Also served in 21st Va. Inf.

**QUINN, JOSEPH P**: Sgt./1st Lt. Enl. on ?. Taken POW on 6/26/62 at Harpers Ferry, WV. Paroled at Johnson's Island, Ohio on 3/14/65. Sent to Point Lookout, Md. for exchange. May have also served with Zarvona's Maryland Zouaves. Res. of Baltimore, Md.

**RANSOM, RICHARD T.**: Pvt. Enl. on 8/9/61 at Brooks Station. Pres. on 10/31/61, 12/31/61, 2/62 and 8/31/64 rolls. Cited for gallantry at Winchester. Discharged by writ of habeas corpus issued by Judge Hallyburton per 10/31/64 roll. Res. of West River, Anne Arundel Co., Md.

**RIDDLE, CHARLES**: Pvt. Enl. on 7/3/61 at Fredericksburg, Va. Pres. on 10/31/61, 12/31/61 and 2/62 rolls. Detailed as teamster from 10/17-11/5/61. AWOL on 8/31/64 roll. Deserted from Petersburg, Va. during 8/64 per 10/31/64 roll. In Gen. Hosp. #8 Richmond, Va. and discharged 8/6/62. Res. of Charles Co., Md.

**RIDGEWAY, MORDICAI**: Pvt. Enl. on ?. Taken POW. Paroled at Jordan Springs, Va. on 8/2/63, then NFR.

**RIDING, JOHN**: Pvt., NFR.

**ROBEY, WILLIAM T.**: Pvt. Enl. on 6/27/61 at Fredericksburg, Va. Pres. through 2/62 roll. KIA on 5/3/63 at Battle of 2nd Fredericksburg, Va.

**ROBINSON, GEORGE W.**: Pvt./Sgt. Enl. on 5/21/63 at Bowling Green, Va. Taken POW at Fredericksburg, Va. on 5/3/63. In Robertson Hosp., Richmond, Va. 8-9/63. WIA at Petersburg, Va. 7/30/64. In Robertson Hosp. during April, May, September to November 1864. Pres. on 12/31/64 roll. on sick furlough on 2/28/65 roll. Paroled at Farmville, Va. late April 1865. Res. of Baltimore, Md.

**RYE, JOHN M**: Pvt. Enl. on 9/7/61 at Brooks Station, Va. Pres. on 10/31/61, 12/31/61 and 2/62 rolls. Deserted from Petersburg, Va. during 8/64 per 10/31/64 roll. Also served in Hampton Legion Light Artillery.

**SANFORD, EDWARD**: Pvt. Enl. on 8/15/61 at Richmond, Va. Pres. on 10/31/61, 12/31/61 and 2/62 rolls. WIA on 6/30/62. Paid $48 on 7/18/62. Also served in Hampton Legion Light Artillery.

**SCHARF, JONATHAN THOMAS**: Pvt. Enl. 8/15/61 at Richmond, Va. Pres. on 10/31/61, 12/31/61 and 2/62 rolls. WIA in leg at Fredericksburg on 5/3/62. Transferred to C.S. navy and served aboard C.S.S. *Patrick Henry* on 6/24/63. Paid $75.28 on 12/15/63. Memoirs of service with the First Maryland Artillery were published in 1992. Author and editor postwar. Wrote *Confederate States Navy*, published by Rogers and Sherwood, New York in 1887; a three-volume *History of Maryland*, published by Tradition Press, Hatboro, Pennsylvania in 1879; and a *History of Western Maryland* in two volumes, published by Everts, Philadelphia Pennsylvania in 1882. Res. of Baltimore, Md.

**SCOTT, GEORGE F**: Corp. Enl. on 7/16/61 at Richmond, Va. Pres. on 10/31/61, 12/31/61 and 2/62 rolls. KIA at Mine Run on 11/27/63. Also served in Hampton Legion Light Artillery.

**SCOTT, THOMAS H.**: Pvt. Enl. 7/16/63 at Richmond, Va. Pres. on all extant rolls through 2/28/65, as well as clothing receipts. Paid $24 on 3/14/64. Probably surrendered at Appomattox C.H. on 4/9/65. Res. of Port Tobacco, Charles Co., Md.

**SERGEANT, HARRY O. C. G.**: Pvt. Enl. on 8/16/61 at Brooks Station, Va. Pres. on 10/31/61, 12/31/61, 2/62 and 8/31/64. Discharged by writ of habeas corpus issued by judge Hallyburton per 10/31/64 roll. Res. of Baltimore, Md. MLCSH.

**SHINBURNE, WILLIAM L**: Pvt. Enl. on 7/26/62 at Gordonsville, Va. Taken POW at Fredericksburg, Va. on 3/2/63. Sent to Fort Delaware, paroled and exchanged shortly thereafter. Cited for gallantry at Winchester. Court-martialed G.O. 17-10, on March 7, 1864. AWOL on 8/31/64. Discharged by writ of habeas corpus issued by Judge Hallyburton per 10/31/64 roll.

**SHUSTER, JOHN M.**: Pvt./Sgt. Enl. on 7/7/61 at Fredericksburg, Va. Pres. on all rolls through 8/31/64. In Gen. Hosp. #9 and the Robertson Hosp. at Richmond as a corp. on 3/10-11/63. Discharged by writ of habeas corpus, issued by Judge Hallyburton per 10/31/64 roll. Took oath as sgt. on 5/15/65. Also served in the Hampton Legion Light Artillery. Res. of Prince George's Co., Md.

**SINDALL, HENRY S.**: Pvt. Enl. on 6/27/61 at Richmond, Va. Pres. on 10/31/61 roll. Absent, detailed at General French's Headquarters on 12/31/61 and 2/62 rolls, then NFR.

**SLATER, WILLIAM J.**: Pvt. Enl. on 6/27/61 at Richmond, Va. Pres. on 10/31/61, 12/31/61 and 2/62 rolls. Also served in Hampton Legion Light Artillery.

**SLEMAKER, JUNIUS**: Pvt. Enl. on ?. Pres. on 10/31/61, 12/31/61 and 2/62 rolls. WIA on 6/30/62. Paid $48 on 7/19/62. In Hosp. #8 and #16 10/13/62 and 11/20/62. Detailed on 9/17/63, (S.O. 221/18); again on 11/18/63 (S.O. 274/16) and 2/18/64 (S.O. 41/19). In Danville, Va. Gen. Hosp. from 4/21/63 to 7/12/63, the furloughed. Detailed to Manchester Woolen Mill, Va. Found to be unfit for field duty on 2/17/64. Also served in Hampton Legion Light Artillery.

**SLOAN, EDWARD O**: Pvt. Enl. on 6/27/61 at Fredericksburg, Va. Pres. on 10/31/61, 12/31/61 and 2/62 rolls. Sprained foot 11/62, admitted to Gen. Hosp. #8. Paid $98 on 7/15/62, including $50 reenlistment bounty. In Gen. Hosps. #8 and #26 during 1-2/63. Found to be incapable of field service on 2/20/63. Paid $22.40 on 3/23/63. Discharged on 2/24/63, then 25 years old, 5'9", dark eyes, auburn hair, occupation clerk.

**SMITH, K.B.**: Pvt. Enl. on 5/15/61 at Culpeper C.H., Va. Transferred from 30th Va. Inf.

**SMITH, P.D.**: Pvt. Enl. on ?. In Gen. Hosp. #9 on 3/22-23/65. Surrendered at Appomattox C.H. 4/9/65.

**SNOWDEN, DeWILTON**: 1st Sgt. Enl. on 7/9/61 at Richmond, Va. Pres. on 10/31/61. Absent assisting at hosp. per 12/31/61 roll. Absent detailed as asst. surgeon at Dumfries Hosp. per 2/62 roll.

**SOMERS, SAMUEL**: Pvt. (Machinist) Enl. on 7/6/61 at Tappannock, Va. by Col. Zarona. Pres. on 10/31/61, 12/31/61 and 2/62 rolls. Paid on 5/15/63.

**STIDHAM, RICHARD**: Pvt. Enl. 8/15/61 at Richmond, Va. Pres. on 10/31/61, 12/31/61 and 2/62 rolls. Severely WIA in the head on 5/3/63 at Hamilton Crossing. In Robertson Hosp. 5/6/63, then NFR. Also served in Hampton Legion Light Artillery.

**STINCHCOMB, JOSEPH E.**: Pvt. Enl. on 7/16/61 at Richmond. Pres. on 10/31/61, 12/31/61 and 2/62 rolls. Given 30-day furlough on 11/14/63. Transferred to Gen. Hosp. #9 on 12/16/63. In Chimborazo Hosp. #4 on 2/1/64, with wound in left ankle, leg ulcerated. Detailed to hosp. on 2/16/64 per S.O. 45/17. In Gen. Hosp. #4 on 8/1/64. Detailed by S. O. at C. S. Arsenal at Richmond, Va. per 8/31/64. Paid $156.13 on 4/5/64. Discharged by writ of habeas corpus issued by Judge Hallyburton per 10/31/64 roll. Also served in Hampton Legion Light Artillery.

**STINE, JOSEPH A.**: Pvt. Enl. on 8/18/61 at Richmond, Va. Pres. on extant rolls through 2/62, then NFR.

**STONESTREET, J. HARRIS**: Sgt./2nd Lt. Enl. on 6/27/61 at Fredericksburg, Va. Pres. as 3rd sgt. on 10/31/61, 12/31/61 and 2/62. Elected 2nd Lt. on 7/25/62. In Charlottesville, Va. Hosp. on 8/11-30/62 with a chest wound. Court-martialed, G.O. 109-6 on 12/26/63. Pres. on all other extant rolls through 2/28/65 as 2nd Lt. Surrendered at Appomattox C.H. on 4/9/65. Also served in Hampton Legion Light Artillery. Res. of Port Tobacco, Charles Co., Md.

**STUMP, GEORGE C.**: Pvt. Enl. on ?. Taken POW on 5/19/63 in Baltimore, Md. Sent to Fort McHenry, Md. on 11/12/63. Released on 5/9/65 per S. O. 89. His case was reviewed by the U. S. Secretary of War. He claimed he was discharged in 7/1862. Described as 5'8", light hair, hazel eyes. Res. of Baltimore Md.

**SUNDERLAND, THOMAS**: Pvt. Enl. on 9/8/61 at Brooks Station. Pres. on all extant rolls through 8/31/64. WIA on 6/30/62. Paid $48 on 7/18/62. Paid $99 on 9/9/62, including $50 re-enlistment bounty. Assigned to extra duty as teamster 1/1-4/22/64. Discharged by writ of habeas corpus issued by Judge Hallyburton. Also served in Hampton Legion Light Artillery.

**SUTHERLAND, L. M.**: Pvt. Enl. 5/21/61 at Alexandria, Va. Pres. on 8/31/64 roll. Discharged by writ of habeas corpus issued by Judge Hallyburton on 10/31/64 roll. On clothing receipt.

**THOMAS, JOHN R.**: Pvt. Enl. on 5/22/64 at Richmond, Va. WIA, flesh wound in face, on 5/31/64. $50 re-enlistment bounty paid on 9/29/64. Pres. on 10/31/64 and 12/31/64 rolls. Absent sick in a Richmond Hosp. on 8/31/64 and 2/28/85 rolls. Paroled on 4/16/65.

**THOMAS, SAMUEL S.**: Pvt. Enl. on 7/25/61 at Richmond, Va. Pres. on 10/31/61, 12/31/61 and 2/62 rolls. Taken POW at Frederick, Md. on 10/3/62. Paroled on 10/15/62. Paid $140, including $50 reenlistment bounty on 12/8/62. Cited for gallantry at Winchester, Va. WIA in face on 6/4/64 at Cold Harbor, Va. Clothing receipts. Absent sick in hosp. On 8/31/64 roll when paid $67.13. Paid $25 on 9/29/64. Discharged by writ of habeas corpus issued by Judge Hallyburton per 10/31/64 roll. Paroled on 4/30/65. Also served in Hampton Legion Light Artillery. Res. of Frederick, Md.

**THOMPSON, C. GRATIO (GRATIOT)**: 2nd Sgt. Enl. on 7/6/61 at Richmond, Va. Pres. on 10/31/61, 12/31/61 and 2/62 rolls as 2nd sgt. Paid $105 on 8/15/62. In Charlottesville Hosp. from 8/27/62 to 1/20/63 for debility. Assigned to duty as acting 2nd lt. and ordnance officer of McGowan's Brigade, A.P. Hill's Division. Also served in Hampton Legion Light Artillery.

**THOMPSON, SAMUEL**: Pvt./Corp. Enl. on 8/14/61 at Richmond, Va. Pres. on 10/31/61, 12/31/61 and 2/62 rolls. Cited for gallantry at Winchester, Va. Also served in Hampton Legion Light Artillery.

**TOLSON, ALBERT**: Pvt. Enl. on 10/6/62 at Bunker Hill. In Charlottesville, Hosp. from 9/25-10/26/61. Severely WIA in arm and shoulder on 5/3/63 at Hamilton Crossing. In Robertson Hosp. 5/6-9/15/63. Paid $24 on 9/3/63. Attached to Charlotte, N. C. Hosp. as courier on 10/31/63. AWOL on 8/31/64. Deserted from Petersburg during 8/64 per 10/31/64 roll. Actually taken POW on 8/27/64 at Washington, D.C. Sent to Fort Warren, Boston Harbor, Boston, MA. His wife Mary applied for his release. Handwritten oath of allegiance dated 8/20/64 says he was from Prince George's Co., Md. Released on oath on 6/2/65. Height given as 5'7 ½". Previously served in Beauregard Rifles.

**TRUMBLE, JOHN D.**: Pvt. Enl. on 12/30/61 at Evansport. Pres. on 12/31/61 and 2/62 rolls. Paid $24 on 3/18/63. Also served in Hampton Legion Light Artillery.

**TUCKER, FRANK E.** Pvt. Enl. on 6/1564. Died on 8/8/64 in Richmond of typhoid fever.

**TUCKER, JOHN W.**: Pvt. Enl. on 6/27/61 at Fredericksburg, Va. Pres. on extant rolls through 2/62. Absent sick in a Richmond Hosp. on 8/31/64 roll. Discharged by writ of habeas corpus issued by Judge Hallyburton per 10/31/64 roll. In Chimborazo Hosps. #2 and #4, Richmond in June, August, September, and October 1864 with typhoid fever and complications. Paid $48 on 9/3/64. Paid $67.13 on 9/28/64. Also served in Hampton Legion Light Artillery. From Caroline Co., Va.

**TYLER, GRAFTON, Jr.**: Pvt. Enl. on 9/16/61 at Brooks Station. Pres. on 10/31/61, 12/31/61 and 2/62 rolls. Discharged on 2/28/63. Also served in Hampton Legion Light Artillery.

**WADE, JOHN R.**: Pvt. Enl. on 7/15/61 at Richmond, Va. Pres. on 10/31/61, 12/31/61 and 2/62 rolls. In Hosp. #13 at Richmond from 12/4-23/62 with intermittent fever. Deserted from Petersburg, Va. per 10/31/64 roll. Also served in Hampton Legion Light Artillery. Res. of Port Tobacco, Charles Co., Md.

**WALLACK, RICHARD L.**: Pvt. Enl. on 11/1/63 at Pisgah. Paid $68.40 on 1/6/64. Absent sick on 8/31/64. Pres. on 10/31/64 roll. AWOL on 12/31/64 roll. Pres. on 2/28/65. Also listed on clothing receipts.

**WALSCH (WALSH), DANIEL**: Pvt. Enl. on ?. Surrendered at Appomattox C.H. on 4/9/65. Res. of Baltimore, Md.

**WARRING (WARING), JOHN L.**: Pvt. Enl. on 6/27/61 at Fredericksburg, Va. Pres. on 10/31/61, 12/31/61 and 2/62 rolls. In Charlottesville, Va. Hosp. 8/11-23/62 with a contusion. Also served in Hampton Legion Light Artillery. Surrendered and took oath on 5/19/65.

**WATERS, JAMES F.**: Pvt. Enl. on 8/15/61 at Richmond, Va. Pres. on 10/31/61, 12/31/61 and 2/62 rolls. KIA on 8/29/62 at 2nd Manassas. Also served in Hampton Legion Light Artillery.

**WATKINS, M. J.**: Rank ?. Political prisoner, 4/7/65 for murder and as a guerrilla. Released from jail on 6/22/65.

**WEBB, LEWIS S.**: Pvt. Enl. on 9/7/62 at Frederick, Md. Pres. on 8/31/64, 10/31/64, 12/31/64, 2//8/65 rolls. Surrendered at Appomattox C.H. on 4/9/65. Res. of Montgomery Co., Md.

**WEEMS. JAMES M**. Pvt. Enl. on 10/18/61 at Evansport. Pres. on 10/31/61, 12/31/61, 2/62, 8/31/64 and 2/28/65 rolls. Discharged by writ of habeas corpus issued by Judge Hallyburton per 10/31/64 roll. Reenlisted. Surrendered at Appomattox C.H., Va. on 4/9/65. Also served in Hampton Legion Light Artillery. Res. of Prince Frederick, Md.

**WILLIAMS, THOMAS**: Pvt. Enl. on 7/22/61. Pres. on 8/31/64 roll. Discharged by writ of habeas corpus issued by Judge Hallyburton per 10/31/64 roll.

**WILLIAMSON, HUGH**: Pvt. Enl. on ?. Discharged on 3/9/63. Paid $27.60.

**WILLS, WILLIAM A.**: Pvt. Enl. on 8/16/61 at Richmond. Pres. on 10/31/61, 12/31/61 and 2/62 rolls. Paid $151.35, including $50 re-enlistment bounty on 10/14/62. Discharged as unfit for debility. Age 50, hazel eyes, grey hair. Also served in Hampton Legion Light Artillery.

**WILSON, A. M.**: Pvt. Enl. on 10/1/62 at Bunker Hill. AWOL on 8/31/64. Deserted from Petersburg in 8/64 per 10/31/64 roll.

First Maryland Artillery

**WILSON, GEORGE W.**: Pvt. Enl. on 10/12/62 at Bunker Hill. In Robertson Hosp. 6/64. Paid $29.10 on 8/15/64. Paid $36 on 9/5/64. Pres. on 8/31/64, 10/31/64 and 2/28/65 rolls, but was AWOL on 12/31/64. Paroled at Farmville, Va. 4/65.

**WILSON, JOHN F.**: Pvt. Enl. on 2/26/63 at Bowling Green. Absent sick on 8/31/64 roll. Taken POW on 10/20/64 or 11/15/64, both Federal records.

**WILSON, M**: Pvt. Enl. on 11/20/64 at Petersburg, Va. Pres. on 12/31/64 and 2/28/65 rolls.

**WILSON, W. W.**: Pvt. Enl. on 10/26/62 at Bunker Hill, Va. In Chimborazo Hosp. #5, Richmond from 4/29 to 5/17/63 with chronic dysentery. Cited for gallantry at Winchester. Paid $24 on 3/31/64. Absent sick on 8/31/64. Pres. on 10/31/64, 12/31/64 and 2/28/65 rolls.

**WILSON, WILLIAM**: Pvt. Enl. on 10/23/64 at Petersburg, Va. Pres. on all extant rolls for time of service. Surrendered at Appomattox C.H. on 4/9/65. Res. of Annapolis, Md.

**WINGATE, THOMAS C.**: Pvt. Enl. on 10/25/62 at Bunker Hill. Pres. on 8/31/64, 10/31/64 and 12/31/64 rolls. AWOL on 2/28/65 roll. Listed on clothing receipts.

**WINTERS, HENRY S.**: Pvt. Enl. on 7/19/61 at Richmond, Va. Pres. on 10/31/61, 12/31/61 and 2/62 rolls. KIA at Fredericksburg, Va. on 10/8/62.

**WOOTTON, WILLIAM T**: Pvt. Enl. on 7/19/61 at Richmond, Va. Pres. on 10/31/61, 12/31/61 and 2/62 rolls. Assigned to Hampton Legion Light Artillery but sent back sick. Paid $48 on 7/18/62. Paid $82.50, including $50 reenlistment bounty on 10/10/62. Cited for gallantry at Winchester. KIA at Winchester, Va. 6/15/63.

**WORTHINGTON, EUGENE**: Pvt. Enl. on 9/8/61 at Brook's Station. Pres. on all extant must rolls. Surrendered at Appomattox C.H. on 4/9/65. Also served in Hampton Legion Light Artillery. From Prince George's Co., Md.

**YATES, JOHN R.**: Pvt. /Corp. Enl. on 7/7/61 at Fredericksburg, Va. Pres. on 10/31/61, 12/31/61, 2/62 rolls. Cited for gallantry at Winchester. Absent sick on 8/31/61 roll. Discharged by writ of habeas corpus issued by Judge Hallyburton per 10/31/64 roll. Listed on clothing receipts. Also served in Hampton Legion Light Artillery.

**YOUNG, ALEXANDER**: Pvt./Sgt. Enl. on 7/26/61 at Richmond, Va. Pres. on 10/31/61, 12/31/61 and 2/62 rolls. Severely WIA in the breast on 6/3/63 at Hamilton Crossing. WIA in left shoulder on 5/3/64 at Cold Harbor. Admitted to Chimborazo Hosp. #5. May have been detailed to procure horses in N. C. in summer of 1864. Also served in Hampton Legion Light Artillery. Res. of Washington, D.C. or Frederick Co., Md.

# Bibliography

## Public Documents

Compiled Service Records of Confederate Soldiers Who Served in Organizations From the State of Maryland. Record Group 109, Microcopy 321, Rolls 9-10, National Archives, Washington, D.C.

Confederate Adjutant and Inspector General's Office, Letters Received, Record Group 109, National Archives, Washington, D.C.

## Manuscripts

Albert, Al James. Unpublished Memoir. Courtesy of the Maryland Historical Society, Baltimore, Maryland.

## Periodicals

*Confederate Veteran*. Nashville, Tennessee, 1892-1932.
*Southern Historical Society Papers*. Richmond, Virginia.

## Published Sources

Edward, Abial Hall (edited by Beverly Hayes Kallgren and James L. Crouthamel). *Dear Friend Anna: The Civil War Letters of a Common Soldier from Maine*. Orono, Maine: University of Maine Press, 1992.

Goldsborough, W. W. *The Maryland Line in the Confederate Army*. Baltimore, Maryland: Guggenheimer,Weil and Co., 1900.

Hartzler, Daniel D. *A Band of Brothers: Photographic Epilogue to Marylanders in the Confederacy*. Bookcrafters, 1992.

Hartzler, Daniel D. *Marylanders in the Confederacy*. Silver Spring, Maryland: Family Line Publications, 1986.

Huntsberry, Thomas V. and Joanne M. *Maryland in the Civil War: The South*. Baltimore, Maryland: J. Mart Publishers, 1985.

Kelly, Tom (ed.) *The Personal Memoirs of Jonathan Thomas Scharf of the First Maryland Artillery*. Baltimore, Maryland: Butternut and Blue, 1992.

Mitchell, Joseph B. *Decisive Battles of the Civil War*. New York: Fawcett Premier, 1955.

Thomas, Dean S. *Cannons: An Introduction to Civil War Artillery*. Gettysburg, Pennsylvania: Thomas Publications, 1985.

U.S. War Department. *The War of the Rebellion: A Compilation of the Official Records of the Union and Confederate Armies*. 128 Volumes. Washington, D.C.: Government Printing Office, 1880-1901.

Wise, Jennings. *The Long Arm of Lee: The Artillery of the Army of Northern Virginia*. Lincoln: University of Nebraska, 1990.

# SECOND MARYLAND ARTILLERY

## Chapter I

## Background

The Second Maryland, or Baltimore Light Artillery was organized in September 1861. Captain John Bowyer Brockenborough commanded the unit until late 1862 and the unit was commanded by Captain William H. Griffin until nearly the end of the war. The battery served primarily with the Army of Northern Virginia, often with cavalry units. The Baltimore Artillery also served as part of the Maryland Line.

There are six extant muster rolls for the Second Maryland Artillery, as follows:

September 17 to October 31, 1861, when located in camp near Centerville, Virginia;

November and December 1861, when no location was given;

December 1862 when located at New Market, Virginia;

To April 1, 1864 when located at Hanover Junction, Virginia;

February 29 to August 31, 1864 when located at Salem Church, Virginia; and

September and October 1864 when posted near Springhill, Virginia.[1]

## Chapter II

## Organization and Training

The Baltimore Light Artillery was mustered into Confederate service in September 1861. On September 17, 1861, it went into camp near Centerville, Virginia. On December 19, 1861, it was designated the Second Maryland Artillery. The initial officers and staff were as follows:

>Captain John Bowyer Brockenborough
>First Lieutenant William Hunter Griffin
>Second Lieutenant William Bennett Bean
>Third Lieutenant James T. Wilhelm

Captain Brockenborough commanded the battery until the last part of 1862. He was promoted to major and later served as acting chief of artillery, First Division, Jackson's Corps and Ordnance Officer on Jackson's staff. W. Hunter Griffin commanded the unit until he was captured at the Battle of Yellow Tavern, on May 11, 1864. Lieutenant Bean apparently commanded the unit until mid-1864. He was succeeded by Lieutenants John McNulty and John W. Goodman. John Goodman replaced McNulty after the Battle of Woodstock on October 9, 1864. Goodman had been commissioned on July 8, 1863, and was shown as third lieutenant on the April 1, 1864, roll and second lieutenant on remaining rolls.

Non-commissioned officers were:

>1st Sergeant James T. Wilhelm, who was elected third lieutenant on November 31, 1861, and promoted to second lieutenant by December 1862 and taken prisoner of war in June 1863.
>2nd Sergeant George Poindexter
>3rd Sergeant John F. Hayden
>4th Sergeant John Powers

## Second Maryland Artillery

5th Sergeant Daniel Malone

1st Corporal William C. Dunn, later served as captain in Co. E, 37th Battalion Virginia Cavalry.
2nd Corporal Patrick Kirby then James O'Grady.
3rd Corporal Lewis F. Talbot
4th Corporal William H. Kendrick

Bugler Charles S. Evans

Commissary Sergeant James Henry Smith, who later served as Quartermaster Sergeant.
Orderly Sergeant William Y. Glen, then William Wirt Robinson who was assigned to duty as acting second lieutenant on March 22, 1865.
Surgeon J. B. Wortham

Many members of the Second Maryland Artillery later served as officers and non-commissioned officers after initially serving as privates:

Joseph A. Bean, 1st Sergeant (1864)
Charles L. Beneke, Corporal
Willoughby H. Brockenborough, Corporal
John Bunting, 6th Corporal (1864)
Andrew J. Byrne, 5th Sergeant (1861)
Chester Charles Burnett, 6th and 7th Corporal (1864)
Charles Harrison Claiborne, Lieutenant (Company G, First S.C. Infantry)
Lewis Clause, Commissary Sergeant (1863)
William S. Ferry, 4th Sergeant
John W. Goodman, Lieutenant (1863)
Harry Marston, 2nd Sergeant (1864)
S. J. Mattison, Ordnance Sergeant (1864)
George McAlwee, 5th Corporal
Matthew McLoid, 4th Corporal
James S. Morrison, 3rd Sergeant
George W. Pembroke, 3rd Corporal
Chris Poehlman, 8th Corporal (1864)
William Quinn, Corporal (1861)
William Wallace, 1st Corporal/Sergeant

## Organization and Training 95

Many members of the unit had special skills or served on details, as follows:

J. B. Armstrong, painter
Chester Charles Burnett, blacksmith
William Campbell, harness maker/teamster
John a. Coleman, harness maker
Joshua Davis, Jr., bugler (1863)/harness maker
W. A. Davis, ambulance driver (1863)/carpenter
Robert E. Fitzgerald, gas fitter
William H. Gaskins, clerk (1863)
Wellington Graham, teamster (1862)
Joseph a. Greenwell, clerk (1863)
Moses Hottinger, teamster (1862)
Michael Irvin, artificer/blacksmith (1861)
G.P. Isreal, telegraph operator (1864)
William Kelly, artificer/blacksmith (1861)
Lewis W. Knight, M.D.
Adolphus Kuble, hospital steward (1863)
William J. Lucas, M.D.
John S. Lynch, M.D., hospital steward (1863)
C. J. Mathews, sail maker
George McAlwee, iron molder
William F. McAvoy, printer
Michael G. Moran, stonecutter
John F. Mudd, blacksmith (1863)
William E. Naylor, blacksmith
Charles Peak Davis, carpenter
William C. Rogers, sailor
William Rucker, teamster
John F. Schenberger, harness maker (1863)
William P. Smith, nurse
Thomas J. Ward, M.D.
Charles E. Whitlock, shoemaker
James T. Wilhelm, M.D.
W. H. Wood, carpenter
Henry Wysing, teamster (1862)

During the winter of 1861-2, the Baltimore Light Artillery remained in camp near Centerville. The unit was one of six artillery companies directed to report to General Joseph E. Johnston at Manassas, Virginia by Special Order No. 170, October 3, 1861. The Baltimore Light Artillery was assigned to the Fourth Brigade, Second Corps, commanded by Brigadier General Elzey by Special Order No. 543, November 25, 1861. An organization report of January 14, 1862, shows the Baltimore Light Artillery in the Potomac District commanded by General P. G. T. Beauregard, Fourth Division commanded by major General E. Kirby Smith in Elzey's Brigade with the First Maryland Infantry, the Third Tennessee Infantry, the Thirteenth Virginia Infantry and the Sixteenth Virginia Infantry.[2]

## Chapter III

## Into the Breech: 1862

The Baltimore Light Artillery remained at Centerville, when General Johnston moved from the area. In early April, the unit saw its first action. Goldsborough described the action:

> Here about the first of April the enemy for the first time heard the bellowing of their loud-mouthed Blakeleys, which were destined to carry death and destruction into their ranks upon more than one bloody field.
>
> It was a lovely afternoon, and fresh in my memory, that the enemy was observed advancing in force towards the river. Their approach had been long expected, and preparations made to receive them. The Baltimore Light Artillery was posted on the extreme right of General Elzey's Brigade, and supported by the First Maryland Infantry. As the dense masses of the enemy came within range, Brockenborough opened with such accuracy of aim as to attract the attention of Elzey, who upon the spot predicted for them a glorious future. For an hour or two the fight was sharp and severe, and most of the enemy's artillery fire concentrated upon the Maryland battery; but they stood their ground and fought their pieces like veterans of an hundred battles. Late in the evening the enemy retired.
>
> Once or twice after, they advanced in small force towards the river, but Brockenborough was ever ready to receive them, and a shell or two sufficed to drive them back.[3]

On April 19, 1862, the unit left for Gordonsville. Due to the poor condition of roads due to heavy spring rains, the trip took three days and nights, and officers and men worked with the horses when wheels sank deeply into the mud. After a short three or four day rest, the battery marched with the rest of General Ewell's Division to join General Stonewall Jackson's Valley Campaign. The following table and map give an idea of the extent of the battery's participation. The following paragraphs describe what happened in chronological order. For this campaign, Ewell's Division was composed of Elzey's, Taylor's and Trimble's Brigades; the Maryland Line, consisting of the First Maryland Regiment and Brockenborough's battery; and the Second and Sixth Virginia Cavalry.

Colonel Stapleton Crutchfield, Jackson's chief of artillery, described the action of May 23 at Front Royal in his official report:

> After a short time Captain Brockenborough's battery came up, and two of his guns having been planted and opened on the enemy, a brisk cannonade of some ten or fifteen minutes was kept up, with no injury to ourselves and no apparent damage to the enemy. At the end of this time the opposing battery drew off and the enemy began his retreat. Captain Lusk's battery having by this time come up, I took from it two rifled guns and started in pursuit.
>
> About a mile or more from the village the enemy had planted a gun and left a few skirmishers on a ridge commanding the bridge over the river, which they had set on fire. A few shells dispersed them, and the fire being extinguished, the bridge was crossed and the pursuit continued. Owing to the jaded condition of our horses and the rapidity of the enemy's movements our artillery did not overtake them again during the chase, and took no further part in the affair.
>
> Both of the guns of the enemy, with their two caissons, were captured by our cavalry, together with seven battery horses and three sets of artillery harness. The harness was turned over to Captain Cutshaw. One gun and caisson were given to Captain Poague in lieu

of a 4-pounder rifled gun belonging to his battery, and the remaining gun and caisson to Captain Brockenborough, to replace one of his Blakeley 12-pounder guns, which had an assembling-bolt in the cheek broken by the strain in its carriage during the firing. Both the captured pieces were 10-pounder Parrott rifled guns. In this affair our guns were badly served and did no execution.[4]

Major General Ewell with Trimble's Brigade, the First Maryland Regiment, Stewart's Cavalry and the batteries of Brockenborough and Courtney, had reached a position about three miles from Winchester by 10 p.m. on May 24, according to General Jackson's official report. Goldsborough wrote:

> Early on the 25th of May, Jackson's army stood in battle array before Winchester, and the engagement soon began. The Baltimore Light Artillery was stationed on the right, and throughout the fight played with much effect upon the enemy's columns. A few days after, at Bolivar Heights, they were engaged for some hours, and finally drove the Federal infantry and artillery from their strong positions.[5]

During the retreat down the Shenandoah Valley, the battery was detailed to support Ashby's and Steuart's Cavalry. Fighting occurred nearly every day. Goldsborough described some of the action:

> At Fisher's Hill a section under Griffin was entirely surrounded and cut off owing to the bad behavior of Steuart's cavalry, which was supporting it, but the gallant fellow drove his pieces through the ranks of the enemy, and reached the main body in safety.
> 
> At the battle of Harrisonburg it supported [Turner] Ashby in his fight with the Pennsylvania Bucktails, and did good service.
> 
> On the 8th of June the division of Ewell was drawn up in line of battle at Cross Keys to dispute the enemy's advance, whilst Jackson crossed his prisoners

and wagon trains over the Shenandoah at Fort [Port] Republic. The ground for the battle had been selected by General Elzey, by order of General Ewell, and a most judicious selection it was, as the result of the fight proved, and for which General Elzey received the thanks of Ewell in his official report.

The Baltimore Light Artillery held the extreme left, supported by the First Maryland Infantry. Theirs was a most exposed position, and upon which was concentrated the fire of several of the enemy's batteries. All day long the battle lasted, and all day long the little battery continued to hurl its shot and shell into the ranks of the enemy. It was a most unequal contest, but stubbornly they held their ground. Generals Elzey and Steuart, who had remained by and watched the battery with painful interest, were both borne wounded from the field. Upon the behavior of that battery perhaps hung the fate of the day, for we were but a handful holding at bay a mighty army. But calmly the officers and men stood to their guns, and although the enemy essayed more than once to drive them from the position, there they remained until night closed upon the combatants, and Jackson's army was saved from the destruction that seemed so imminent.

As a reward for the gallantry displayed in this fight, General Dick Taylor presented the battery with two of the splendid brass Napoleons which his brigade captured next day at Port Republic. "I want you to have them," he said, "for from what I saw of you yesterday, I know they will be in good hands."[6]

After a rough start, the Baltimore Light Artillery performed very well in the Valley Campaign. Nearly all the officers who commanded units that the battery served under were very complimentary. Major General Ewell wrote that the battery had been "under my observation since the campaign opened, and I can testify to their efficiency on this as on former occasions." Brigadier General Winder wrote, "A section of Brockenbrough's battery joined me just as the retreat commenced and was ably handled."

Colonel Bradley T. Johnson, commander of the Maryland Line, writes, "It is my duty to notice the precision and gallantry with which Captain Brockenborough served his guns." As noted, General Richard Taylor gave the battery two brass Napoleons for the performance in the Battle of Cross Keys.[7]

During the Valley Campaign, the Baltimore Light Artillery lost two of its "loud-mouthed" Blakeley 12-pounder guns. As previously noted, one of these guns was replaced with a 10-pounder Parrott rifled gun because an assembly bolt in the cheek of one of the Blakeleys was broken by the strain on its firing at Front Royal on May 23, 1862.

Colonel Stapleton Crutchfield noted, "In the retreat of Col. Z. T. Conner from Front Royal, the Blakeley gun belonging to Captain Brockenborough's battery was by some means lost." The official return of casualties at the Battle of Cross Keys and the engagement at Port Republic show that the battery had two men killed in action.[8]

After the end of the Valley Campaign, the battery went into camp near Weyer's Cave, about five miles from Port Republic. Here the unit received new harness and fresh horses. The Baltimore Light Artillery had a break in action of about nine days, June 10-18, 1862.

Next came participation in the Seven Days Battles around Richmond. On June 19, 1862, the Baltimore Light Artillery set out for Richmond with the rest of Jackson's troops. For these battles, the battery was still in Ewell's Division, as part of the Maryland Line. In fact, Major General Ewell's Division Artillery consisted of the batteries of Brockenborough, Carrington and Courtney. The first action was skirmishing the night of May 26, 1862, near Gaines' Mill. The Baltimore Light Artillery participated with the following regiments: First Maryland, Sixth Louisiana, Thirteenth Louisiana.

Colonel Stapleton Crutchfield reported on the artillery operations for the next day's battle (Gaines' Mill or Cold Harbor), May 27, 1862.

> About 5 p.m. or perhaps a little later, the batteries of Captains Brockenborough, Carrington and Courtney were ordered in near the left to engage the enemy's guns, then firing heavily on our infantry. They went up in good style and under a hot fire; but so soon as they engaged the batteries of the enemy the fire of the latter

grew wild and did very little damage. Our own practice was good, and our batteries were soon enabled to fire advancing by half to the enemy's rapid retreat. The lateness of the hour, together with the smoke of the battlefield, ignorance of the ground beyond, the jaded condition of the horses, and the fact that the road was so obstructed as to forbid the rest of our artillery from closing up to the front, where alone it could be brought into action, effectually prevented that rapidity of pursuit and concentration of fire which a subsequent acquaintance with the nature of the ground and other circumstances proved would have resulted in extreme loss to and doubtless rout of the enemy.[9]

Goldsborough reported on this battle also, as follows:

The battle here was very unequal, for the enemy had greatly the advantage in artillery and position, and soon succeeded in disabling a number of Jackson's pieces. In a short time the Jeff Davis Mississippi Battery was torn to pieces and the Baltimore Light Artillery ordered to take its place, immediately under the eye of Jackson himself. Gallantly the Marylanders responded to the order, and dashing at a full run across the field, unlimbered and opened fire.

The author was standing close beside General Jackson when the battery went forward, and he shall long remember the look of anxiety with which he watched it, and well he might, for upon the success of that battery much depended. For a while the air was filled with exploding, crashing shells, and the horses and men fell rapidly before that withering fire, which was directed with almost the precision of a rifle shot. Away went a limber chest high in the air, scattering death and destruction around. "We are not close enough," said the brave Brockenborough. "Limber to the front, forward, gallop!" rung out his sharp command, and in an instant the battery was in position at point blank range. Fiercely those guns were then worked, despite the iron hail that plowed up the ground around them, and in a few minutes Brockenborough had the satisfaction of seeing the enemy retire precipitately, leaving the ground covered with dead and dying men and horses, and shattered carriages and dismounted guns. It was French's famous battery they had encountered, but French's no longer, save in name.[10]

Goldsborough's narrative continued, as follows:

On the morning of the 29th, the battery accompanied Ewell's division to Dispatch Station on the York River Railroad, where a few shots were exchanged with the enemy, when Ewell retraced his steps, and moved towards Malvern Hill.

In the afternoon of the 1st of July, the battle of Malvern Hill began, and soon raged fiercely. The enemy had been enabled to reach the heights of Malvern where he posted sixty guns, which swept every foot of ground around. In vain did the heavy masses of infantry rush with desperate valor upon these guns, but it was only to be driven back, leaving the ground covered with heaps of dead and mangled men. In this unequal contest artillery was not available, for not a position was to be had. Two or three times the Baltimore Light Artillery tried it, but was as often compelled to hastily withdraw, and when night ended the conflict, Malvern Hill was not yet won.[11]

According to official reports, the Baltimore Light Artillery had one man killed in action and another wounded at the Battle of Malvern Hill. There are no other reported losses for the unit in the Seven Days Battles. The battery probably participated in skirmishing on July 4, in the woods in front of Westover Church. Colonel Bradley T. Johnson reported that the Maryland Line had some "sharp skirmishing" there at that time.[12]

Next came a chance for rest and relaxation. The Valley Campaign and the Seven Days Battles had taken their toll on the

Maryland Line. Recruiting and reorganizing were also needed, as noted by Goldsborough:

> For this purpose the First Maryland Infantry and Baltimore Light Artillery were ordered to Charlottesville, where they remained a month, when they were once more ordered to join Jackson, who was about to make his great movement to the rear of Pope's army at Manassas. Alas! The two commands did not journey together far, for at Gordonsville an order overtook Colonel Johnson requiring him to at once disband the First Maryland, and the order was reluctantly obeyed.
>
> The separation was affecting to the greatest degree, and the little battery pursued its way with sad and lonely hearts. It was like severing the ties that bind brother to brother, for in the series of battles in which they had participated side-by-side, the conduct of each had inspired the other with confidence and respect. "With the First Maryland in support," I heard Captain Brockenborough say, "I know I am always safe." And so it was, for one would never desert the other while life lasted.[13]

Goldsborough then reported on the next movements of the Second Maryland Artillery:

> On the morning of the 19th of August, the battery reached Orange Courthouse, where, much to the joy of all, it was attached to Starke's Louisiana Brigade. An affinity had long existed between the Maryland and Louisiana troops, and they commanded the other's fullest confidence. In fact, they seemed nearer akin, for in both there was that sprightliness, dash and vim not so noticeable in troops from other states.
>
> With three days' rations in haversacks, Brockenborough, on the 21st, moved towards the Rappahannock, where he found the enemy occupying the north bank in force. A severe artillery fight immediately began, and was maintained for some

hours. The battery pitted against Brockenborough was Company M, United States Regular, which, towards nightfall, he succeeded in silencing and driving back with the loss of many men and an exploded caisson. On the morning of the 22nd, the artillery was thrown across the river, but soon after encountered the enemy in heavy force, and was compelled to recross after a desperate struggle. In this affair the Baltimore Light Artillery suffered a loss of four men killed— Irvin, Cox, Bradley and Reynolds—and several severely wounded.[14]

Brigadier General William B. Taliaferro, commanding Jackson's Division, also reported on the action at Cunningham's Ford on the Rappahannock.

> On approaching this ford I discovered the enemy on the opposite bank (in what force I could not tell, their infantry holding the edge of a cornfield and a skirt of woods which approached the river bank and the brows of the hills overlooking the ford. I could not discover their batteries, but supposed they would soon be exhibited. I halted the troops under cover of the woods and ordered to the front, under charge of Major L. [M.] Shumaker, my chief of artillery, the long-range guns of Brockenbrough, Wooding, Poague and Carpenter. These pieces, having been placed in position, soon developed the position of the enemy's batteries, and after a short resistance silenced their guns, blowing up one of their caissons and dispersed in confusion their infantry. By direction of the major-general the infantry was kept back, while a cavalry force was posed over the ford to reconnoiter. This force under Major-General Steuart, re-enforced by a section of Brockenbrough's and Wooding's batteries, remained over the river some two hours, capturing a number of prisoners and many arms, which had been abandoned in their haste to escape the severity of our shelling. Some time after this the enemy was discovered moving

large masses up the river from below us. Here, the cavalry having retired, his batteries were again placed in position near the ford and a large party of skirmishers thrown out to the riverbank above and below the ford. I at once detailed a sufficient force of sharpshooters from the Third Brigade to hold the river bank, with whom and the enemy an animated skirmish was kept up during the rest of the day.

Toward night the enemy re-enforced his skirmishers with a brigade of infantry, when I directed Major Shumaker to open upon them with his pieces, which, although it drew upon our artillerists a heavy fire, which was continued as long as it was light enough to distinguish objects, had the effect of driving them back in confusion. Our batteries then replied to those of the enemy with deliberation and vigor until dark.

On the following morning I was directed to hold the ford until the other divisions of General Jackson's corps had passed to my left in the direction of Farley Ford, on the Hazel River, and then to follow with my division. I had again on the morning of the 22d a warm artillery fight with the enemy, resulting, as on the day previous, according to his published reports, in very considerable slaughter to the enemy. Our loss was privates 20 killed and wounded and no officers.[15]

The next action was the Battle of Second Manassas. It was not easy to get there, as noted by Goldsborough:

Brockenborough, finding it impossible to cross at that point [Cunningham's Ford], moved up to Hanson's Ford, where a crossing was effected, and he then pursued his way through Orleans, Salem and Thoroughfare Gap and reached Manassas on the 26th, having marched fifty miles in two days, with nothing for his men or horses to eat save the green corn gathered along the road. Here at Manassas, though, was found in the captured trains and sutler's stores all they could have desired, and for hours they reveled in the good things their new commissary had so bountifully supplied, and over Rhine wine and lobsters forgot for the time the privations of the past few days. From Manassas, Jackson moved on to Centerville, but finding the enemy there in force, he retraced his steps to Manassas, closely pursued, and formed his line of battle about sunset on the 28th, upon the ground occupied by the enemy in the battle of July 1861.

Colonel Stapleton Crutchfield reported on the battle:

> Early on Friday, the 29th, the enemy renewed the attack over nearly the same ground, while our troops occupied pretty generally the same position. Their infantry being repulsed by ours, artillery was thrown out in front of our right to complete it. The batteries of Captains Poague, Carpenter, Dement, Brockenbrough and Latimer, under Major Shumaker, were so engaged, facing obliquely toward Groveton, while the battery of Captain Braxton was placed farther to our right, bearing on the road from Groveton to Warrenton, in case the enemy should advance from that direction rather in rear of the other batteries.[16]

Goldsborough also reported on the battle:

> The engagement immediately commenced, and raged with great fury for some time, but the enemy was repulsed in every assault, and driven back with heavy loss. Colonel Stephen D. Lee then put the several batteries in position along the crest of a commanding hill and there awaited the attack sure to be renewed next day.
> About 2 o'clock on the 29th heavy columns emerged from the woods in Jackson's front and advanced boldly to the attack, but the storm of grape and canister which tore through their ranks was more than flesh and blood could withstand, and they were driven back with dreadful slaughter. But again and again did those devoted columns reform and return to

the attack with undiminished ardor, but the same terrible fire greeted them and strewed the ground with dead and dying.

But nevertheless Jackson's situation was a most critical one. With but a handful of worn and weary troops he was battling with ten times his numbers, which must necessarily soon wear him out and exhaust his ammunition; but as the hearts of his men were sinking within them, they were cheered by the clouds of dust that arose in the distance and heralded the approach of their great chieftain, Lee, with the veterans of Longstreet's corps. At night the battle ceased, and the weary troops threw themselves upon the ground to seek a little repose before the work of death and destruction should be resumed on the morrow.[17]

The battle continued the following day. Colonel Crutchfield reported.

On Saturday, the 30th instant, this army corps occupied still the same position. About 3 p.m. the enemy attacked along our front, having advanced from the direction of Centerville. In this attack his line exposed its left flank to batteries on the rising round from our right cross to the Groveton and Warrenton Pike. Accordingly, the batteries of Captains John R. Johnson, D'Aquin, [W. H.] Rice, [George W.] Wooding, Poague, Carpenter, Brockenbrough and Latimer were so placed (in all eighteen guns), their right joining the left of General Longstreet's batteries, that their fire was directed upon the last line of the enemy's forces, which was broken under it just as it nearly reached the edge of the woods and never reformed within their range. As soon as it was observed to be giving way I ordered forward Captain [Lieutenant] Garber's battery of four guns at a gallop to move down into the plain below, so as to get an enfilading position on their other lines when they should be repulsed from the woods in which they were engaged with our infantry, and so endeavor to convert the repulse into a rout. Just as the battery was getting into position and the enemy began to fall back from the woods Brigadier-General Early's brigade charged from the woods, and effecting a change of front perpendicularly forward to the left, formed a line between the battery and the enemy, so that the former could not fire. The same movement checked also the fire of all the short-range runs from the hill, and so they were withdrawn, and the others, viz, those of Captains Brockenbrough, Latimer and D'Aquin, were at once moved round to the range of hills to the right of the Groveton and Centerville road, where the enemy were concentrating a very heavy fire of artillery on General Longstreet's line. Here they engaged the enemy's batteries for the remainder of the fight.[18]

Goldsborough's account of the second day's fighting reads:

At the break of day on the morning of the 30th of August, the troops were aroused from their slumbers and ordered to prepare for the great and decisive battle at hand. But hour after hour passed by, and except an occasional picket shot, all else was still. It was, though, but the calm which precedes the storm, for suddenly dense masses of the enemy emerged from the woods and moved at the double quick upon Jackson's lines. It was a grand sight to see those three lines rush forward in the most beautiful order. For a minute a death-like silence prevailed, when the very earth was made to tremble by the roar of Stephen D. Lee's thirty-six pieces of artillery, fired at point blank range. The slaughter was appalling, and whole ranks melted away in an instant, but the brave survivors closed up their decimated columns, and despite that awful fire pressed on until they encountered the infantry posted in the railroad cut in front, where for a time the fight was waged hand-to-hand. At length they began to break and to retreat, and the batteries, which had been silent for

> some time, owing to the proximity of the struggling columns of infantry, again belched forth into the fleeing mass their deadly discharges of grape, which was continued until the fugitives reached the shelter of the woods from which they had emerged.
> Of the several batteries under General Lee that day not one was worked more fiercely than the Baltimore Light Artillery, and none contributed more to the defeat and destruction of the enemy.[19]

The Baltimore Light Artillery had two guns disabled during this battle. One burst and the vent piece of another was burned out.

Next came the Maryland Campaign. The artillery of Jackson's Division for this campaign consisted of the following batteries, commanded by Major L. M. Shumaker:

> Carpenter's Alleghany Virginia Artillery
> Brockenborough's Baltimore Maryland Light Artillery
> Wooding's Danville Virginia Artillery
> Caskie's Hampden Virginia Artillery
> Raine's Lee Virginia Artillery
> Poague's Rockbridge Virginia Artillery.

The Baltimore Light Artillery was in the advance portion of Lee's Army and was supported on the march by the 15th Louisiana Infantry commanded by Colonel Edmund Pendleton. The battery went through Leesburg and crossed the Potomac at White's Ford (now White's Ferry) on September 5. Goldsborough's description of events continued.

> On the 6th of September the battery passed through Frederick City and encamped on the suburbs. Many were the congratulations the brave fellows received from the citizens, and during the three days they remained their wants were abundantly supplied.
> Leaving Frederick City, the battery passed through Boonsboro, Middletown and Williamsport, where they re-crossed the Potomac, and on the 12th entered Martinsburg.[20]

Into the Breach: 1862  111

The battery was joined by Colonel Pendleton's 15th Louisiana Infantry shortly after 2 p.m. on September 13, 1862. Colonel Pendleton reported on the ensuing action:

> At that hour we were ordered to move by an unfrequented road to our left and almost at right angles with the Charlestown road, to a position nearer the Potomac, supporting the Baltimore battery of light artillery, commanded by Captain Brockenborough and attached to this brigade, which opened upon the enemy and continued its fire until dark, the enemy responding, but without damage to us.
>
> Shortly before dawn we resumed our position of the evening before, again supporting the Baltimore battery, which reopened its fire and delivered a few telling shots, some of them, I regret to say, after the besieged hoisted the white flag. It is but justice, however, to add that from the position we occupied the flag was imperceptible, nor were we aware of the surrender until a message was received from the major-general commanding, directing a cessation of fire.
>
> It gives me pleasure to be able to say that not a single casualty of any kind is to be reported in this brigade on the occasion, although the result was so glorious to our arms.[21]

Then it was on to Harpers Ferry, as reported by Goldsborough:

> From thence it moved toward Harper's Ferry, when upon arriving at Loudon Heights, Brockenborough was assigned a position, from which, at early dawn of the 15th, he opened, along with other batteries, a terrific fire upon the enemy's entrenched position on Bolivar Heights. The batteries were worked furiously for an hour, when just as the Confederate infantry were put in motion to storm the works, a white flag fluttered in the breeze, and Harper's Ferry surrendered with its twelve thousand troops, and artillery and supplies in abundance.

But there was heavy work yet to be done, for General Lee with a portion of his army was confronting the overwhelming masses of McClellan at Sharpsburg, and no time was to be lost in reaching him. The surrender had, therefore, scarcely been effected when the troops were dispatched to his aid. By a forced night march Jackson's artillery reached Sharpsburg on the 16th, and was immediately assigned a position on a range of hills rather northwest of the town.[22]

The Baltimore Artillery was in the "left wing" at Sharpsburg and was equipped with one 3-inch rifle, one 12-pounder howitzer and two Blakeley rifles. The morning of September 17, 1862 opened with dawn skirmishing, followed by an artillery duel. Enemy artillery on the opposite side of Antietam Creek was responded to "by the batteries of Poague, Carpenter, Brockenborough, Raine, Caskie and Wooding." Goldsborough provided an excellent description of the action:

> Soon after sunrise slight artillery skirmishing commenced along the lines, which increased in volume until the air seemed filled with exploding shells. Upon the position held by the batteries of Brockenborough, Carpenter and Poague, Moody, Raine and Caskie was opened a terrific fire, which was promptly returned and the enemy's batteries several times compelled to change position. This continued for two hours, when it became evident that the infantry was massing for a charge. The position was of the most vital importance, for should the enemy succeed in gaining possession of this point and turning Lee's left flank, he would be irretrievably lost. His orders to General Jackson were, therefore, to, "Hold the range of hills to the last."
>
> McClellan's advance upon this point was gallantly met by Jackson's veteran infantry, and for some time the fighting was of the most determined character; but at length the immense superiority of numbers prevailed, and Jackson's troops gradually fell back

across the turnpike, past the Dunkard Church, and through the woods, and appeared upon the plain beyond. Most beautifully did the heavy columns emerge from the woods and move forward upon the batteries quietly awaiting their near approach. "Do not pull a lanyard," said Brockenborough, who was temporarily in command of the whole, "until you get the command." Nearer and nearer those solid columns approached, and amid loud huzzas rushed forward at the double quick. It was a moment of dreadful suspense. On, on, they came! "Will Brockenborough never give the command?" Yes; he now has them at the muzzles of his guns, and the next instant the command, "Fire!" was heard above the exultant cheers of the advancing columns, and twenty-four pieces of artillery, double-shotted with canister, belched forth their deadly contents into the very faces of the assailants.

The scene that was presented as the smoke lifted beggars description. The ground was literally covered—nay, piled—with the slain and maimed of the enemy, and the survivors were in full retreat. They were soon reformed, however, and again moved boldly to the attack, but only to be again mercilessly slaughtered and driven back. A third time they essayed, but with the same result, when, a disordered mass of fugitives, the survivors sought the shelter of the woods from which they had but a few minutes before emerged, confident of success.

The fighting ended at nightfall. The Baltimore Light Artillery had performed very well. Captain Brockenborough was promoted to Major as a result of his actions in the campaign. Jackson's infantry had held. Both armies faced each other on the eighteenth, but no action occurred. Burial parties were, however, very busy. That night Lee's Army re-crossed the Potomac River near Shepherdstown.

During the movement from Harper's Ferry to Sharpsburg a caisson belonging to the Baltimore Light Artillery was lost due to the extreme exhaustion of the horses—the horses and caisson both rolled down a cliff on the side of the road. L. M. Shumaker, Major and Chief of Artillery, Jackson's Division, in his report of September 22, 1862, noted that Brockenborough's battery had one three-inch rifle and one twelve-pounder howitzer present for duty and one ten-pounder Parrott and one Blakeley rifle absent. He also noted that Brockenborough's battery needed the following—fourteen horses, three guns and caissons, four wheel harness sets and fifteen lead harness sets. S. Crutchfield, Colonel and Chief of Artillery, Valley District, forwarded Shumaker's report with his own comments of the same date. He added the following to his report:[23]

> Captain Brockenborough can work the three guns he asks for by turning in his howitzer, and I would be glad to see him get Napoleons. I do not request it, though, if you need them more elsewhere, especially if other batteries can furnish the teams. One of his guns, a 12-pounder Blakeley, he reports disabled. The stock was broken in the battle of Sharpsburg, and it was sent to Winchester. If it can be repaired there, or the gun put on another carriage, I would be glad to get it back, and then, by giving Captain B[rockenborough] two Napoleons and allowing him to turn in his howitzer, he would have a capital battery of four guns, two of them rifles.[24]

Crutchfield also added, referring to the Baltimore Light Artillery, "This is one of our best companies."[25] Goldsborough had the following to report after the campaign:

> Soon after the battle of Sharpsburg, the Baltimore Light Artillery, now under command of Captain W. H. Griffin, was ordered to join the cavalry and infantry of the Maryland Line, then in camp near Newmarket, in the Valley of Virginia. Here they passed the fall and winter months quietly in camp, and in early spring were again prepared, with recruited ranks and renewed equipments, to enter the field.[26]

Goldsborough, however, was not fully correct. It is known that the Baltimore Light Artillery, along with the rest of the Maryland Line, remained at Winchester, Virginia until the day before the surrender and evacuation on December 4, 1862. Also, the Baltimore Light Artillery participated in the "battle" of Moorefield on January 2, 1963.

The fighting of 1862 took its toll on the battery: five men killed in action, eleven others wounded and six more taken prisoner. Resupply of equipment did occur. The Baltimore Light Artillery received thirteen overcoats, seventy-five jackets and thirty-five pair of socks on December 5, 1862.[27]

## Chapter IV

## Continuing the Fight: 1863

In January 1863, the Baltimore Light Artillery had three officers and fifty-seven men present for duty, an aggregate present of seventy-two and a total of 102 present and absent.[28] It was equipped with three pieces of artillery. It was also in action, not just resting and surviving the winter.

On January 2, 1863, the Baltimore Light Artillery was part of Brigadier General William E. "Grumble" Jones' force marching on Moorefield, along with the following units: 6th Virginia Cavalry, 7th Virginia Cavalry, 12th Virginia Cavalry, 17th Battalion Virginia Cavalry, Chew's Battery, 1st Battalion Maryland Cavalry and the 1st Battalion Maryland Infantry. Even the official reports of the resulting fighting hint that the whole affair was a fiasco.

General Jones stated that his forces reached their destination by 7 a.m. on January 3 via a forced march, cavalry and artillery. The following excerpts from General Jones' official report of January 6, 1863, described the action:

> Hoping to overcome the force at Moorefield before the arrival of that from Petersburg, the attack was made at once. Being wholly unacquainted with the topography of the country, I trusted the placing of my artillery of Captain Harness of the Seventeenth Battalion Virginia Cavalry, a resident of that vicinity and once a captor of the town. The hills selected on each side of the Petersburg road are so distant that our six pieces, with their defective ammunition, were no match for the two of the enemy. Nearly all our shots fell far short, while theirs either passed over or struck in our midst. In the meanwhile the force at Petersburg, timely warned of our approach, came within striking distance and

opened on our rear. Though they reached us with ease, they were out of our range. The two wings of my command were too far apart for mutual support, and the ground between was swept by both batteries of the enemy. Unable to unite my own forces, I could prevent the union of the enemy's. I could not expect re-enforcements in 24 hours; my adversaries might receive assistance from New Creek in less time. With my right wing I determined to hold my position, which commanded the road up the South Fork and prevented a junction of the two hostile forces, while Colonel [R. H.] Dulany should march by a road west of the Moorefield and Petersburg pike on the latter place, whence he could cross Middle Mountain to the South Fork in my rear. I retained my position about two hours, when, my battery having expended the last of its well-husbanded, worthless ammunition, and when Colonel Dulany was so far on his way as to be out of danger, I retired up the South Fork.[29]

General Jones even claimed success! He continued:

We claim a partial success, for we killed 1 man, captured 99 (among them 1 captain and 2 lieutenants), 51 horses, 18 sets of harness, and 5 wagons, which we burned, and 1 portable bake-oven, which was brought off, and caused the enemy to burn from $15,000 to $20,000 worth of stores. A knowledge of the ground would have enabled me to capture in detail both garrisons and the first re-enforcement. In my entire ignorance of the country I was compelled to trust to others, and lost the rich fruits of hard labor.[30]

Confederate losses were miniscule, "1 horse killed and 2 wounded."[31]

General Jones' report led to the two replies given below. The first was prepared by J. Gorgas on January 16, 1863, who wrote:

Officers are always ready to praise when they succeed and to blame when they fail. Colonel Cabell, of the artillery, at Fredericksburg, complimented our ammunition yesterday. Every effort is constantly made to overcome the many obstacles we have had to contend with in the production of the laboratory, and I am quite as much inclined to blame General Jones' artillerists as he is to blame my ammunition. Without wishing to detract from his skill as an officer, I may be allowed to state that he is known to be very apt to find fault. His depreciation of the ammunition is, however, taken in good part, and will only stimulate the endeavor to improve where there is still much room for improvement.[32]

The second item was prepared by General R. E. Lee and sent to Grumble Jones on January 13. General Lee wrote:

Your report of your expedition to Petersburg and Moorefield, on the 2d instant, has been received. I am much gratified to hear of your success, and of the good conduct of your officers and men. I wish you to continue your efforts, to watch well your opportunities, and drive the enemy from the valley, if possible.[33]

Federal reports estimated the strength of Jones' force at 3,000 and took credit for running him off.

In February 1863 the Baltimore Light Artillery had its first significant desertions. The following men deserted in early February and were taken prisoner on February 7-8 in Winchester, Virginia: Thomas Anderson, J. B. Armstrong and Samuel B. Hardy.

General Jackson's letter of February 28, 1863, to General Robert E. Lee said that Brockenborough's promotion was favored over Chew's by Colonel Crutchfield.[34] Brockenborough was detailed as Chief of Artillery, First Division, Jackson's Corps on the December 1862 roster.

Rest, relaxation and refitting continued through March and early April 1863.

On April 21, General Grumble Jones' command left camp at Lacey Springs, Rockingham County, in compliance with General R. E. Lee's instructions. Jones was ordered to move in conjunction with General John D. Imboden into Northwest Virginia to destroy the Baltimore and Ohio Railroad. The first three days to Moorefield were especially arduous, owing to the road conditions caused by bad weather. Upon reaching the South Branch of the Potomac, it was discovered the water had risen, forcing a detour by Petersburg. The command reached Moorefield unchallenged.

Moving on, Federal forces were first engaged at Greenland Gap. The Federal picket was captured. The Federal reserve retired to a log church and surrounding houses. The rest of the log structures were secured by the Confederates, and the sharpshooters secured the woods and hillside on the left. Winchester's mounted rifles, under Captain John Chapman, were dismounted and thrown to the right, also performing as sharpshooters. They were able to penetrate close to the buildings, securing the stone works and reconnoiter the enemy's position. White's and Brown's Battalions were dismounted to storm the log structures. They rushed the house and were fired upon from twenty yards. After dark the storming party crossed a stream and attempted to surround the houses. Not informing their comrades of their movements and due to the lack of visibility, they were fired upon not only by the Federals, but by two of their own companies, the 7th Regiment and the 34th Battalion.

The bulk of the command moved on to Rowlesburg arriving at the Cheat River around 2 p.m. The pickets were captured and intelligences received that the garrison was held by only three hundred men. Their garrison was then ordered to be charged by Lieutenant Colonel Marshall with the 7th Virginia Cavalry and Colonel Lunsford Lomax with the 11th Virginia Cavalry as support. A portion of Witcher's Battalion with eighty sharpshooters from the 11th Virginia Cavalry were sent under the command of Captain Weems, to the east end of the railroad bridge at Rowlesburg and to fire it. Colonel Green was sent to storm the pickets about a mile above the town and leave them for the regiments in his rear. If, during his advance, a heavy force was encountered, he was to dislodge them with sharpshooters and proceed. Jones remained at the bridge of the northwest grade to guard the rear if attacked.

Jones was less than pleased with the lack of efficiency his orders were executed. Colonel Green was stopped by less than twenty men and Captain Weems "attacked with only twenty-eight men leaving the remainder of his command to guard his rear against an imaginary foe." Though the bridge and trestlework was destroyed at the Cheat River, Jones was frustrated. He was not only frustrated with the failure of each attack. Also he found himself without forage as well as not having heard from General Imboden.

The next morning, the command left for Evansville. Rations and forage were secured and couriers were sent to General Imboden. Jones also sent out scouts to gather information. To insure that news would not spread along the railroad, a force was sent to Independence and the bridge was destroyed. Not hearing from Imboden, Jones decided to search for Colonel Harman. About midnight Jones went into camp, anticipating a junction with the Colonel.

At daylight, Harman appeared giving details of the success he and McDonald had achieved at Oakland and Altamont. With both forces united, the entire command marched on Morgantown. Jones' men fed their horses, rested until dark, and then began the march to Fairmont. Jones ordered the men into camp at 9 p.m. and did not resume the march until 1 a.m. The command advanced on Fairmont after a detour at Buffalo Creek. Entering the town from the west, the command found a Federal force occupying the hills commanding the road. Jones sent them through the woods on the right to flank the Federal position. The command entered the town at a charge and Colonel Harman secured the suspension bridge over the river where he and a portion of White's Battalion crossed. The Federal force divided, with one part retreating up the east bank of the river and the other part retreating up the west bank.

Both forces rejoined at the bridge to fend off the Confederates. After ascertaining the Federal position, Jones initiated a simultaneous attack on both sides of the river. The vigorous Confederate attack only met moderate resistance. The Federals produced a white flag and 260 prisoners were surrendered. As soon as their arms were stacked, a train arrived from Grafton, providing Federal artillery and infantry. The Confederate troops on the west bank of the river were shelled as the Federal infantry was moved forward to recapture the railroad bridge. Colonel Harman met the infantry and Lieutenant Colonel Marshall placed his horses behind a hill for protection and ordered his men to use the captured arms.

Colonel Harman informed Jones, he could capture the entire command but Jones, whose main objective was the bridge, ignored the troops and exerted his entire energy in destruction of the bridge. The engineer, Lieutenant Williamson, assisted by Captain John Henderson, took charge of the working parties.

The bridge was made of iron; three spans, each three hundred feet long. More than two years were required for its construction. After dark, the "magnificent structure" tumbled into the river. Colonel Harman's skill and daring were praised by Jones again, but he was also disappointed in Colonel Green again.

The command began the march again, in search of General Imboden. They camped after a couple of hours marching to resume early the next morning. They then crossed the Monongahela River, went up Simpson's Creek and the Maryland Cavalry under Major Brown captured the force at Bridgeport. The Confederates also destroyed a bridge to the left of town, ran a captured train into a stream, and burned the trestles. Jones ordered the command into camp after marching until sometime after dark.

When a few miles from Buckhannon, on May 2nd, Jones received intelligence that Imboden was there ready to move on Weston. After exchanging information, original plans were altered due to deviations that had already occurred. Jones and Imboden discussed the attack on Clarksburg and believing such an attack would be dangerous, they agreed Imboden should move south and Jones was to march on the Northwestern Railroad toward Parkersburg.

On May 6, 1863, the movement began. Colonel Harman was detached in command with the 11th and 12th Virginia Cavalry Regiments and the 34th Battalion and ordered to move on West Union. Jones took the remainder of the command to the Parkersburg Pike to attack the railroad at Cairo. Harman and his detachment sent out skirmishers while he sent other parties to burn the two bridges to the right and left of town. Jones met with equal success at Cairo. The guard surrendered without firing a shot. Three bridges and a tunnel cribbed with wood were burned.

Jones' command then moved on Oiltown on May 9. A decision was made to destroy the oil stored there, however the troops were ignorant of the oil's explosive and flammable properties. Five

Confederates were reported to have approached a large oil storage tank that was one-third full with oil, while its upper portion was surcharged with gas generated by the oil. One of the troops climbed the ladder to the tank and dropped a burning torch inside. The tank exploded killing the five instantly covering them with flaming oil.

After leaving Oiltown, the command marched by Glenville and Sutton to Summerville. At Summerville, Jones' and Imboden's commands were again reunited. The two exhausted cavalry commands began moving homeward. The Second Maryland Artillery was back in the Shenandoah Valley by mid-May.

General Ewell described the first steps in the campaign in the official report:

> On the 13th, I sent Early's division and Colonel Brown's artillery battalion (under [W. J.] Dance), to Newtown, on the Valley pike, where they were joined by the [First] Maryland Infantry Battalion, Lieutenant-Colonel [J. R.] Herbert, and the Baltimore Light Artillery, Captain [W. H.] Griffin. General Early was directed to advance toward the town [Winchester] by the Valley pike.
>
> At Winchester, the Maryland Battalion was attached to General Steuart's brigade, and the Baltimore Light Artillery to Colonel Brown's battalion, with which they served with their usual gallantry throughout the campaign.[35]

General Early described what happened at Winchester on June 14, 1863, in his official report. The plan was to leave part of the force in position "to amuse the enemy and conceal the movement upon his flank and rear" and attack from the flank and rear. Early wrote:

> After receiving final orders from General Ewell, I replaced the skirmishers of Hays' and Smith's brigades by others from Gordon's brigade, and leaving General Gordon, with his brigade, the Maryland battalion, and two batteries of artillery (the Maryland battery and [A.] Hupp's battery, of Brown's battalion) to amuse the enemy and hold him in check in front, I moved with

Hays', Hoke's and Smith's brigades, and the rest of Jones' and Brown's battalions of artillery, to the left (west), following the Cedar Creek turnpike for a short distance, and then leaving that and passing through fields and the woods, which I found sufficiently open to admit of the passage of artillery, thus making a considerable detour, and crossing the macadamized road to Romney about three miles west of Winchester and a half mile from a point at which the enemy had had a picket the night before.[36]

The plan worked very well. The Federal commander, General Milroy, abandoned Winchester that very night, leading to the battle on June 15, already described, in which Lieutenant Contee's section of the First Maryland Artillery performed so effectively and admirably. Goldsborough also described the sequence of events for June 13-14 for the Baltimore Light Artillery, as follows:

On the 13th of June the infantry and artillery of the Maryland Line, with one company of its cavalry, all under the command of Lieutenant-Colonel James R. Herbert, moved towards Winchester, near which place they were to unite with the division of General Early, which was moving across from Front Royal. Near Kernstown a body of Milroy's cavalry was encountered, but a shot from the battery scattered them in all directions. A short time after, Early camp up and proceeded to form a line of battle. The enemy soon made his appearance in force, and opened a severe fire upon Griffin from his batteries, which was vigorously responded to, and in a little while the enemy were driven beyond Kernstown. Early, as soon as he had formed his line of battle, moved forward, and by a spirited charge of Gordon's Brigade, drove him into his strong works to the left of Winchester.

The next afternoon Hay's Louisiana Brigade was moved around to the enemy's right with orders to charge a strong line of works whilst the artillery opened upon him in front. Griffin was posted on a commanding hill a little to the left of the pike, and threw his first shell into the very centre of the Star fort. Finding he had the exact range, he commenced a furious fire, which threw the enemy for a moment into the greatest confusion, and greatly assisted Hays in his movement upon their right. The fire was soon spiritedly returned by the Federal Maryland battery and continued until night, when Milroy evacuated his fortifications and attempted to escape with his army, but in this he was successful in reaching Harper's Ferry with a few of his troops.[37]

The Baltimore Light Artillery again performed extremely well. Goldsborough described this also:

> The precision and effect with which the guns of the Baltimore Light Artillery were served upon this occasion elicited the highest praise from General Gordon, to whose brigade it was temporarily attached, and as a mark of the high esteem in which he held the battery, he procured them permission from General Ewell next morning to select from among the captured guns the best pieces, to take the place of their own, which were greatly inferior.
>
> The day after the Battle of Winchester, the corps of General Ewell took up its line of march toward the Potomac. The Baltimore Light Artillery was directed by subordinate officers to report to General Nelson of the reserve artillery. The order occasioned the greatest surprise and indignation throughout the command, for always before they had led the advance and covered the retreat. Such an indignity, as they considered it, could not be tamely submitted to, and a protest was immediately drawn up and forwarded to General Ewell, who at once ordered the battery to join Albert G. Jenkins' brigade of cavalry, which was the van of the army in the invasion of Pennsylvania.
>
> The battery crossed the Potomac on the 18th of June and that day joined Jenkins, when the whole

command moved rapidly forward in the greatest good humor. Many were the jokes they practiced, and many the quaint sayings peculiar only to the soldier. "Take them mice out of your mouth," one would bawl out, as an officer with a well-waxed mustache rode by; "Taken 'em out, no use to say they ain't thar, for I see their tails sticken' out." And as another came along, but a short time in the service, and wearing a "boiled shirt," and white collar, his ears were sure to be assailed with, "Say, mister, how long did you have to soldier afore one of them things growed 'round your neck?" and a staff officer, with handsome cavalry boots, would be requested by a dozen voices to "Come out of them thar boots, for it's too soon to go into winter quarters."[38]

Then it was on to Pennsylvania with the cavalry. The route was from near Hagerstown to near Greencastle, up the Cumberland Valley to Shippensburg, on to Carlisle and Mechanicsburg and to the Susquehanna River. Then the forces withdrew toward Gettysburg. After fighting at Gettysburg, the Baltimore Light Artillery returned to Virginia via Hagerstown, participating in a severe cavalry fight at Hagerstown.

The *New York Herald* of Thursday, June 18, 1863, reported on the first portion of the campaign in Pennsylvania:

The Harrisburg Telegrams<br>Harrisburg, June 16, Midnight

Two of our reporters have just returned from in front of the rebel pickets, who are picketed forty-seven miles from Harrisburg, at Scotland Bridge, which they burned this morning. A party of fifteen set fire to the bridge. The rebels are encamped at three points around Chambersburg, and are thirty-five hundred strong, under General Jenkins. The rebels say that a brigade under General Rhodes is coming, and that they have seized two hundred horses to mount their infantry. The rebels have fifteen pieces of artillery.

Goldsborough also described this action:

> The command of Jenkins pursued its march rapidly through Maryland, and struck the Pennsylvania line near Greencastle. Thence their way lay up the Cumberland Valley to Shippensburg, where a halt was made for a short time to allow the tired troops to partake of the delicious apple-butter, ham, bread, etc., furnished them in abundance by the startled inhabitants. Whilst thus enjoying themselves to their hearts' content, the cry of "Yanks" was raised, and in an instant the scene changed. Cavalrymen sprang to their horses, and artillerymen to their guns, but the wary enemy could not be induced to come within range of Griffin's Parrott's, but retired towards Carlisle, followed leisurely by Jenkins.
>
> Upon arriving within sight of that town, the Yankee flag was found defiantly flying from the public buildings, when Jenkins, supposing the enemy to be there in force, prepared to attack. Placing two pieces of artillery in a position to rake the main street, and disposing of his other troops in the most available manner, he demanded the surrender of the town. It was not long before a deputation of the "solid" citizens made their appearance, and surrendered the place, of which General Jenkins at once took possession.

William Hunter Griffin, Captain, Second Maryland Artillery
(Illustration by Jeff Sherwood)

After remaining at Carlisle one day, during which time they were bountifully supplied with provisions and forage by the citizens, the command moved in the direction of Harrisburg. At Mechanicstown a small body of cavalry were encountered, but a shot from Griffin caused them to beat a hasty retreat. Upon reaching the Susquehanna, the Confederate commander found the opposite side of the river strongly fortified, but he at once opened fire from his batteries, which was promptly responded to. This continued until late in the afternoon, when the enemy's infantry advanced in force, and a severe skirmish ensued, which lasted until after night. General Rhodes (I have forgotten to mention the fact that Jenkins and Rhodes united their forces at Carlisle) having accomplished his purpose, that night withdrew in the direction of Gettysburg.[39]

Then it was on to Gettysburg.

On the morning of July 2, Jenkins' brigade advanced into the valley between Seminary Ridge and the mountain range held by the Federals. Jenkins' Brigade was ordered to a wooded area that had been a section of the previous day's battlefield. There was a relative silence with the occasional report from a gun. General Jenkins, becoming impatient, decided to reconnoiter to determine the cause of the delay, taking his staff, he headed south on the Harrisburg road cross Rock Creek, and spotted Blacker's Knoll on the right. Jenkins reached the crest of the hill and discovered a commanding view. He was using his field glasses to survey Union positions when a courier arrived, delivering orders from General Ewell directing Jenkins to occupy the position to the left of Johnson. Almost immediately after the message was delivered, a shell, fired from Cemetery Hill, exploded nearby. Several other shots were fired, with the fourth or fifth round exploding directly overhead. Shell fragments killed Jenkins' horse and knocked Jenkins unconscious. No others being injured, members of the small staff grabbed Jenkins and headed down the northeast slope of the hill. The untimely injury undoubtedly thwarted Lee's plans and weakened the Confederate attack against the Federal right flank at Culp's Hill.

The brigade mounted at 4 a.m. on July 3, advancing to the extreme left. The object was to "flank the enemy's army and cut off its way of retreat." So in effect, Steuart's plan was linked to that of the Army of Northern Virginia. Steuart hoped to attack the Federal rear and turn the right flank, simultaneous with General George Pickett's infantry charge on the Federal center. After marking about two and a half miles on the Yorktown pike, General Steuart joined the brigade as Witcher related, "Steuart himself rode with me out to the field at the head of the command." The command turned right, passing the Stallsmith farm to "a commanding ridge that completely controlled a wide plain of cultivated fields stretching toward Hanover on the left, and reaching to the base of the spurs among the enemy held positions." The location Steuart described became known as the East Cavalry Battlefield. The ridge was known as Cress Ridge. Being covered with woods, the Confederate presence was concealed. Shortly after arrival, Steuart directed one of Griffin's (the Baltimore Light Artillery) guns to fire a shot in each compass direction. This was possibly to inform Lee that he was in position and ready to attack. Others have considered the shots to have been employed to induce the Federal cavalry to reveal their position. About 300 or 400 yards from the foot of the hill on the plains below was located a farm owned by the Rummel family. Standing on the farm was a large frame barn, called the Rummel barn. Just southeast of the barn was the dwelling house and a couple of other buildings in a cluster together. A lane passed by the house, on down past the springhouse. Steuart placed two brigades on the left (Lewis and Hampton) and two on the right (Chambliss and Jenkins/). The 34th Battalion was directed by General Steuart to dismount about 8 a.m. and at 10 a.m. Steuart ordered them forward to the left of the Rummel barn. The command passed by the barn and fence that ran in line with the barn. Moving another hundred yards, the 34th took position behind a second fence that ran parallel with the first.

Only a portion of Jenkins' Brigade was designated to engage the enemy: five companies of the 34th Battalion (332 men) with four companies of the 16th Virginia Cavalry (about eighty men) under Major James Nounnan and four companies of the 14th Virginia Cavalry (not more than 150 men) under Major Benjamin Franklin

Eakle. The balance of the 16th Virginia, which was placed under command of Colonel Milton J. Ferguson since General Jenkins' absence, was on the Fairfield road. The 17th Virginia Cavalry under the command of Colonel William H. French and the 14th Virginia under Lieutenant Colonel John A. Gibson were guarding prisoners captured the first day. The two companies of the 36th Battalion Virginia Cavalry were under Captain Cornelius T. Smith (thirty men) and Captain James B. Morgan were merely pickets, and not engaged, guarding the roads on the right and left—to protect the 34th's flanks with a space of five hundred or six hundred yards between Witcher's left. The only part of Jenkins' brigade that was actually engaged was Jackson's Battery and the Baltimore Light Artillery. Witcher's front was three hundred or perhaps four hundred yards long, the right in front of the barn and the left under Captain Baldwin and Chapman with companies A and B resting upon the spring house and bushes. No other part of Jenkins' Brigade was on the field except the Baltimore Light Artillery, which was silenced and knocked to pieces almost as soon as it engaged. Steuart placed another battery on the left, but it didn't take position until after 10 a.m. The battery had six pieces but no more than two could be used at a time. The Confederate battery was about one-fourth mile north of the barn and formed a line with the barn and Pennington's Union battery.

The 34th had only gotten in position, when they were attacked furiously by the 1st New Jersey and 3rd Pennsylvania who were dismounted. Witcher's adjutant was shot down early in the action at the springhouse. Others of his command were killed in his presence. The 34th, contrary to popular myth, was not withdrawn, nor were they equipped with just ten rounds of ammunition. Witcher's Battalion, alone, fought the Federals who were attacking from behind a fence in front of Witcher's line. The Federals were stubbornly held off until about noon.

The men had not drawn ammunition for several days, thus their stores were rapidly becoming exhausted. Witcher ordered them to retire slowly behind the stone fence in their rear, placing their right behind the Rummel barn and the left resting upon a road.

Many of Witcher's men occupied the Rummel Barn, cutting rifle loopholes in the siding planks from which to fire their Enfields.

These men served as sharpshooters until a Federal shell tearing through the upper rafters dislodged them.

After fighting with the cavalry at Gettysburg, the Baltimore Light Artillery helped cover the rear of Lee's retreating forces. In particular, covering the wagon trains and infantry moving through "bottlenecks," such as mountain passes, was their major concern. Goldsborough described how they did it:[40]

> At a point near Mount Zion the enemy had so stationed his guns as to completely command the road through the gap over which a column of infantry must pass. There was but little time to spare, for the enemy were pressing them hard. Captain Griffin was ordered to place his guns in position, and if possible silence the battery. It seemed a desperate undertaking, but there was no alternative. Quickly the brave fellows ran their guns to within point blank range, and opened a deadly fire. It was promptly returned, and a heavy artillery duel continued for some time, when the enemy's battery was driven from its position, and the infantry and wagon train passed in safety. I have heard it asserted by old soldiers that this was one of the most desperate artillery fights they ever witnessed. And the Marylanders had ever reason to be proud of their victory, for it was their old antagonist, Battery M, of the regular artillery, that they had again measured strength with.[41]

In the vicinity of Hagerstown and Boonesborough/Funkstown, Maryland, the Baltimore Light Artillery participated in a severe running cavalry fight. Official reports indicate that Griffin's battery had three men wounded in action in this engagement. After crossing the Potomac, the battery went to Fredericksburg and then Culpeper Courthouse. The battery had at least three men taken captive during the retreat from Gettysburg.

The Baltimore Light Artillery had a good period of rest, relaxation and recovery during August 1863. Like all good things, it did not last. The Baltimore Light Artillery was soon to go into action at Culpeper Courthouse. This was well described by Goldsborough:

> On the 10th of September Meade became restive, and General Lee moved forward to give him battle if he desired it. Beckham was ordered to advance and take position with his artillery near Muddy Creek. In a short time the enemy appeared in force, and a sharp artillery fight ensured. The enemy then threw forward his infantry, and compelled Beckham and his supports to fall back to the vicinity of Culpeper Courthouse. The artillery was here ordered to take a position and "hold it." The fighting soon became fierce, and the Baltimore Light Artillery was exposed to the severest part of it, but they gallantly held their ground for some time, despite the fire of six pieces that were playing upon their three. But this could not last long, for all support had been withdrawn, and the enemy's dismounted men were advancing in heavy force. It seemed scarcely possible to save the battery, but the brave fellows had been in such scrapes before, and they determined to hold on to their pieces as long as there was hope. Retiring through the town, they had nearly accomplished their purpose of escaping, when a body of the enemy charged up a cross street and captured the rear gun, with Lieutenant John McNulty and nine men attached to it. The remaining guns were safely taken off the field.
> 
> The next morning the enemy made their appearance in considerable force, and the battery was able to repay them for the rough treatment received the day preceding, for as a body of cavalry were engaged in drill, entirely ignorant of the close proximity of the Baltimore battery, it opened upon them with deadly effect at very close range.[42]

A dozen officers and men of the Baltimore Light Artillery were captured at Culpeper Courthouse, also called the Battle of Brandy Station. They were: Privates Walter Bell, George W. Clotsworthy,

James O. Cosgriff, James A. Duncan, John G. Gatchell, N. E. Ladde, William Paine, James Roane, Corporal James O'Grady, Musician, Lieutenant John McNulty, W. Texas and Corporal William Wallace.

The last action for the Baltimore Light Artillery in 1863 occurred at Bethel Church near James City on October 10, 1863. General J. E. B. Steuart, in his official report of February 13, 1864, and General P. M. B. Young, in his official report of December 8, 1863, both described the affair. Steuart's and Young's descriptions are similar. Basically two pieces of horse artillery under Captain Griffin occasionally fired on enemy batteries from a position near the village.

Goldsborough also described the "demonstration" and wrote:

> After the affair at Mine Run, which soon followed that at Culpeper Courthouse, the battery was detached from the main army, and temporarily assigned to duty with General Young's Brigade of cavalry. On the 9th of October that general crossed the Rapidan, and advanced by way of Madison Courthouse. His progress was slow, as the march was by circuitous and concealed side roads in order to avoid the observations of the enemy. On the 10th Young met the advance of the enemy at James City, without an intimation of his approach, and their bands were regaling the citizens with patriotic airs, when a shot from Sergeant Harry Marston's gun of the Baltimore Light Artillery, plunged into their midst, and abruptly terminated the musical entertainment for that evening at least. In a short time a battery was brought up and a severe artillery fight ensued. Soon another made its appearance and opened as enfilading fire upon Griffin, but, notwithstanding, he stubbornly held his position. Whilst this was going on a large force of the enemy's skirmishers attacked the Confederate flank, and threw the cavalry into some confusion by their unexpected onset from this quarter. Griffin at the instant wheeled his pieces and opened with grape and canister upon this new enemy. This checked them until the supports came

Continuing the Fight: 1863 135

up, when the enemy were compelled to retreat precipitately.[43]

Goldsborough mentioned that a sharp engagement took place near Brandy Station on October 12, 1863, but details are lacking. On October 31, 1863, the Maryland Line, again including the Baltimore Light Artillery, was ordered to Hanover Junction by W. H. Taylor in Special Order 269.[44] At this time the Maryland Line was organized and commanded as follows:

> Maryland Line, Colonel Bradley T. Johnson
> First Maryland Infantry Battalion, Colonel J. R. Hebert
> First Maryland Cavalry Battalion, Lieutenant Colonel R. Brown
> Baltimore Maryland Light Artillery, Captain W. H. Griffin.

Department of Richmond returns for November 30, 1863, for the Baltimore Light Artillery show four officers and fifty-eight men present for duty, an aggregate of seventy-three present, one hundred present and absent and three pieces of field artillery.[45] The battery had at least four men wounded in action and at least fifteen captured during 1863.

## Chapter V

## At It Again: 1864

The Baltimore Light Artillery spent the winter and early spring of 1864 at Hanover Junction and was again with the Maryland Line. The following information from the Department of Richmond returns gives a picture of the battery's strength at this time:[46]

| Date | Present for Duty | Aggregate Present | Present and Absent | Artillery Pieces |
|---|---|---|---|---|
| 2/10/64 | 66 | 76 | 100 | 3 |
| 3/31/64 | 66 | 79 | 103 | 4 |
| 4/20/64 | 70 | 80 | 104 | 4 |
| 5/10/64 | 75 | 87 | 96 | 4 |

Recruiting was continuing and men were transferred from other units and returning from prison camps. In fact, during April, May and June 1864, at least twelve men were transferred from other units and at least fifteen men were enlisted into the unit, ten at Hanover.

At this time the Maryland Line consisted of, and was commanded by the following:

>Maryland Line, Colonel Bradley T. Johnson
>2nd Maryland Infantry, Captain J. P. Crane
>1st Maryland Cavalry, Lieutenant Colonel R. Brown
>2nd Maryland Artillery, Captain W. H. Griffin
>Cooper's Virginia Battery, Captain R. L. Cooper

The Second Maryland Artillery had the following officers and staff in April 1864:

>Captain W. H. Griffin
>1st Lieutenant W. B. Bean
>2nd Lieutenant J. T. Wilhelm, who was absent as a prisoner of war

3rd Lieutenant John W. Goodman
1st Sergeant J. A. Bean
2nd Sergeant Harry A. Marston
3rd Sergeant James s. Morrison
4th Sergeant William S. Ferry
1st Corporal William Wallace, who was absent as a prisoner of war
2nd Corporal James O'Grady, who was absent as a prisoner of war
3rd Corporal George W. Pembroke
4th Corporal Matthew McLoid
5th Corporal George W. McAlwee
6th Corporal John Bunting
7th Corporal Chester C. Burnett
8th Corporal J. F. Hayden
Bugler Joshua Davis, Jr.
Commissary Sergeant Lewis Claus
Quartermaster Sergeant James H. Smith
Orderly Sergeant William W. Robinson
Ordnance Sergeant William Quinn
Surgeon J. B. Wortham

In early May 1874, it was time to return to the field. Goldsborough described what occurred:

> On the 10th of May 1864, whilst encamped at Wickham's Park, the battery was ordered by General J. E. B. Steuart, to move up along the Rivanna and join the forces there awaiting to intercept Sheridan, who was advancing towards Richmond. Reluctantly Colonel Johnson suffered it to go, for during the winter and spring he had reorganized and equipped it with much care; but the exigency of the occasion compelled him to acquiesce, General Steuart assuring him he would "borrow" it for but a few days, and "return it in good condition."
>
> On the 11th the battery took position at Yellow Tavern and soon after the enemy made his appearance in force. A heavy encounter ensued, when the battery

was retired about half a mile. For a time there was a lull in the fighting; but upon the arrival of General Steuart it was ordered forward, supported by the cavalry and took position to the left of the Brook turnpike, directly in Sheridan's front. The battle was then renewed with great fury. Sheridan brought three batteries to bear on Griffin at a range of not over eight hundred yards and the rain of shot and shrapnel became terrific, but the brave fellows never flinched, and served their guns with great effect. Hour after hour this savage fight was waged, but no man faltered at his post, although the groans of the wounded and dying and the shrieks of maimed and disemboweled horses, were enough to appall the stoutest heart. But General Steuart was there, watching with an anxious eye that little command, upon which so much depended, and they fought on, undismayed, despite the frightful scenes around them. At length the enemy massed a heavy body of cavalry, determined, at any sacrifice, to capture the guns that were making such dreadful havoc in their ranks. A charge was made upon him, when Griffin resorted to grape and canister. At every discharge whole companies melted away and the enemy fell back in confusion. But again they advanced, and the Confederate cavalry giving away at the instant, the battery was left at the mercy of the enemy, who dashed upon it; but there the brave men continued to stay determined to remain at their posts to the last, for all knew the vital importance of the position; and as the enemy pressed on they were met with that never ceasing hail of canister, until they reached the guns and rode over the men, and sabered and captured them at their pieces. Steuart had witnessed it all whilst rallying his broken cavalry, when seizing the colors of the First Virginia, he rode forward exclaiming, "Charge, Virginians, and save those brave Marylanders!" Alas! It was his last command on the field of battle, for at the instant he received a pistol shot, and was conveyed mortally wounded from the field, when his men precipitately retreated.

Nevertheless, in the confusion and excitement of the moment, Lieutenant McNulty, with some of the gallant fellows, actually drove two pieces off in triumph, despite the efforts of the enemy to prevent them.

In this desperate battle at Yellow Tavern, the battery suffered the loss of many men and horses, and two guns, and its brave commander was a prisoner in the enemy's hands.[47]

Goldsborough continued his account of the Second Maryland Artillery's participation at Yellow Tavern by giving an account of "individual heroism." He wrote:

During the hottest of the fight Private John Hayden was struck by a piece of shell and dreadfully mangled and would have bled to death in a few minutes had not the surgeon of the battery, Dr. Wortham, carried him on his back into the woods and stanched the hemorrhage. In a short time the enemy had possession of the field, but carefully concealing himself and his charge until they had passed on, he that night carried Hayden to a place of safety, where he eventually recovered.

With the two guns saved from the wreck of the battery, Lieutenant McNulty crossed the Chickahominy, closely pursued and took position on the right of the road, commanding the bridge, where, by a vigorous fire, he checked the enemy's advance and covered the retreat. McNulty then pushed on to the Old Church and joined the main body, which had been there reassembled.[48]

The Second Maryland Artillery lost twelve men at Yellow Tavern, two wounded in action and another ten were captured including Captain Griffin.

After the disaster at Yellow Tavern, the battery returned to Hanover Junction. In late June the unit was ordered to report for

## At It Again: 1864

service under General Jubal Anderson Early. Part of Early's forces had been operating primarily in the Shenandoah Valley and the whole force was about to invade Maryland and threaten Washington, D.C.

The Second Maryland Artillery marched for six days, waited for four days at Waynesboro, Virginia, and then joined Early's troops for the raid on Washington. The battery was now commanded by First Lieutenant W. B. Bean, since Captain Griffin's capture at Yellow Tavern. The unit was attached to General Bradley T. Johnson's Cavalry Brigade, which was leading the way.

For this campaign, Brigadier General Bradley T. Johnson's Cavalry Brigade was made up of the following units, officially:

- 1st Maryland Cavalry Battalion
- 8th Virginia Cavalry
- 21st Virginia Cavalry
- 22nd Virginia Cavalry, which was shown as a part of this organization, but recollections of members of the regiment show it was really part of John McCausland's Brigade.
- 34th Virginia Cavalry Battalion, which was detached and operating in Southwest Virginia and never served with Bradley Johnson
- 36th Virginia Cavalry Battalion

The overall mission of Early's force was to threaten Washington, D.C., and thus relieve some of the pressure on Lee's forces at Richmond and Petersburg. Johnson's mission, which he considered to be nearly impossible, was to free Confederate prisoners at the Point Lookout prison camp. Johnson had about 1,500 men and was to be joined by a naval task force of about 1,000 men, in an attempt to free an estimated 10,000 prisoners. Word of this mission apparently leaked out and the mission was scrubbed while Johnson's force was at Beltsville, still some eighty miles from Point Lookout.

Next came the raid itself. Washington Hands described what took place:

> On the morning of the 4th of July, Johnson approached Martinsburg, when he was charged by about six hundred of the enemy's cavalry, which for a moment

created some confusion in his ranks; but a few well directed discharges of spherical-case from Bean caused them to beat a precipitate retreat.

The command then pushed on and entered Martinsburg, when they came suddenly upon a battalion of women, dressed in their holiday attire, drawn up on the sidewalks, as though bent on preventing Johnson from taking possession of the town, or at least their wagon train, laden with ice cream, confectionery, etc.; for the fair and unfair dames, damsels and sweethearts of the troopers were about to celebrate the great national holiday by a picnic, when surprised by the naughty rebel Johnson, upon whom they at once opened such a fusillade of invectives in bad and not very choice English as to compel him and his command to retire in disgust, leaving them masters of the field.

From Martinsburg Johnson moved to Shepherdstown and crossed the Potomac into Maryland and took position on Catoctin Mountain, where he encountered a force of the enemy with artillery, but Bean soon drove them off, when they retired to Frederick City, closely pursued by Johnson's cavalry. Here, being reinforced, they made a stand within the confines of the city, and opened fire from their battery, protected by the houses. The fire was not returned for some time, as Johnson was loath to open his guns upon defenseless women and children, but finally forbearance ceasing to be a virtue, he opened his battery and a sharp artillery fight continued until night, when Johnson retired to the mountain to await Early's arrival.

Early having at length come up, Johnson, with his cavalry, and a section of the artillery under command of Lieutenant J. McNulty, proceeded to destroy the railroad bridges at Cockeysville, and this accomplished, he made a rapid move around Baltimore, and struck the Washington branch of the

Baltimore and Ohio Railroad at Beltsville, where a large body of the enemy's cavalry was met, which, after a few shots from the battery and a charge from the cavalry, broke and fled towards Washington in the utmost confusion. The battery, with Johnson's cavalry, covered Early's retreat from Washington though it was but seldom brought into requisition until the army reached Poolesville, where the enemy made a vigorous attack, but were kept in check by Johnson's cavalry and artillery until the whole army had crossed in safety.[49]

The Second Maryland Artillery had two men wounded in this action, William Forner on July 23 near Middletown, and Joseph Greenwell, who already had an artificial right leg due to his wounds at Sharpsburg. Nine men were captured during or just after the raid:

> Stockdale Fletcher, on July 7, 1864, near Frederick, Maryland;
> William Duvall on July 12, 1864, near Beltsville, Maryland;
> William Hart on July 16 near Rockville, Maryland;
> Robert Hawthorne on July 10 at Rockville, Maryland;
> John Lynch on July 11, 1864, at Frederick, Maryland;
> H. G. Richardson on July 16, 1864 near Rockville, Maryland;
> Adam Schaffer on July 16, 1864, near Rockville, Maryland;
> Albert Wheeler and Michael Shield were probably both taken prisoner on July 12 near Snicker's Gap, Virginia.

On July 24, Early's Valley Army defeated Averell's Federals at Kernstown. Neither McCausland's nor Johnson's Brigades were called into this action and Confederate losses were light. After the engagement at Kernstown, Federal forces retired to Maryland Heights and Harper's Ferry. On July 26, Early moved his infantry to Martinsburg. The Valley Army's cavalry moved to the Potomac River where the nearby Baltimore and Ohio Railroad was wrecked. Early noted that several private homes and other private property had been destroyed by Federals. Then, to use his words:

I came to the conclusion it was time to open the eyes of the people of the North to this enormity, by an example in the way of retaliation. I did not select the cases mentioned, as having more merit or greater claims for retaliation than others, but because they had occurred within the limits of the country covered by my command and were brought more immediately to my attention.

McCausland's and Johnson's Brigades rode north to bring Early's retribution demands to the residents of Chambersburg, Pennsylvania. In addition to the cavalry, Jackson's Horse Artillery rode with McCausland and Griffin's Baltimore Light Artillery rode with Johnson. Early took sole responsibility on himself and reported that McCausland was only following orders when he put the town to the torch. Early, however, gave these Northerners an opportunity the Federal armies never offered their Southern counterparts. The understanding was if the town fathers would come up with $500,000 in U.S. greenbacks or $100,000 in gold the Confederate raiders would ride south and all would be well. If payment was not made then the town would burn. It seemed quite equitable from the Southern point of view. In the Northern mind, however, it would create immense wrath toward Early's army and the commitment of considerable Federal resources to stop him, at almost any cost.

To execute the plan, McCausland and Johnson, with their 2,600 men crossed the Potomac River on July 29, at McCoy's Ferry near Clear Springs above Williamsport, Maryland. To generate a diversion, Early took his remaining cavalry and infantry toward Federal positions at Harper's Ferry. On the 30th, Chambersburg was reached and Early's ultimatum was promptly delivered. Early's July 29, 1864, message to "the Municipal Authorities of Chambersburg, Pennsylvania" read:

> The houses of Andrew Hunter, Esq., Alexander R. Boteler, Esq., and Edmund I. Lee, Esq., citizens of Jefferson County, Virginia having been burned by order of the officer commanding the Federal Forces in the Department called the "Department of Virginia" I have directed that your town pay for the said houses to

be handed over to the owners the sum of $100,000 in gold or $500,000 in current Northern funds.

In default of the payment of this money your town is directed to be laid in ashes in retaliation for the burning of said houses, and other houses of citizens of Virginia by Federal authorities.

Chambersburg's authorities called McCausland's hand and lost. They said they did not have the money. It is possible that they thought that the Averell's force would come to their aid in time to prevent the destruction. It is possible that they thought the threat was a bluff, since Confederate forces generally had acted in a gentlemanly manner on previous raids. In fact, if the decision had been left to Bradley Johnson, it would not have been carried out. McCausland, however, obeyed Early's orders and laid waste to the town.

Reverend B. S. Schneck, resident of Chambersburg's environs, noted, "Soldiers exhibited their proficient training by immediate and indiscriminate robbery. General Bradley Johnson reported, "Every crime in the catalogue of infamy has been committed, I believe, except murder and rape.... Thus the grand spectacle of national retaliation was reduced to a miserable huckstering for greenbacks." Confederate cavalrymen destroyed 537 buildings in the town, evaluated at more than $1.2 million, in a methodical manner. They kindled a fire before one building and moved on to the next on the street and duplicated the process.

Washington Hands described the action around Chambersburg from the perspective of a cannoneer:

> On the 29th of July General Johnson was ordered by General Early to accompany McCausland into Pennsylvania and exact a stipulated sum of money from the citizens of Chambersburg, or in case of their not complying with that demand to burn the town. The Baltimore Light Artillery was attached to the brigade and the whole crossed at McCoy's Ferry and proceeded on their way. Before day on the morning of the 30th the advance approached Chambersburg and

after feeling the place with a few shells, and finding no enemy, the town was entered and burned.[50]

The cavalry brigades camped for an evening at McConnellsburg on July 30. On the 31st, the McCausland-Johnson team moved to Hancock, Maryland. McCausland ordered Johnson, only slightly his junior, to ransom the town for $30,000. Johnson refused, claiming the town could not raise that amount. McCausland and Johnson ended their feuding when a mutual enemy, Federal cavalry, arrived on the scene. The combined Confederate forces moved on to Bevansville, reaching that point at 3 a.m. on August 1. At dawn they shifted position to their next objective.

The second goal of the mission was to ransom the town of Cumberland, Maryland. This town was more heavily fortified than Chambersburg. It was decided that the mission could not be accomplished and Cumberland was by-passed. Averell's Cavalry was in pursuit, so the Confederates moved to Old Town, Maryland, arriving at dawn on August 2. The Confederates withdrew toward Hampshire County, crossing to the south bank of the Potomac near South Branch. Johnson and McCausland's men succeeded in capturing the garrison there and partially destroyed the rail bridge over the Potomac. On August 4, McCausland advanced on New Creek with the purpose of destroying the Baltimore and Ohio Railroad there. McCausland's men encountered a small Yankee force and attacked their right flank. McCausland then led his men to Old Fields just above Moorefield in Hardy County. Washington Hands wrote:

> Retracing his steps to Virginia by way of Cumberland, McCausland arrived at that place late in the afternoon of the next day and found his situation a critical one. [Federal Brigadier General Benjamin Franklin] Kelly, with a large force, was in his front, strongly posted behind breast-works, and Averill was rapidly coming up in rear, and to avoid the former he was compelled to move to the left and take a different road from the one he had intended; but as there was not a man in his command who knew the country, this was not to be easily accomplished. After some delay, Colonel Harry

At It Again: 1864    147

Gilmore settled the question by seizing a Union man who was familiar with the different roads and fords, and with a cocked revolver at his head compelled him to pilot the way. In the night, four miles from Cumberland, McCausland's advance encountered the enemy, who were, after a brisk skirmish, driven back, when McCausland determined to await the morning to ascertain his position.

At the dawn of the day the enemy was discovered in line behind the crest of a range of hills between the canal and river, when McNulty was ordered to post his guns, and open the fight, whilst the cavalry dismounted and crossed the canal on a bridge hastily constructed by Captain Welsh of the First Maryland Cavalry, when the enemy retired. But a more formidable obstacle then presented itself in the shape of an iron clad battery mounted on an engine upon the railroad, whilst the cars to which it was attached were loop-holed for musketry, and the banks of the railroad, which formed an excellent breastwork, were lined with infantry. A very strong blockhouse that commanded every approach to the ford, was also found strongly garrisoned.

Colonel Harry Gilmore was at once ordered to carry the ford, which he attempted in most gallant style, but was unable to reach the opposite bank owing to the dreadful enfilading fire opened upon him.

Lieutenant McNulty was then directed to take position with his pieces, and open on the iron-clad. Quickly moving his guns to an open field, and but two hundred yards from the enemy, he unlimbered at this much exposed point, and called upon his best gunner, George McElwee, to bring his piece to bear upon the formidable looking mass of iron before him. The brave fellow, despite the shower of bullets to which he was exposed, coolly sighted his piece and fired, and when the smoke cleared away McNulty had the satisfaction of seeing the huge monster enveloped in steam, for the shot had directed by the unerring aim of McElwee had pierced the boiler, and it lay a helpless wreck upon the track. His next shot was as effective, and entered one of the portholes, dismounting the guns and scattering death and destruction around, when the enemy along the bank broke and fled.

But there was yet the blockhouse to dispose of before the command could resume its retreat, and minutes were becoming precious. An hour was consumed in discussing the matter before anything definite was determined upon, when General Johnson suggested that an attempt be made to get a piece of the artillery across the river. The suggestion was instantly adopted, and under cover of the bank, though subjected to a severe fire, the piece was started over in a full run and unlimbered in the river, and taken to its bank by hand, when, at the instant a demand for the surrender of the blockhouse was complied with, and McCausland was safe.

At Moorefield [August 7, 1864], soon after, McCausland was surprised in camp by Averill, when thirteen men of the Baltimore Light Artillery were sabered and captured at their guns endeavoring to load them, and two pieces were lost.[51]

McCausland and Johnson were still feuding, when they camped at Moorefield. Johnson's Brigade took positions on the north bank of the South Branch of the Potomac, near Romney Road. McCausland's Brigade camped on the south bank closer to the town of Moorefield. Averell's Cavalry, seeking revenge for Chambersburg, were still in pursuit. It is clear that the Southerners knew they were being chased, but they probably did not know how close the Federals were. This led to further charges and counter charges between McCausland and Johnson. Each suggested investigation of the other for dereliction of duty. Neither man was subjected to a standard inquest. Johnson got the worst of it and was informally reprimanded for not maintaining an effective watch. McCausland, though not completely vindicated, was able to sustain an effective command until the war's end. Johnson was not.

Averell's men captured the Confederate pickets and sentries without an alarm being given. The Federals astonished the sleeping Southerners before first light on August 7. McCausland's and Johnson's Brigades were routed—420 men taken prisoner, 400 mounts lost, as well as the loot taken from Chambersburg. John H. Bobbitt of Company G, Twenty-second Virginia Cavalry formerly of Grayson County, Virginia, wrote from Greensburg, Indiana, in 1902, "The name of Moorefield, a town in Hardy County, W. Va., is suggestive of a conflict never to be forgotten by the members of McCausland's Brigade of Virginia Cavalry and the sister brigade commanded by Gen. Bradley T. Johnson...."[52]

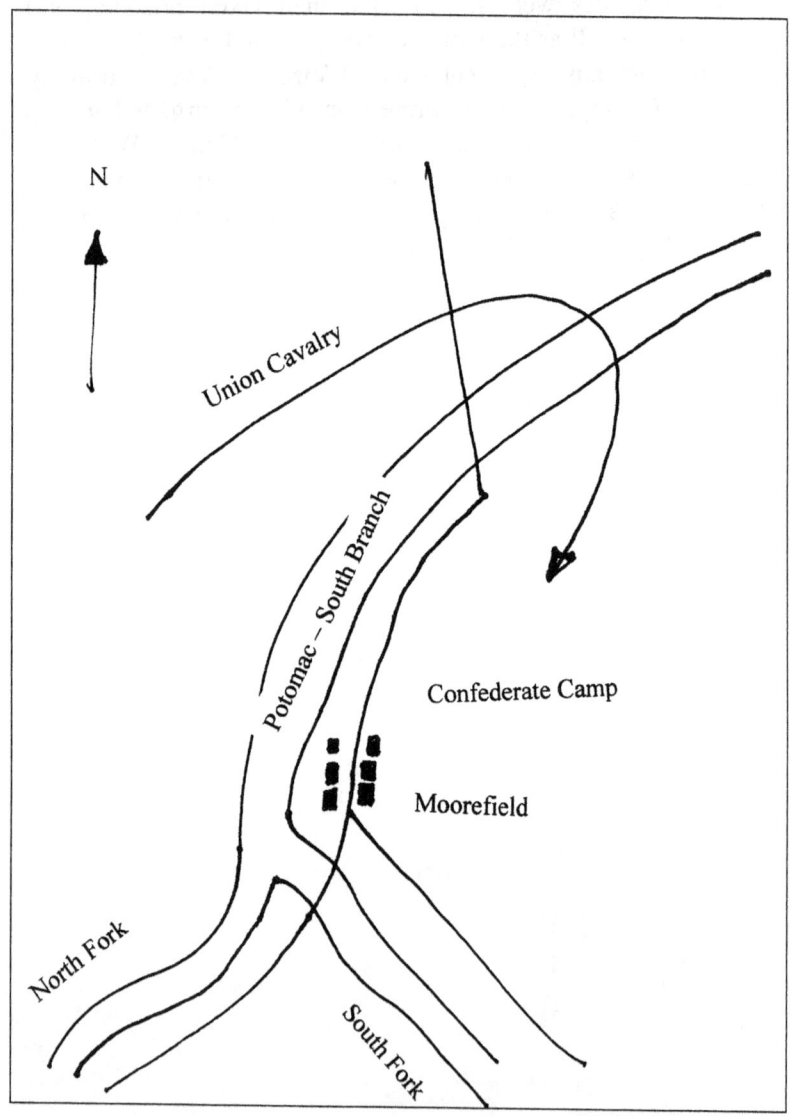

Battle of Moorefield, August 7, 1864

Joshua Hickman of the Second Maryland Artillery was killed during the action. Battery members Corporal George McAlwee and Private William Rogers were wounded, and the following men are known to have been captured: 5th Corporal George McAlwee, 6th Corporal John Bunting, Privates Martin Beane, Charles Beucke, J. Bukey, John Coleman, W. A. Davis, Robert Fitzgerald, Albert Holland and William Rogers.

Lieutenant William Bean tendered his resignation on August 9 and Early had him arrested on the 22nd. Lieutenant John McNulty, who had escaped from Johnson's Island on February 9, 1864, and was serving as an aide on General Johnson's staff, replaced him. The unit gained replacements from transfers and horses and guns from the reserve artillery.

Old Jubilee reported in his memoirs that on August 9, 1964, General Imboden reported that the Federal Sixth and Nineteenth Corps and Crook's Corps were at Harper's Ferry. They were under a new general to them, Philip "Little Phil" Sheridan. General Alfred T. A. Torbert was given overall command of the Federal cavalry. On August 10, Early's troops moved from just east of Winchester to cover the Charlestown and Berryville roads. On the twelfth McCausland's and Johnson's Brigades joined the rest of the army at new positions near Fisher's Hill. Another substitute affected the battery; General Lunsford Lomax replaced General Robert Ransom, disabled by disease, as commander of Early's cavalry.

Early's troops clashed with the Yankees at Newtown on August 11. The Confederates, neither defeated nor victorious, withdrew to a defensive line on Fisher's Hill. Union skirmishers crossed Cedar Creek on the fourteenth, but were pushed back with little inconvenience to the Confederates. On August 17, Johnson and McCausland went back into action and pursued the Yankees to Kernstown. Johnson's Brigade clashed with Federal horsemen. Johnson was reinforced by Gabriel Wharton's infantry brigade and S. D. Ramseur's infantry and the three won the field before darkness fell. The Second Maryland Artillery lost no one during these operations.

Lomax's cavalry division marched to Martinsburg, then to Shepherdstown, and to Charlestown, arriving on August 21. Early established camp at Cameron for the night. The Confederates made a concerted demonstration near the Federal's front from August 22-24. This was according to Early to "amuse the Federals" in front of Charlestown. On August 22, Union pickets were forced through Charlestown, Johnson's Brigade on the left flank of the army. McCausland's Brigade supported Joseph B. Kershaw's Infantry Division during these operations. On the August 26, the main body of the army moved to Leetown, and on the 27th to Bunker Hill. Anderson's infantry and McCausland's cavalry moved to Stephenson's Depot. Federal pressure forced the Cavalry advance guard to move back across the Opequon Creek on August 28, where "a brisk skirmish occurred." A second skirmish occurred across the stream on the 29th, when the Federal cavalry crossed and pushed the Confederate horsemen back. Early brought up his infantry and forced them back across. An artillery duel was fought, and some elements of the Valley army pursued the Federals through Smithfield towards Charlestown.

Johnson's Brigade, guarding supply trains at Bunker Hill on September 2, was routed as were their associates in Vaughn's Cavalry Brigade. The Confederate Cavalry were reinforced by Robert E. Rhodes' Infantry Division, and soon compelled the Yankees from the field. On September 5, Lomax's cavalry was rescued again by Rhodes' infantry.

On September 10, 1864, Lomax's Cavalry Division pursued Federals through Martinsburg and across Opequon Creek. On September 12, most of Early's units had returned to Bunker Hill and to Stephenson's Depot. Over the next week there was nearly constant skirmishing with Federal units operating in the northern Valley. All of these actions were a prelude to the Third Battle of Winchester. The Valley Army's cavalry units were reduced by battle, the rout at Moorefield and reassignments.

General Early divided his force on September 18, sending about half of his men toward Martinsburg, West Virginia. Averell's forces were operating in that area and he sent word to Sheridan that the Confederates had separated. General Lee had ordered Anderson's division back to Richmond, diminishing the Valley Army to less than 15,000 men. Sheridan did not pass up the opportunity.

On the morning of September 19, Early's cavalry crossed the Opequon Creek, and undertook to safeguard all crossings of the stream.

After resting and refitting, the Second Maryland Artillery was called back into action in late September, to help Early drive Sheridan's forces up the Shenandoah Valley. On the eighth and ninth of October, the battery was heavily involved in the action sometimes called the "Woodstock Races."

By September 28, Early sent Lomax's Cavalry to "watch the right flank and rear." The balance of the Army simultaneously moved toward Rockfish Gap. On September 29 and 30 the Army rested near Waynesboro. On October 1, 1864, the Army moved to Mount Sidney and remained there until October 6. On the eighth, Lomax's Cavalry skirmished at Tom's Brook with Federal cavalry. Sheridan's Yankees were engaged in burning and pillaging the Valley. Little Phil Sheridan told his cavalry commander, Torbert, to whip the Confederate horse soldiers "or get whipped." On October 8, Rosser's Cavalry Division was on the south bank of Tom's Brook. Custer faced him on the north. Lomax's division was stationed at the town of Woodstock.

Torbert deployed his men early on October 9, crossing Tom's Brook at the Valley Pike. Charles Russell Lowell's Brigade charged to the left, Thomas Devin took the center and James Kidd's Brigade moved with Custer on the Back Road. Mudwall Jackson's Brigade opposed Lowell and Bradley Johnson's Brigade opposed Devin's men. Artillery support was provided to the Confederates by McNulty's Maryland battery of four cannon. The Southern horsemen possessed only Enfield rifles, which severely limited their ability to fight while mounted.

The Union charge broke through the Southern center and W. L. Jackson's men broke as well. Devin's troops laid waste to Johnson's left. With Johnson's collapse, Confederate cavalry resistance ceased. McNulty's field artillery fired "grape and canister" before the Federal advance. The Confederate cavalry retreated in considerable disorder through and around Woodstock. The Second Maryland Artillery abandoned its cannons, and joined in the withdrawal. The disorganized evacuation, in reality another rout, ended at the infantry lines, twenty-six miles south of the morning's positions. Lomax in his report noted, "I was unable to rally this command." The Federals called the engagement the "Woodstock Races."

Washington Hands described what transpired from the artilleryman's point of view:

> Slight skirmishing ensued between the pursued and pursuers until the former reached Fisher's Hill, where they met their infantry, when [Major General Lunsford] Lomax, in command of the cavalry, retired to the vicinity of Woodstock. At daylight next morning, the 8th of October, Lomax and Rosser moved to attack on the left the enemy, who had advanced to Maurytown. Rosser was ordered to attack and Lomax took the right, forming his troops on both sides of the Valley pike. The Baltimore Light Artillery, under McNulty, was stationed on an eminence north of the town. The fight soon began with great fury, Lomax and Rosser attacking simultaneously, and the enemy was driven back some distance. Heavy reinforcements coming to the support of the enemy, he reformed his broken columns, and the fight was waged with redoubled fury. Towards noon Rosser, on the left, was overwhelmed and soon after the heavy columns massed in front of Lomax, attacked furiously, and drove that General back in the utmost confusion.
> 
> During this time the gallant McNulty and his brave command were hurling death and destruction into the ranks of the enemy, but to no avail. With the retreat of the cavalry under Lomax, McNulty limbered up and suddenly fell back, unlimbering at every available point, and opening his fire upon the pursuing foe, thus enabling the cavalry to escape. In this manner the village of Woodstock was reached. Still through its streets he continued to pour into the faces of the advancing enemy destructive discharges of grape and canister. But the gallant little battery was doomed, for the enemy pressed upon them in overwhelming numbers, and still they disdained to abandon their

pieces. Beyond the town they made one more effort to stay the dense masses which almost enveloped them, but even as the gunners were ramming home the last double charge of canister, they were captured and cut down in the act.

Twenty-three men and the four guns fell into the hands the enemy. Lieutenant McNulty... with the balance of his men fought their way through and escaped.[53]

The following men of the Second Maryland Artillery were captured at Woodstock on October 9: 6th Corporal Chester Burnett, Privates Harry Arens, H. V. Barry, Richard Biscoe, George Christy, George Clotworthy, Matthew Coffee, Charles Evans, Robert Hunt, Edward Hynes, A. Kernan, Lewis Knight, Daniel Lynch, Robert McCubbin, James Rhiems, William Reimes, G. W. Richardson, Joseph Sullivan and William Tarr.

After this battle, the battery fought no more in 1864. The unit simply went into winter quarters near Fishersville. Four conscripts were received in October and on October 31 only sixty-eight officers and men were present. Many of the regiments in Lomax's Division could muster barely more than one hundred men at the time. At this time no less than fifty-three were prisoners of war. On October 31, 1864, the battery's officers and staff consisted of:

Jr. 1st Lieutenant John McNulty
2nd Lieutenant John Goodman
1st Sergeant Joseph Bean
2nd Sergeant Harry Marston
3rd Sergeant James Morrison (POW)
4th Sergeant William Ferry
1st Corporal William Wallace (POW)
2nd Corporal George Pembroke
3rd Corporal Matthew McLoid
4th Corporal George McAlwee (POW)
5th Corporal John Bunting (POW)
6th Corporal Chester Burnett (POW)
7th Corporal John Hayden
8th Corporal Chris Pochlman

Bugler, Joshua Davis, Jr.
Commissary Sergeant Lewis Claus
Quartermaster Sergeant James Smith
Orderly Sergeant William Robinson
Ordnance Sergeant Samuel Mattison
Surgeon J. B. Wortham

In his after-action report on the "Woodstock Races," Lomax noted that the four pieces of artillery were lost due to the "miserable condition of the horses" from the Baltimore Battery, "which had just been newly equipped for the field."[54] However, Lomax also noted that the officers and men did all they could to save their pieces after their horses gave out, unlimbering and firing until the enemy reached them.

Early put his Shenandoah Valley army in motion again on October 12. The main Confederate infantry force marched from Rude's Hill to Woodstock where they camped for the night. Lomax's cavalry were located in the Luray Valley. On October 13 the infantry and artillery forces gathered on the south bank of Cedar Creek. When the Valley Army took up these positions a brisk skirmish ensued. The Second Maryland Artillery was not an active participant.

## Chapter VI

## Faithful to the End: 1865

The Second Maryland Artillery spent the winter of 1864-5 relatively uneventfully. The hard fighting of 1864 had taken its toll: one man was killed in action, six men were wounded and fifty-five were taken prisoner.

The Second Maryland Artillery had been attached and loaned out so often that higher headquarters did not seem to know where it belonged. The Army of Northern Virginia table of organization for January 31, 1865, placed it in an unnamed Cavalry Artillery battalion, along with J. H. McClanahan's Virginia Battery.[55] The Army of the Valley Organization of the same date showed the battery again, as follows part of the Lomax Horse Artillery with Captain Warren S. Lurty's Virginia battery.[56]

In early 1865 the beleaguered Confederacy did not have the resources to fully reequip the Second Maryland Artillery. Guns, horses, men and equipment were all in short supply. In Special Orders No. 13, Headquarters Artillery, Army of Northern Virginia, dated March 22, 1865, Brigadier General and Chief of Artillery W. W. Pendleton directed consolidation of the Second Maryland Artillery with Chew's battery. The order read:

> 3. The armament, horses, and equipment and transportation of Chew's battery, McIntosh's battalion, will also be turned over to Lieut. Co. C. M. Braxton, and Captain Chew will proceed with his men to Richmond and report to Lieutenant Colonel Chew, commanding horse artillery, for orders in connection with his consolidation with Griffin's battery, Breathed's battalion. Chamberlayne's battery, Owen's battalion, will report for duty to Colonel McIntosh in place of Chew.[57]

At about the same time, Longstreet had another use for the men of the Second Maryland Artillery. He wrote General Lee on March 20, 1865:

> I presume that the enemy's next move will be to raid against the Danville railroad, and think that it would be well if we begin at once to make our arrangements to meet it. In order that we may get the troops that may be necessary to meet such a move I would suggest that we collect all the dismounted men of General Fitz Lee, Rosser, and Lomax and put them behind our strongest lines, and draw out a corps of infantry and hold it in readiness for the raid. General W. H. F. Lee's dismounts might also be used behind our works to hold the enemy in check. I think that our infantry may be able to overtake the raiding column. If we can get a large cavalry force I think that we would surely be able to destroy the raiding force.[58]

Second Lieutenant John Goodman, commanding the battery since early 1865, was dropped on March 2, 1865. This was probably due to his letter of resignation of September 4, 1864, in which he protested the "many individual acts of robbery and pillage" that took place in Maryland during Early's raid.

On March 22, 1865, Orderly Sergeant William Wirt Robinson was assigned to duty as Acting Second Lieutenant. He probably commanded the unit until the end of the war, less than three weeks away.

Washington Hand's words end this history of the Second Maryland Artillery:

> Soon after the disastrous fight at Maurytown, Goodman was ordered to Fishersville, where the little left of Early's artillery were preparing their winter quarters. Whilst here every effort was made to procure guns, horses, etc., for the battery, to replace those lost in their last fight, but without success, for the Confederate Government had none to spare. But the brave fellows were ready for any duty that might be assigned them, and when Sheridan, in March,

threatened Lynchburg, they gladly obeyed the summons to repair to that place and assist in its defense in any capacity. But their services were not required, and they were in a few days ordered to Petersburg, to man the fortifications there.

When the great crash came, and the little army under General Lee was forced to retreat before Grant's overwhelming masses, along with the rest was to be found the remnant of the Baltimore Light Artillery—one day fighting as infantry and the next as cavalry, or assisting some battery in trouble. Noble fellows, like their comrades of the Maryland Line, they were true to the cause they had espoused to the last, and, like the infantry and cavalry, were determined to fight on whilst a ray of hope remained. Alas! That last ray disappeared with Lee's surrender at Appomattox Courthouse, and when told they were disarmed, and no more to be led against the enemy, these veterans, who had unhesitatingly faced death in all its dreadful shapes on so many bloody fields, wept like children. Surely Maryland should be proud of her "Young Line" in the Confederate States Army, as she was of the "Old" in the days of the Revolution.[59]

## Chapter VII

## Statistical Summary

At least 230 men served in the Second Maryland Artillery. Since the unit was also called the Baltimore Light Artillery, it comes as no surprise to find that most of the men came from Baltimore, Maryland.

The year of enlistment is known for 189 men and is broken down as follows:

| 1861 | 1862 | 1863 | 1864 |
|---|---|---|---|
| 85 | 58 | 24 | 22 |
| 45% | 31% | 13% | 12% |

Most of the men of the battery enlisted in Virginia as shown below:

| Virginia | Maryland | Alabama | Georgia | Tennessee |
|---|---|---|---|---|
| 175 | 9 | 3 | 1 | 1 |
| 93% | 5% | 2% | ½% | ½% |

Four of the nine men who enlisted in Maryland, mustered in service in Frederick and two others enrolled in Baltimore.

Richmond was the most common place for the 175 Virginia enlistments:

| | | |
|---|---|---|
| Richmond | 112 | 64% |
| Charlottesville | 11 | 6% |
| Hanover | 10 | 6% |
| Rappahannock | 6 | 3% |
| Harrisonburg | 5 | 3% |
| Other | 22 | 13% |

These other enlistments included: Centerville, 3; Bunker Hill, 3; Baskerville, 2; Woodstock, 2; Ashland, 1; Brandy Station, 1;

Edinburg, 1; Fairfax, 1; Glouster, 1; Gordonsville, 1; Lacy Springs, 1; Lexington, 1; Mt. Crawford, 1; Martinsburg, 1; Petersburg, 1; and West Point, 1.

As expected, most of the men came from Maryland, as shown:

| Maryland | Virginia | D.C. | Ireland | Other |
|---|---|---|---|---|
| 114 | 6 | 4 | 3 | 7 |
| 85% | 4% | 3% | 2% | 5% |

Other places of residence included one man each from Alabama, Kentucky, Louisiana, Tennessee, Texas, Mississippi and, believe it or not, Michigan.

Of the 114 known Marylanders, most were from Baltimore County.

| Baltimore Co. | St. Mary's Co. | Carroll Co. | Talbott Co. | Other |
|---|---|---|---|---|
| 75 | 14 | 5 | 3 | 16 |
| 66% | 12% | 4% | 3% | 16% |

The other categories include two men each from Anne Arundel, Charles, Frederick, Hartford, Queen Anne, Prince George's and Somerset Counties. One man came from Kent, Montgomery and Washington Counties.

Statistical Summary

As shown on the following table, the Second Maryland Artillery had at least seven men killed in action, at least twenty-six were wounded in action and at least eighty-three men were taken prisoner during the war. At least fifty-five men were taken prisoner during 1864, when infantry and cavalry support was not as sound as it had been in 1862 and 1863.

| Date | Engagement | KIA | WIA | POW | Total |
|---|---|---|---|---|---|
| 5-6/62 | Valley Campaign/ Malvern Hill | 1 | 4 | 7 | 12 |
| 6/27-7/3/62 | Seven Days | | 5 | | 5 |
| 8/22/62 | Cunningham's Ford | 4 | 2 | | 6 |
| 9/17/62 | Sharpsburg, MD | | 4 | | 4 |
| 11/30/62 | -- | | | 2 | 2 |
| 2/7/63 | Winchester | | | 3 | 3 |
| 7/1-5/63 | Gettysburg, PA | | 3 | 3 | 6 |
| 9/13/63 | Culpeper C.H. | 1 | | 12 | 13 |
| 5/11/64 | Yellow Tavern | | 2 | 10 | 12 |
| 7/1-20/64 | Early's Raid | | 2 | 9 | 11 |
| 8/7/64 | Moorefield | 1 | 2 | 10 (13) | 16 |
| 10/9/64 | Woodstock | | | 19 (23) | 23 |
| | Other | | 2 | 8 | 10 |
| | Total | 7 | 26 | 83 (90) | 123 |

## Second Maryland Artillery

The Second Maryland (Baltimore Light) Artillery strength figures are given in the next table. As can be seen, the overall strength of the battery did not vary much throughout the war. Morale must have been quite good, as desertion was quite rare. Also, it is very clear that losses were compensated for by enlistments and transfers.

| Baltimore Light Artillery Strengths | | | | |
|---|---|---|---|---|
| Date | Present for Duty | Aggregate Present | Present & Absent | Artillery Pieces |
| 10/31/61 | 76 | 76 | 76 | - |
| 12/31/61 | 63 | 63 | 75 | - |
| 1/63 | 60 | 72 | 102 | 3 |
| 11/30/63 | 62 | 73 | 100 | 3 |
| 2/10/64 | 66 | 76 | 100 | 3 |
| 3/31/64 | 66 | 79 | 103 | 4 |
| 4/20/64 | 70 | 80 | 104 | 4 |
| 5/10-31/64 | 75 | 87 | 96 | 4 |
| 8/31/64 | 79 | 84 | 127 | 2 |
| 10/31/64 | 68 | 70 | 138* | - |

The significant losses for the Second Maryland Artillery are given in the next table. Note that no one was transferred to another unit or was retired. Also, nobody left under a writ of habeas corpus. Most discharges were for physical disability. The AWOL entry refers to those individuals whose last roster entry was AWOL.

| Significant Losses | | |
|---|---|---|
| KIA | 7 | 3% |
| WIA | 26 | 11% |
| POW | 83 | 36% |
| Deserted | 7 | 3% |
| Detailed | 16 | 7% |
| Discharged | 11 | 5% |
| Died of Disease | 4 | 2% |
| Died of Wounds | 2 | 1% |
| Dropped | 2 | 1% |
| AWOL | 8 | 3% |

* Fifty-three of these men were absent, prisoners of war.

S. Fletcher escaped from Point Lookout, Maryland, on October 18, 1864, after being a prisoner of war there for three months. Lieutenant John McNulty escaped from Johnson's Island by assuming another prisoner's identity.

Point Lookout was the most common destination for prisoners taken from the Second Maryland Artillery and received twenty-nine men before the war was over. Camp Chase became the temporary home of fourteen men, Elmira, New York, received thirteen, Ford Delaware, five, the Old Capitol Prison in Washington, D.C., held six and Johnson's Island, Ohio, held two. In addition to the listed camps and prisons, there was one prisoner at Fort Monroe, Fort McHenry and Wheeling. Many men taken prisoner during 1862 were paroled or exchanged without being sent to camps or prisons.

| Prisoner of War Statistics | | |
|---|---|---|
| Paroled | 11 | 13% |
| Exchanged | 32 | 39% |
| Released on oath | 34 | 41% |
| Died in prison | 2 | 2% |
| Escaped | 2 | 2% |
| Unknown | 2 | 2% |

The following list gives the trades and occupations of members of the Second Maryland Artillery, where known and in order by number per occupation: Clerk, eight; Teamster, six; Blacksmith, five; Physician, five; Student, five; Carpenter, four; Harness maker, four; Seaman, four; Farmer, three; Merchant, three. The following occupations and trades had one person each: gas fitter, iron molder, laborer, mechanic, painter, plasterer, printer, sail maker, shoemaker, stone cutter and telegraph operator.

See the introduction to the roster of the First Maryland Artillery. Similar comments and abbreviations apply to this roster.

# NOTES

[1] Compiled Service Records, (CSR) Second Maryland Artillery.
[2] OR, Vol. V, 1030.
[3] Goldsborough, 276.
[4] OR, Vol. XI, 560.
[5] Goldsborough, 276.
[6] Goldsborough, 277.
[7] OR, Vol. XII, 780, 742, 818.
[8] OR, Vol. XII, 727, 718.
[9] OR, Vol. XII, 725.
[10] Goldsborough, 278.
[11] Goldsborough, 278.
[12] OR, Vol. XI, 622.
[13] Goldsborough, 279.
[14] Goldsborough, 279.
[15] OR, Vol. XII, 654-5.
[16] OR, Vol. XII, 652.
[17] Goldsborough, 280.
[18] OR, Vol. XII, 653.
[19] Goldsborough, 280-281.
[20] Goldsborough, 280-281.
[21] OR, Vol. XIX, 1016.
[22] Goldsborough, 282.
[23] OR, Vol. XIX, 964.
[24] OR, Vol. XIX, 964.

[25] OR, Vol. XIX, 964.

[26] Goldsborough, 283.

[27] CSR, Second Maryland Artillery.

[28] OR, Vol. XXI, 602.

[29] OR, Vol. XXI, 747.

[30] OR, Vol. XXI, 748.

[31] OR, Vol. XXI, 748.

[32] OR, Vol. XXI, 748.

[33] OR, Vol. XXI, 749.

[34] OR, Vol. XXI, 644-6.

[35] OR, Vol. XXVII, 440.

[36] OR, Vol. XXVII, 461.

[37] Goldsborough, 283.

[38] Goldsborough, 284.

[39] Goldsborough, 285.

[40] Goldsborough, 285.

[41] Goldsborough, 285.

[42] Goldsborough, 286.

[43] Goldsborough, 286.

[44] OR, Vol. XXXIII, 1090.

[45] OR, Vol. XXXIII, 856.

[46] OR, Vol. XXXIII, 1058, 1247, 1299; OR, Vol. XXXVI, 988.

[47] Goldsborough, 287-288.

[48] Goldsborough, 288.

[49] Washington Hands' Civil War Notebook, used by permission of the Maryland Historical Society (Hereafter cited as Hands), 107-108.

[50] Hands, 108.

[51] Hands, 109-110.

[52] Weaver, Jeffrey C. 22nd Virginia Cavalry, 44.

[53] Hands, 111.

[54] OR, Vol. XLIII, 613.

[55] OR, Vol. XLVI, 1178.

[56] OR, Vol. XLVI, 1184.

[57] OR, Vol. XLVI, 1334.

[58] OR, Vol. XLVI, 1329.

[59] Hands, 112.

# COMPILED SERVICE RECORDS ROSTER

## Second Maryland Artillery

**ANDERSON, THOMAS**: Enl. on ?. Deserted, taken POW at Winchester, Va. on 2/7/63, sent to Camp Chase, Ohio. Described as 6' ½", age 23, dark eyes, dark hair. Released on oath on 3/27/63. Res. of Prince George's Co., Md., occupation clerk.

**ARENS (ARENDTS), HARRY**: Enl. on 6/1/64 at Richmond. Pres. on 8/31/64. Taken POW on 10/9/64 at Woodstock, Va., sent to Harper's Ferry, then to Point Lookout, Md. Exchanged on 3/14/65. Paroled at Lynchburg, Va. on 4/13/65.

**ARMSTRONG, J. B.**: Enl. on ?. Taken POW at Winchester, Va. on 2/8/63, then age 25, 5' 6 ½", blue eyes, light hair, painter, res. of Texas. Sent to Camp Chase, Ohio where held until released on oath on 3/5/63.

**BANNER, CHARLES**: Enl. on 8/15/61 at Richmond. Pres. on 10/31/61 and 12/31/61 rolls. AWOL on 12/62 roll.

**BARRY, (BONEY) H. (HUGH) V.**: Enl. on 6/1/64 at Richmond, Va. Pres. on 8/31/64 roll. Taken POW at Woodstock on 10/9/64, sent to Harper's Ferry on 10/20/64, then to Point Lookout, Md. where held until released on oath on 5/12-14/65. Res. of Emmitsburg, Frederick Co., Md.

**BEAN, JOSEPH A.**: Pvt./1st Sgt. Enl. on 8/15/61 at Richmond, Va. Pres. on 10/31/61 roll as pvt. Absent sick in Hosp. in Richmond, Va. on 12/31/61 roll. Pres on 4/1/64 as 1st sgt. Pres. on 8/31/64 and 10/31/64 rolls. Surrendered at Appomattox C.H. Paroled on 4/22/65 at Harper's Ferry. Res. of Great Mills, St. Mary's Co., Md. Age 25, 6', brown hair, hazel eyes.

**BEAN, WILLIAM BENNETT**: 2nd Lt./1st Lt. Enl. on 8/15/61. Pres. on 10/31/61 and 5/11/62 as 2nd lt. Absent sick on 12/31/61 roll. Pres. on 12/62 roll as jr. 1st lt. Pres. On 4/1/64 roll. Absent, in arrest by order of Maj. Gen. J. A. Early, 8/22/64 per 8/31/64 and 10/31/64 rolls. Bean tendered his resignation on 2/19/63, 2/22/64 and 8/9/64. Res. of St. Gregor's, St. Mary's Co., Md.

**BEANE, MARTIN**: Enl. on 2/16/64 at Hanover Junction, Va. Pres. on 4/1/64 roll. Taken POW on 8/7/64 at Moorefield, Va. Released on oath on 8/17/64, sent to Philadelphia, Pa. He was paid $50 bounty.

**BELL (BEALL), WALTER**: Enl. on ?. Taken POW at Culpeper C.H., Va. on 9/14/63, sent to Point Lookout, Md. on 9/26/63 where he died on 11/28/63. He previously served in Holbrook's Independent Light Artillery.

**BEUCKE (BUCK), CHARLES L.**: Pvt./Corp. Enl. on ?. Taken POW at Moorefield, Va. on 8/7/64, sent to Harper's Ferry, then to Wheeling, W Va., then to Camp Chase, Ohio. Paroled on 2/25/65. Res. of Baltimore, Md., age 26, 6'3", blue eyes, black hair, farmer. Paid $109 on 3/29/65.

**BRADLEY THOMAS J.**: Enl. on 8/15/61 at Richmond, Va. Pres. on 10/31/61 and 12/31/61 rolls, then NFR.

**BREADON, BRANSON**: Enl. on 3/31/62 at Rappahannock Station, $50 bounty paid. NFR.

**BRISCO, RICHARD CLARK**: Enl. on 2/11/61 at Baltimore, Md. Taken POW at Woodstock, Va. on 10/9/64, sent to Point Lookout, Md., where held until released on oath on 4/17/65. He previously served in Co. F, 1st S. C. Light Artillery, MLCSH.

**BROCKENBOROUGH, JOHN BOWYER**: Capt./Major, Enl. on 8/15/61 at Richmond, Va. Previously served as 1st lt. in the 1st Rockbridge Virginia Artillery, where he enl. on 4/29/61. Slightly WIA in the face at 1st Manassas with this battery. Paid $65.33 on 10/26/61. Pres. on 10/31/61 roll. Paid $280 on 12/19/61. Absent sick furlough at home on 12/31/61 roll. Paid $420 on 3/31/62, paid $140 on 5/31/62. Recommended by officers commanding batteries in battalion. Lee Battery – Capt. Raine, Hampden Artillery – Capt. Caskie, Lusk's Battery – Capt. Donald in Letter to Lt. Gen. T. J. Jackson dated 11/11/62 for promotion to major. Brig. Gen. J. R.

Jones, commanding division wrote a similar letter to Sec. of War Randolph on 11/18/62. Later served as Ordnance Officer, Jackson's staff. Paid $280 on 10/32/62, $560 on 12/31/62, paid $162 on 8/31/64, 9/31/64 and 10/31/64. Retired from service on 3/24/64 for disability. B. 4/6/1836 in Lexington, Va. Attended Washington College 1855-56. Graduated from U. Va. in 1857, graduated from Washington College in 1859 with LL.D. degree. Occupation – attorney. Antebellum res. of Rockbridge Co., Va. Had law practice at Lynchburg, Va. 1864–86, when appointed Special Agent for Dept. of Interior by Pres. Cleveland. Moved to Baltimore, Md. in 1900. Died at Evanston, Wyoming on 11/15/1901. Buried in Loudon Park Cem., Baltimore, Md. Bro. of Willoughby H. Brockenborough.

**BROCKENBOROUGH, WILLOUGHBY NEWTON**: Enl. on 4/29/61 at Lexington, Va. in the 1st Rockbridge Artillery as pvt., and was promoted to 3rd Corp., but was reduced to ranks by 4/22/62. Transferred to the Second Maryland Artillery on 5/26/62. Pres. on 4/1/64. Taken POW at Yellow Tavern on 5/11/64, sent to Fort Monroe and then to Fort Delaware by 6/23/64. Brown hair, blue eyes, 5' 11 ½". Released on oath on 6/12/65. B. ca 1843 in Lexington, Va., student, age 17, 1860 Lexington, Va. census. Attended Washington College 1867-8. Antebellum res. of Rockbridge Co., Va. Lawyer in Columbia, Mo. in 1904.

**BROOME, ROBERT**: Enl. on ? Paroled at Appomattox C.H., Va. on 4/10/65

**BROWNE, W. H.**: Enl. on 5/5/61 at Fairfax Station, Va. in the 17th Va. Inf. Transferred to the Second Maryland Artillery on 5/2/64. Taken POW at Yellow Tavern, Va. on 5/11/64, sent to Fort Monroe on 5/17/64 and then to Elmira, N.Y. on 8/17/64. Exchanged on 10/29/64. Res. of Baltimore, Md.

**BRYNE, ANDREW J.**: Pvt./Sgt. Enl. on 8/15/61 at Richmond, Va. Appointed 5th sgt. on 10/31/61. Pres. on 10/31/61 and 12/31/61 rolls, then NFR. Later served in Co. A, Davis' Maryland Cavalry.

**BUCKEY, J.**: Enl. on 7/17/64 at Poolsville, Md. Taken POW at Moorefield, Va. on 8/7/64.

**BUNTING, JOHN**: Pvt./Corp. Enl. on 10/28/61 at Richmond, Va. In Gen. Hosp. No. 18, Richmond, Va. on 11/24-12/12/61. Absent sick in hosp. on 12/31/61 roll. Pres. on 10/31/61, 4/64 (as 6th Corp.) rolls. Taken POW at Moorefield on 8/7/64. Age 20, 5' 7", brown eyes, dark hair, occupation clerk. Sent to Harper's Ferry and then to Camp Chase, Ohio on 8/11/64 and then to Point Lookout, Md. on 3/4/65. Paroled on 4/20-24/65. Res. of Baltimore, Md.

**BURGESS, JOHN W.**: Enl. on 6/13/62 at Port Republic, Va. Pres. on 4/1/64 and 8/31/64 rolls. $50 bounty was paid. Paroled at Lynchburg, Va. on 4/16/65. Res. of Hancock, Washington Co., Md.

**BURKE, WILLIAM**: Enl. on 2/6/62 at Richmond, Va. AWOL on 12/62 roll. $50 bounty paid. Res. of Carroll Co., Md.

**BURNETT, CHESTER CHARLES**: Pvt./Corp. Enl. on 8/15/61 at Richmond. Pres. on 10/31/61, 12/31/61, 4/1/64 (as 7th corp.), 8/31/64 and 10/31/64 (as 6th corp.). But was taken POW at Woodstock, Va. on 10/9/64, sent to Point Lookout, Md. where held until exchanged on 3/17/65. Paid $9.20 on 8/23/63 for extra duty as blacksmith and paid $26 on 3/12/64.

**CALLIGAN (CALLINGHAM), JOHN T.** Enl. on 4/ /62 in Purcell's Battery of Pegram's Battalion. Transferred to Second Maryland Artillery in 4/64. Taken POW before reporting at New Market, Va. Sent to Camp Chase, Ohio in 5/64. Exchanged in 3/65. Took oath on 5/1/65. Res. was corner of 4th and D St., East Washington, D.C.

**CAMPBELL, WILLIAM**: Enl. on 4/1/64 at Hanover Junction, Va. Pres. on 4/1/64 roll. Detailed as harness maker for the company on 8/31/64 roll. Detailed as teamster on 10/31/64 roll.

**CANE, JAMES**: Enl. on ?. Took oath at Fort Delaware on 8/10/62. NFR.

**CARR, JOHN C.**: Enl. on 9/17/61 at Richmond, Va. Pres. on 10/31/61 and 12/31/61 rolls. Sick in hosp. on 12/62 roll. In hosps. 10-11/62 and 1/63 for rheumatism. Discharged on 5/29/63. Taken POW at Harrisburg, Va. on 6/6/62. Paroled at Winchester, Va. on 7/3/62. Paid $30 on 12/5/62. Aged 29, 5' 9", blue eyes, dark hair, laborer. Native of Galway, Ireland.

**CECIL, JAMES**: Enl. on ?. AWOL on 12/62 roll. Also served in 4th Maryland Light Artillery. Res. of St. Mary's Co., Maryland.

**CHAMBERS, JOHN EDWARD**: Enl. on 2/1/61 at Baltimore, Md. Pres. on 10/31/64 roll. Taken POW at Staunton, Va. and paroled on 5/1/65, age 24, 5' 8", black hair, dark eyes. Res. of Baltimore, Md. Previously served in Rhett's 1st S.C. Heavy Artillery. MLCSH.

**CHARLOTTE, GEORGE W.**: Enl. on 4/30/63 Harrisonburg. Pres. on 4/1/64 and 8/31/64 rolls. Deserted per 10/31/64 roll.

**CHRISTY, GEORGE W**: Enl. on 4/13/64 at Hanover Junction, Va. Pres. on 8/31/64 roll. Taken POW at Woodstock, Va. on 10/9/64, sent to Point Lookout, Md. on 10/13/64. Died of scurvy on 4/1/65, buried in grave #1388. Res. of St. Mary's Co., Md.

**CLAIBORN, CHARLES HARRISON**: Enl. on ?. AWOL on 12/62 roll. Also served as lt. in Co. G, 1st S.C. Inf. Res. of Baltimore, Md.

**CLARK, CHARLES J.**: Enl. on ?. AWOL on 12/62 roll. Taken POW at Strausburg, Va. on 6/22/62, exchanged at Aiken's Landing, Va. on 6/26/62. Also served in Co. I, 56th Va. Inf.

**CLAUS, LEWIS (LOUIS)**: Pvt./Commissary Sgt. Enl. on 8/15/61 at Richmond, Va. Pres. on 10/31/61, 12/31/61, 4/1/64, 8/31/64 and 10/31/64 rolls. In Gen. Hosp. #21 Richmond 2/26-3/16/62 with rheumatism, 7/8-14/64 with consumption, and 9/28-10/13/62 with wound. WIA on 9/17/62 at Sharpsburg on the back of the left hand. Acting Company Commissary 4/30-8/31/64.

**CLEAL, CHARLES**: Enl. on 8/15/61 at Richmond, Va. Pres. on 10/31/61 roll. Absent sick in hosp. on 12/31/61 roll. Paid $147 on 9/2/62, including a $50 bounty. Detached on 12/62 roll. In Chimborazo Hosp. #3, Richmond from 9/23-11/8/63 with diarrhea. Pres. on 4/1/64 roll. Deserted on 5/25/64 near Ashland, Va. per 8/31/64 roll.

**CLEARY, J. H.**: Enl. on ?. Taken POW at Woodstock, Va. on 6/2/62. Exchanged at Aiken's Landing, Va. on 8/5/62, NFR.

## Second Maryland Artillery

**CLIFFORD, HENRY A.**: Enl. on ?. Took oath on 4/25/65. Farmer/seaman. May have also served in the C.S. Navy. Res. of Baltimore, Md.

**CLOTHWORTHY, GEORGE W.**: Enl. on 8/15/61 at Richmond, Va. Pres. on 10/31/61 and 12/31/61 rolls. AWOL on 12/62 and 4/1/64 rolls. Pres. on 8/31/64 roll. Taken POW at Woodstock, Va. on 10/9/64. Sent to Point Lookout, Md. where he was held until exchanged on 2/10/65. Also taken POW at Culpeper, Va. on 9/14/63, sent to Point Lookout, Md., exchanged at some point. Took oath on 4/15/65 at Richmond. Arrested on 4/25/65. Res. of 76 N. Howard St., Baltimore, Md.

**COFFEE, MATTHEW J.**: Enl. on 6/13/62 at Richmond, Va. Pres. on 4/1/64 and 8/31/64 rolls. Taken POW at Falling Waters, Md. on 7/14/63. Sent to Point Lookout, Md. where held until exchanged on 12/24/63. Taken POW at Woodstock, Va. on 10/9/64, sent to Point Lookout, Md. where held until exchanged in 2/65. At Camp Lee, Va. on 2/20/65.

**COLEMAN, JOHN (JAMES) A.**: Enl. on 2/17/62 at Richmond, Va. Taken POW at Moorefield, Va. on 8/7/64, sent to Camp Chase, Ohio on 8/12/64 and then to Point Lookout, Md. on 3/18/65. Present at Camp Lee, Va. on 3/28/65. Res. of New Orleans, La. or Baltimore, Md. 5' 4 ¼", age 26, grey eyes, auburn hair, occupation harness maker. He also served in Letcher's Virginia Light Artillery. MLCSH.

**COSGRIFF, (COSGROVE) JAMES O**: Enl. on 8/15/61 at Richmond, Va. Pres. on 10/31/61 and 12/31/61 rolls. In hosp. on 4, 5, 6-8/62. Paid $122 on 11/6/62. Ordered to report from hosp. on 12/1/62 per 12/62 roll. Taken POW on 9/13/63 at Culpeper C.H., sent to Old Capitol Prison, Washington, D.C., released on oath on 12/17/63.

**COX, GEORGE**: PWR only

**COX, WILLIAM HENRY HARRISON**: PWR only

**CRISALL, I**: Enl. on ?. Paroled at Lynchburg, Va. on 4/16/65.

**DAVIS, JOSHUA Jr.**: Pvt./Bugler. Enl. on 3/17/62 at Richmond, Va. Declared unfit for field duty, detailed to work in harness shops

10/23/62 until returned to the company as bugler on 3/1/63. Pres. on 4/1/64. In hosp. 6/19-8/30/64. Absent sick on 8/31/64 roll. Absent sick on 10/1-15/64 with fever. On leave on 10/31/64 roll. Paroled at Lynchburg, Va. Res. of Princess Anne, Somerset Co., Md.

**DAVIS, W. A.**: Enl. on 3/15/62 at Richmond, Va. Detailed as ambulance driver 4/10/63 per 4/1/64 roll. Paid $.25 per day as ambulance driver, 3rd qtr. 1863. Taken POW at Moorefield on 8/7/674, sent to Camp Chase, Ohio on 8/2/64 and then to Point Lookout, Md. on 3/18/65. Age 26, 5'7", dark eyes, light hair, carpenter. Pres. at Camp Lee, Va. on 3/28/65. Res. of Montgomery Co., Md.

**DEMPSEY, JOSEPH**: Enl. on 10/28/61 at Richmond, Va. Pres. on all rolls and clothing receipts.

**DOSENBERRY (DUSENBERG), H. BOWIE**: Enl. on 6/27/62 at Richmond. Transferred from Lee Virginia Light Artillery. Pres. on 10/31/64 roll. Paroled on 5/13/65. Also served in Breathed's Battery. Res. of Baltimore, Md.

**DUNCAN, JAMES A.** Enl. on 4/1/63 at Harrisonburg, Va. Taken POW at Culpeper C.H. on 9/13/63, sent to Point Lookout, Md. where held until exchanged on 12/24/63. Paid $130.78 on 1/6/64. AWOL on 4/1/64 roll. Pres. on 8/31/64 and 10/31/64 rolls. Paroled at Lynchburg, Va.

**DUNN, WILLIAM**: 1st Corp. Enl. on 8/15/61 at Richmond, Va. Pres. on 10/31/61 and 12/31/61 rolls. Later served as Capt. Co. E, 37th Battalion. Va. Cav. Res. of Baltimore, Md.

**DUVALL, WILLIAM G.**: Enl. on 3/21/62 at Richmond, Va. Pres. on 4/1/64 roll. Taken POW at Beltsville, Md. on 7/12/64 on a raid toward Baltimore. Sent to Elmira, N.Y. on 7/25/64. Paroled on 3/10/65. Res. of Johnson's Store, Anne Arundel Co., Md.

**EARNEST, J. THOMAS**: Enl. on 7/1/62 at Charlottesville, Va., $50 bounty paid. Paid $24 on 5/12/63. In hosp. 4/6/64 to 1/5/65 with syphilis and gonorrhea. Paroled at Lynchburg, Va. on 4/16/65.

**EDELL, H. J.**: Enl. on 8/15/61 at Richmond, Va. Pres. on 10/31/61, 12/31/61 and 4/1/64 rolls. In Chimborazo Hosp. #5 from 7/14-12/12/62 for gonorrhea and syphilis. Taken POW on 5/11/64 at

Yellow Tavern, Va., sent to Fort Monroe, Va. on 5/15/64 and then to Elmira, N.Y. on 8/17/64, where held until paroled on 3/10/65. Res. of Baltimore, Md.

**EVANS, CHARLES S.** Bugler/Pvt. Enl. on 8/15/61 at Richmond, Va. Pres. on 10/31/61 roll. Sick on 12/31/61 roll. Pres. on 4/1/64 and 8/31/64 rolls. Taken POW at Woodstock, Va. on 10/9/64, sent to Harper's Ferry and then to Point Lookout, Md. on 10/13/64, where held until released on oath on 6/5/65.

**FARMER, JAMES A.** Enl. on 10/20/61 at Richmond, Va. Pres. on 10/31/61 and 12/31/61 rolls. Paid $85 on 10/6/62. Taken POW at Winchester, Va., sent to Fort McHenry, Md. on 8/13/62 and then to Fort Delaware on 8/25/62. Paroled there on 9/16/62, exchanged at Aiken's Landing, Va. on 10/3/62. NFR.

**FARR, FRANCIS MARION**: Enl. on 5/28/64 at Hanover C. H. Pres. on 8/31/64. Deserted while under arrest per 10/31/64 roll. Res. of Havre de Grace, Harford Co., Md.

**FAUCETT, JAMES A.**: Enl. on 7/1/63 at Winchester, Va. Pres. on 4/1/64, 8/31/64 and 10/31/64 rolls. Paroled at Lynchburg, Va. on 4/16/65. Res. of No. 14, Low St., Baltimore, Md.

**FERRY, WILLIAM S.**: 4th Sgt. Enl. on 4/25/62 at Richmond, Va. Pres. on 4/1/64 roll. Absent, acting aide on Gen. Bradley T. Johnson's staff per 8/31/64 roll. Paroled at Lynchburg, Va. on 4/16/65. Res. of Baltimore, Md.

**FITZGERALD, ROBERT E.**: Enl. on 8/22/62 at Richmond, Va. Taken POW at Moorefield on 8/7/64, sent to Wheeling, W.Va. Age 23, blue eyes, dark hair, 5'7". Sent to Camp Chase, Ohio where held until released on oath on 2/14/65. Previously served in 20th Va. Light Artillery. Res. of Washington, D.C. Occupation gas fitter.

**FITZPATRICK, JOHN D.**: Enl. on 8/15/61 at Richmond, Va. Pres. on 10/31/61 and 12/31/61 rolls. Taken POW at Harrisonburg, Va. on 6/6/62, exchanged at Aiken's Landing, Va. on 8/5/62, then NFR. Later served with Zarvona's Maryland Zouaves.

**FLETCHER, STOCKDALE (SOLOMON) D. (J.) (G.)**: Enl. on 4/30/63 at Harrisonburg, Va. Paid $62.98 on 11/27/63. Pres. on 4/1/64 roll. Paid $24 on 4/16/64. Taken POW on 7/7/64 near

Frederick, Md., sent to Fort McHenry, Md. on 7/16/64 and then to Point Lookout, Md. on 7/21/64 where held until he escaped on 10/18/64. Paroled on 4/24/65. Res. of Carroll Co., Md.

**FORNER, WILLIAM**: Enl. on 8/15/61 at Richmond, Va. Pres. on 10/31/61, 12/31/61 and 4/1/64 rolls. Absent, WIA near Middletown, Va. on 7/23/64 per 8/31/64 roll. In hosp. at Lynchburg per 10/31/64 roll. Res. of Pikesville, Baltimore Co., Md.

**FORT, D.**: Enl. on ?. Absent sick on 12/62 roll, then NFR. Also served with Maryland's Guerilla Zouaves.

**FREDERICK, ADOLPHUS**: Enl. on 2/26/62 at Richmond, Va. In hosp. 9/28-11/5/62 for debility, but deserted from the hosp. on 11/1/62, returned 11/4/62. Paid $24 on 11/5/62. Taken POW at Yellow Tavern, Va. on 5/11/64, sent to Fort Monroe on 5/17/64 and then to Elmira, N.Y. on 8/15/64, where held until released on oath on 5/17/65. 5'9", dark hair, blue eyes. Res. of Baltimore City, Md.

**GARDNER, ELIJAH F.**: Enl. on ?. On 10/31/64 roll. Paroled at Charlottesville, Va. on 5/17/65.

**GASKINS, WILLIAM H.**: Pvt./Clerk. Originally Enl. in 39th Va. Inf. Found suitable duty with the Second Maryland Artillery and $50 bounty paid 3/17/63. Discharged for disability on 8/20/63, then age 43, 5'6", blue eyes, occupation clerk. Served as clerk, detailed to A.A.G. Office of Gen. Elzey March, April and June 1863. Paid $7.70 on 4/30/63, $7.75 on 3/31/63, $12 on 4/24/63, $24 on 3/31/63, $12 on 4/30/63, $12 on 6/4/63, $31 on 6/6/63, $24 on 8/1/63 and $296 on 6/30/64.

**GATCHELL, JOHN G.** Enl. on 5/1/63 at Richmond, Va. Taken POW at Culpeper C.H. on 9/13/63, sent to Old Capitol Prison on 9/15/63 and then transferred to Point Lookout, Md. on 9/26/63. Sent to Elmira, N.Y. on 8/14/64 where held until paroled on 8/14/64. Paroled at Harrisonburg, Va. on 5/2/65, age 30, 5'9", brown hair, grey eyes. Res. 219 Garden St., Baltimore, Md.

**GEGAN, H. W.**: Enl. on 7/20/63 at Richmond, Va. Transferred from Co. B, Gilmore's Bn. Cav. On 4/21/64. Pres. on 8/31/64 and 10/31/64 rolls. Paroled at Lynchburg, Va. on 4/16/65. Res. of Baltimore, Md.

**GIBSON, EDWARD**: Enl. on 4/1/64 at Gordonsville, Va. Transferred from Johnson's Battery. Pres. on 10/31/64 roll. Paroled at Lynchburg, Va. on 4/16/65. Res. of Talbot Co., Md.

**GIBSON, FAYETTE**: Pvt./Corp. Enl. on 7/11/62 at Richmond, Va. Transferred from Johnson's Battery. In hosp. 7/8-8/5/63 as Corp., Co. A, Steuart Horse Artillery. Pres. on 10/31/64. Paroled at Lynchburg, Va. on 4/16/65 as a corp. Res. of St. Michaels, Talbot Co., Md. MLCSH.

**GLENN, WILLIAM Y.** Pvt./Orderly Sgt. Enl. on 10/25/61 at Richmond, Va. Pres. on 10/31/61 and 12/31/61 rolls. Appointed orderly sgt. on 11/30/61 at a pay rate of $21 per month. Res. of Baltimore, Md.

**GOODMAN, JOHN W.**: Pvt./Lieutenant. Enl. on 8/15/61 at Richmond, Va. Pres. on 10/31/61 and 12/31/61 as pvt. In hosp. 4/19-5/13/62 with diarrhea and 9/29-11/1/63 with syphilis. Discharged for disability on 1/10/63, then age 25, 5'10 ½", blue eyes, dark hair, occupation clerk, paid $70. Commissioned 3rd lt. on 7/8/63. Paid $90 on 2/6/64. Pres. on 4/1/64 roll as 3rd lt. Pres. on 8/31/64 and 10/31/64 rolls as 2nd lt., but had submitted his resignation on 9/4/64. Absent on 12/31/64 roster of officers of Lomax's Horse Artillery. Dropped from rolls on 3/2/65. Paroled on 4/21/65 at Winchester, Va. Res. of 241 S. Pace St., Baltimore, Md.

**GORDON, WILLIAM J.**: Enl. on 5/1/64 at Hanover C.H., Va. Pres. on 8/31/64 and 10/31/64 rolls.

**GORE, JOHN W.**: Enl. on?. Taken POW on 7/19/63 in Berkeley Co., Va. Sent to Camp Chase, Ohio on 7/30/63. Released on oath on 1/16/63. Age 43, light hair, blue eyes, 5' 11". Res. of Talbot or Baltimore Co., Md.

**GRADY, JAMES O.**: Enl. on 8/15/61 at Richmond, Va. Pres. on 10/31/61 and 12/31/61 rolls. $50 bounty paid. Paid $99 on 10/16/62 and $24 on 11/3/62. Also served in Co. E, 1st Va. Inf. Possibly the same as James O'Grady.

**GRAHAM, WILLINGTON**: Enl. on ?. Detailed to extra duty as teamster 7/1-11/1/62. AWOL on 12/62 roll.

**GREENWELL, JOSEPH A.**: Pvt./Clerk. Enl. on 6/25/62 at Richmond, Va. WIA at Sharpsburg, Md. on 9/17/62, right leg amputated. Taken POW at Sharpsburg on 9/19/62, exchanged at Fort Monroe on 7/6/63. Found unfit for field service. Detailed and served as clerk in Provost Marshall's Office, Richmond as clerk in the passport office from 11/63 to 3/64. Paid $25.50 on 7/12/63, $69.88 on 1/15/64, $30 and $90 on 3/15/64. Then detailed to serve as clerk in the Engineer Bureau, S.O. 61, 3/4/64 per 4/1/64 roll. Paid $92 on 5/2/64, $24 on 5/4/64, $24 on 6/1/64, $24 on 7/11/64 and $276 on 9/16/64. Obtained artificial leg and rejoined unit. WIA on 6/21/64. Res. of Great Mills, St. Mary's Co., Md.

**GRIFFIN, WILLIAM HUNTER**: 1st Lt./Capt. Enl. on 8/15/61 at Richmond, Va. Pres. on 10/31/61, 12/31/61, 12/62, 4/1/64 as capt. Paid $100 on 12/14/61, 1/25/62 and 2/2/62. Taken POW at Yellow Tavern, Va. on 5/11/64. Sent to Fort Delaware on 6/25/64 then to Hilton Head, SC on 8/20/64. Sent to Fort Pulaski, Ga. on or about 10/20/64 and then back to Fort Delaware on 3/12/65. Released on oath on 6/16/65. Dark hair, hazel eyes, 5' 10 ½". Res. of Southampton Co., Va. or Baltimore, Md.

**GRUBB, H. C.**: Enl. on 3/6/62 at Richmond, Va. Pres. on 4/1/64, 8/31/64 and 10/31/64 rolls. $50 bounty paid. Hospitalized at Harrisonburg, Va. on 3/2/63 with pneumonia at Charlottesville 8/29-9/21/63 for treatment of wounds, place WIA not stated; Gen Hosp. #9, Richmond, Va. 10/30-31/63; Chimborazo No. 2 10/31/63-1/25/64, 1st and 4th fingers of left hand amputated. Paroled at Lynchburg, Va. on 4/16/65..

**GUYTHER, JAMES (JACK) W.**: Enl. on 8/15/61 at Richmond, Va. Pres. on 10/31/61 and 12/31/61 rolls. In Gen. Hosp #21 9/27-11/16/62, in Camp Winder Hosp. 11/16/62-2/28/63 for debility. Shown as age 19 on hosp. rolls. Absent WIA on 12/62 rolls. Pres. on 4/1/64 and 8/31/64 rolls. AWOL on 10/31/64 rolls. Paroled as a deserter at Washington, D.C. on 3/6/65. Res. of St. Mary's Co., Md.

**HAMMER, FRANCIS H.**: Enl. on 10/20/61 at Richmond, Va. Pres. on 10/31/61 and 12/31/61 rolls. MWIA at some point, died of wounds at Charity Hosp., Gordonsville on 9/22/63.

**HAMMETT, DANIEL**: Enl. on 8/15/61 at Richmond, Va. Pres. on 10/31/61, 4/1/64 and 8/31/64 rolls. Absent sick on 12/31/61 rolls. AWOL on 10/31/64 roll. Paid $48 on 3/31/64. Deserted with Jeremiah Artis of the 2nd Maryland Inf., reported at Baltimore, Md. Wrote letter stating that he left the battery on 9/1/64 between Harrisonburg and Staunton. Res. of St. Gregor's, St. Mary's Co., Md.

**HANDS, WASHINGTON**: Enl. on 8/1/64 at Macon, Al. Pres. on 10/31/64 roll. Paroled at Lynchburg, Va. on 4/15/65. B. 1840. Res. of 36 N. Exeter St., Baltimore, Md. D. 1914. Wrote several articles for the *Confederate Veteran*, Vol. VI, December 1898; Vol. VII, January and February 1899.

**HARDY, SAMUEL B.** Enl. on ?. Deserted, taken POW at Winchester, Va. on 2/7/63. Sent to Atheneum Prison, Wheeling, W. Va. on 2/11/63, sent to Camp Chase, Ohio on 2/12/63 where held until released on oath on 3/20/63. Light hair, 5' 6 ½", age 26, plasterer. Res. of Baltimore Md.

**HARPER, JOHN**: Enl. on?. Taken POW at Strausburg, Va. on 11/11/64, sent to Harper's Ferry on 11/18/64 and then to Point Lookout, Md. where held until released on the oath on 6/14/65.

**HARRINGTON, S. W.**: Enl. on 8/15/61 at Richmond, Va. Pres. on 10/31/61 and 12/31/61 rolls. Paid $122, including $50 bounty on 11/5/62. Absent WIA on 12/62 roll. Discharged on 2/4/63 because he was a minor and had been wounded twice in the same foot. Enlisted as a minor, 16 years old. Res. of Baltimore, Md.

**HART, WILLIAM E.**: Enl. on 3/1/63 at Edinburg, Va. Pres. on 4/1/64 roll. Taken POW near Rockville, Md. on 7/16/64. No Federal record of incarceration. Res. of Kent Co., Md. MLCSH

**HAWTHORNE, ROBERT**: Enl. on ?. Taken POW in Harrison Co., W. Va. on 7/23/63. Sent to Camp Chase, Ohio on 7/30/63, then transferred to Fort Delaware on 2/29/64. Another record indicated he was taken POW at Rockville, Md. on 7/10/64, sent to Elmira, N.Y. where held until released on oath on 5/17/65, dark hair, blue eyes, 5'9½". Res. Detroit, Michigan.

**HAYDEN, JOHN F.**: Sgt./Corp. Enl. on 8/15/61 at Richmond, Va. Pres. on 10/31/61 and 12/31/61 rolls as 3rd sgt. WIA on 7/3/62. In Gen. Hosp #21 7/3-26/62. Paid $26 on 3/21/64. Pres. on 4/1/64 roll as 8th corp. Extensively WIA on 5/11/64, shell wound in thigh and wrist. In Chimborazo Hosp. #2 5/17-8/15/64. Pres. on 8/31/64 roll as 8th corp. Pres. on 10/31/64 roll as 7th corp. Occupation mechanic. Res. of Baltimore, Md.

**HEAPHY, JOHN**: Enl. on 8/1/64 at Mt. Crawford. Pres. 8/31/64 roll. Also served in C.S. Navy.

**HEITZELBARGER, S.V.**: Enl. on 7/18/63 at Richmond, Va. Transferred from 2nd Co., Richmond Howitzers by S.O. 93. In gen. hosp. 5/9-10/64 and 5/31-6/1/64, in Chimborazo Hosp. 6/1-3/64 with rheumatism. Had been in Castle Thunder and volunteered in Winder Legion for defense of Richmond against the 1864 Sheridan Raid. Deserted and took oath near Washington per 8/31/64 roll.

**HENNICK, MARION**: Enl. on 8/15/61 at Richmond, Va. Pres. on 10/31/61 and 12/31/61 rolls. AWOL on 12/62 roll, then NFR.

**HERON, A.**: Enl. on 9/1/64 at Winchester, Va. Pres. on 8/31/64 and 10/31/64 rolls.

**HICKMAN, JOSHUA**: Enl. on 11/10/62 at Richmond, Va. Pres. on 4/1/64 roll. Taken POW at Moorefield, Va. on 8/7/64 per 8/31/64 roll, but listed as KIA on 10/31/64 roll. Hospitalized for rheumatism 3/18-29/64 in Chimborazo Hosp. #2.

**HOLLAND, ALBERT G.**: Enl. on 2/18/62 at Richmond, Va. Transferred from Purcell's Virginia Artillery Battery per S.O. 98, 4/1/64. Taken POW at Moorefield, Va. on 8/7/64, sent to Camp Chase, Ohio via Wheeling. Transferred to Point Lookout, Md. on 3/18/65. Exchanged, at Camp Lee, Va. on 3/28/65. Paroled at Appomattox, C.H., Va. on 4/9/65. On list of men on duty with the Quartermaster and Ordnance Dept. of Artillery Ordnance Train, 1st Corp. Took the oath and was released on 511/65. Age 22, 5' 4 ½", grey eyes, dark hair, clerk. Res. of 382 13th St., Washington, D.C.

**HOTTINGER, MOSES**: Enl. on 9/1/62 at Rappahannock, Va. Pres., detailed as teamster per 12/62, 4/1/64, 8/31/64 and 10/31/64 rolls.

## Second Maryland Artillery

**HOWARD, WILLIAM**: Enl. on 10/31/61 at Centerville, Va. AWOL on 12/31/61 roll then NFR.

**HUNTER, ROBERT**: Enl. on 10/25/61 at Richmond, Va. Pres. on 10/31/61, 12/31/61, 4/1/64 and 8/31/64 rolls. WIA in 7/62. In Danville, Va. Hosp. 7/9-8/2/62. In Charlottesville, Va. Hosp. 8/4-11/62. Taken POW at Woodstock, Va. on 10/9/64, sent to Harper's Ferry and then to Point Lookout, Md. Exchanged there on 2/13/65. At Camp Lee, Va. on 2/17/65.

**HURST, WILLIAM**: Enl. on 10/8/61 at Richmond, Va. Pres. on 10/31/61 and 12/31/61 rolls. In Gen. Hosp. No. 21, 7/9-21/62 with typhoid fever, died on 7/21/62.

**HYNES, EDWARD**: Enl. on 8/1/62 at Charlottesville. Pres. on 4/1/64 and 8/31/64 rolls. WIA on 5/12/64. Taken POW at Woodstock, Va. on 10/9/64, sent to Point Lookout, Md. via Harper's Ferry, exchanged on 10/30/64. Res. of Mobile, Alabama.

**IRVIN, JOHN**: Enl. on 10/28/61 at Richmond, Va. Pres. on 10/31/61 and 12/31/61 rolls. KIA on 8/22/62 at Cunningham's Ford.

**IRVIN, MICHAEL**: Artificer/Pvt. Enl. on 10/28/61 at Richmond, Va. Pres. on all rolls. Detailed as blacksmith on last two rolls. Asst. blacksmith on 12/62 roll. Paroled at Lynchburg, Va. on 4/16/65.

**ISREAL, G. P.**: Enl. on 4/19/61 at Martinsburg. Transferred from Lee's Maryland Light Artillery, Alexander's Artillery Battalion, S.O. 93. Detailed as telegraphic operator on 8/31/64 and 10/31/64 rolls.

**JACKSON, HENRY INLOES**: Enl. on 5/1/64 at Hanover C.H. Pres. on 8/31/64 and 10/31/64 rolls. Died of peritonitis 2/27/65.

**JOHNSON, CHARLES W.**: Enl. on 7/27/62 at Charlottesville, Va. WIA per 12/62 roll. Hosp. at Charlottesville 9/29-10/27/62 with sounds; in Howard's Grove Hosp. 11/13-12/11/62 with syphilis; in Chimborazo No. 5, 12/11-15/62 with syphilis; in Eastern District Hosp. 3/12-17/63. Discharged on 1/3/63, age 36, 5'6", blue eyes, dark hair, native of Ireland, boat hand. Paid $49.80 on 1/3/63.

**JOHNSON, GEORGE M.**: Enl. on 10/1/62 at Winchester, Va. Paid $48 on 7/31/63. Pres. on 4/1/64, 8/31/64 and 10/31/64 rolls.

Compiled Service Records Roster 185

**JOHNSON, THOMAS SOMERVILLE**: Enl. on 9/1/62 at Frederick, Md. Paid $74, including $50 bounty on 11/10/62. WIA by shell in both thighs in 11/63, sent to Gen. Hosp. #9 11/26/63. In Chimborazo Hosp. #4, 11/27/63-1/12/64. Pres. on 4/1/64 roll. Paid $48 on 5/6/64. Absent detailed in Ordnance Dept. at Hanover Junction, Va. on 8/31/64 roll. Pres. on 10/31/64 roll. Paroled at Lynchburg, Va. on 4/16/65. Res. of Hill St., Baltimore, Md. MLCSH.

**JONES, WILLIAM**: Enl. on 4/1/64 at Hanover Junction. Pres. on 4/1/64, 8/31/64 and 10/31/64 rolls. In Chimborazo Hosp #5 6/5-7/9/64 with an abscess of the right foot.

**KELLY, WILLIAM**: Artificer/Pvt. Enl. on 8/15/61 at Richmond, Va. Pres. on 10/31/61 and 12/31/61 rolls. WIA in 7/62. In Gen. Hosp. #21 7/3-14/62. Asst. blacksmith 7/1-11/1/62. AWOL on 12/62 roll. Res. of Princess Anne, Somerset Co., Md.

**KENDRICK, WILLIAM H.**: Corp. Enl. on 8/15/61 at Richmond, Va. Pres. on 10/31/61 rolls and 12/31/61 rolls as 4th corp., then NFR.

**KERMAN, A. (JAMES L.)**: Enl. on ?. Taken POW at Woodstock on 10/9/64, sent to Point Lookout via Harper's Ferry on 10/20/64, released on oath on 5/13/65. Res. of 49 Pearl St., Baltimore, Md. Occupation clerk.

**KING, JAMES A.**: Enl. on 8/1/63 at Richmond, Va. Pres. on 4/1/64 roll. Taken POW at Yellow Tavern, Va. on 5/11/64, sent to Fort Monroe, Va. on 5/17/64, then transferred to Elmira, N.Y. on 8/15/64. Released on oath on 6/14/65. Auburn hair, hazel eyes, 5'9½". Res. of Baltimore, Md.

**KIRBY, PATRICK**: Corp./Bugler. Enl. on 8/15/61 at Richmond, Va. Pres. on 10/31/61 rolls as 2nd corp. Absent sick on 12/31/61 roll. WIA on 6/30/62, ball fractured tarsal bones of left foot. Hospitalized at Charlottesville, Va. 10/24/62-1/22/63. In Chimborazo Hosp. #5 7/64 with debility. Retired for disability on 3/15/65. Then age 22, 5'7", grey eyes, dark hair, occupation clerk. Res. of Baltimore, Md.

**KNIGHT, JOHN H.:** Enl. on 8/15/61 at Richmond, Va. Pres. on 10/31/61 and 12/31/61 rolls. AWOL on 12/62 roll. Took oath on 4/16/65. Occupation carpenter. Lived between Main and Carey, Darlington, Harford Co., Md.

**KNIGHT, LEWIS (LOUIS) W., M.D.:** Enl. on 8/5/63 at Richmond, Va. Paid on 5/4/64. Pres. on 8/31/64 roll, transferred from Gilmore's Cav. Battn. by S.O. 93. Taken POW at Woodstock, Va. on 10/9/64, sent to Harper's Ferry and then to Point Lookout, Md. 10/13-4/64. Released on oath on 5/3/65. Res. of Baltimore, Md.

**KNOX, WILLIAM FRANCIS:** Enl. on 5/28/64 at Ashland, Va. Pres. on 8/31/64 and 10/31/64 rolls. Res. of Baltimore, Md. MCLSH.

**KUBLE, ADOLPHUS:** Pvt./Hosp. Steward. Enl. on 10/15/61 at Richmond, Va. Pres. on 10/31/61 and 12/31/61 rolls. Pres. detailed as hosp. steward on 9/1/63 per 4/1/64 roll. Appointed Hosp. Steward, Johnson's Brigade per last two rolls.

**LADD, N.E.:** Enl. on 4/30/63 at Harrisonburg, Va. Taken POW at Culpeper C.H., Va. on 9/13/63. Sent to Old Capitol Prison, released on oath on 11/5/63.

**LANIER, JAMES B.:** Enl. on 10/16/61 at Richmond, Va. Pres. on 10/31/61 and 12/31/61 rolls. In Gen. Hosp. #21 in 3/62, syphilis. Paid $67.50 on 6/16/61. Discharged for disability from tertiary syphilis, age 22, 5'8", blue eyes, light hair, clerk.

**LEGG, E.A.:** Enl. on 6/15/62 at Charlottesville. $50 bounty paid. Paid $24 on 10/10/62 and $66.27on 9/13/64. Absent WIA on 12/62 roll. Arm amputated at some point. Absent on 4/1/64 roll with certificate of permanent disability. Black hair, blue eyes, 5'8". Res. of Alexandria, Va. Age 26. Paroled on 5/17/65.

**LINDENBORNE, PHILIP:** Enl. on 8/1/62 at Charlottesville, Va. WIA 9/62. In hosp. 9/29-11/5/62 at Charlottesville, Va. for treatment. Pres. on 4/1/64, 8/31/64 and 10/31/64 rolls. Paroled on 4/20/65 at Mt. Jackson, Va. Age 28, 5'8", brown hair, blue eyes.

**LONG, EDWARD S.:** Enl. on 7/1/62 at Charlottesville. Pres. on 4/1/64, 8/31/64 and 10/31/64 rolls. Res. of Baltimore, Md.

**LOWNDS (LOWDES), JAMES A.**: Enl. on 9/1/62 at Winchester, Va. Paid $24 on 4/12/63. Discharged for disability on 12/3/63, age 24, 5'6", blue eyes, dark hair, clerk. Paid $109.18 on 12/3/63.

**LUCAS, WILLIAM J. (M.D.?)**: Pvt./Orderly. Enl. on 11/30/61 at Centerville. Pres. on 12/31/61 roll. In Gen. Hosp. #21 4/62. In Charlottesville, Va. hosp. 6/62 with debility. Paid $14.40 on 10/31/62. Detached on 12/62 roll. Later served as orderly to General Steuart.

**LYNCH, DANIEL**: Enl. on ?. Taken POW at Woodstock, Va. on 10/9/64, sent to Harper's Ferry and then to Point Lookout, Md. on 10/20/64. Released on oath on 12/10/64. Also served in Lucas' 15th S.C. Heavy Artillery.

**LYNCH, JOHN STEVENS (M.D.)**: Pvt./Hosp. Steward. Enl. on 5/1/63 at Harrisonburg. Detailed as hosp. steward 6/15-8/31/63. In Staunton Gen. Hosp. 12/63. Discharged on certificate of disability on 3/19/64. 5'8", hazel eyes, dark hair. Physician. Paid $83.77 on 3/24/64. Taken POW on 7/11/64 at Frederick, Md. Sent to Elmira, N.Y. on 7/15/64. Sent to Point Lookout, Md. for exchange on 10/29/64. Also served as lt. in Co. C, 6th Alabama Inf. Res. of St. Mary's Co., Md.

**MAHARD, WI8LLIAM**: Enl. on 8/15/61 at Richmond, Va. Pres. on 10/31/61 and 12/31/61 rolls. AWOL on 12/62 roll. In Charlottesville, Va. hosp. 10/1-17/62 with chronic rheumatism. Taken POW at Bolivar Heights, Va. on 11/30/62. Also served in Holbrook's Independent Maryland Light Artillery.

**MALLORY, MAT**: Corp. Enl. on ?. Paroled at Charlottesville, Va. on 5/22/65. Also served in Breathed's Battery, Steuart Horse Artillery.

**MALONE, DANIEL**: Pvt./Sgt. Enl. on 8/15/61 at Richmond, Va. Pres. on 10/31/61 roll as 5th sgt., then NFR.

**MALONEY, JAMES**: Enl. on 10/16/61 at Richmond, Va. Pres. on 10/31/61. Absent sick on 12/31/61 roll. In Gen. Hosp. #21 3/-4/22/62. Discharged on 4/29/62 for extreme youth, age 15 and delicate condition.

**MARSHALL, PETER B.:** Enl. on 4/1/64 at Hanover Junction. Pres. on 8/31/64 roll. Detailed on 10/1/64 per 10/31/64 roll. Paroled on 5/29/65.

**MARSTON, FREDERICK A.:** Enl. on 6/25/62 at Richmond, Va. $50 bounty paid. Paid $24 on 3/21/64. Pres. on 4/1/64 and 10/31/64 rolls. Absent on 7 days leave on 8/31/64 roll. Paid $53.06 on 8/31/64 roll. Paroled at Lynchburg, Va. on 4/16/65. Also served in Zarvona's Maryland Zouaves.

**MARSTON, H. A.:** Sgt. Enl. ?. Pres. as 2nd sgt. on 4/1/64, 8/31/64 and 10/31/64 rolls. Paroled at Lynchburg, Va. on 4/16/65.

**MATHEWS, C. J.:** Enl. on ?. Taken POW at Kernstown, Va. on 1/25/63. Sent to Camp Chase, Ohio via Wheeling on 2/13/63. 5'5½", 19 years old, dark eyes, auburn hair, sail maker. Released on oath on 3/26/63. Res. of Baltimore, Md. Also served in Edelin's Heavy Artillery.

**MATTISON, SAMUEL J.:** Pvt./Ord. Sgt. Enl. on 9/1/62 at Bunker Hill, Va. WIA in 8/63, in Gen. Hosp. #21, 9/7-18/63 and then to Chimborazo Hosp. #1 9/18-12/3/63 with paralysis. Pres. on 4/1/64, 8/31/64 and 10/31/64 rolls. Appointed ord. sgt. on 10/1/64. Paroled on 5/1/64 then age 28, 5'5", brown hair, grey eyes. Res. of Baltimore, Md. or Tobaccostick, Dorchester Co., Md.

**McALWEE (McALEVEE, McELWEE), GEORGE W.:** Corporal. Enl. on 4/25/62 at Richmond, Va. Pres. on 4/1/64 roll as 5th corp. WIA and taken POW at Moorefield, W. Va. on 8/7/64. Sent to Wheeling on 8/10/64. Then age 25, 5'11", grey eyes, dark hair, iron molder. Res. of Washington, D.C. Sent to Camp Chase, Ohio on 8/12/64. Transferred to Point Lookout, Md. for exchange on 3/18/65. Paroled at Lynchburg, Va. on 4/16/65. MLCSH.

**McAVOY, WILLIAM F:** Pvt. Enl. on 3/14/62 at Richmond, Va. $50 bounty paid. Detailed to Office of State Printer, Columbia, S.C. in late 1862 and early 1863. Pres. on 12/62, 4/1/64, 8/31/64 and 10/31/64 rolls. Surrendered at Appomattox C.H., Va. on 4/10/65. Res. of Baltimore, Md.

Compiled Service Records Roster 189

**McCLELLAN, SAMUEL**: Pvt. Enl. on ?. AWOL on 12/62 roll. $50 bounty paid. He also served in Holbrook's Independent Maryland Light Artillery.

**McCLUBBIN, ROBERT W.**: Pvt. Enl. on 9/1/62 at Bunker Hill, Va. Pres. on 4/1/64 and 8/31/64 rolls. Taken POW at Woodstock on 10/9/64. Sent to Point Lookout, Md. on 10/10/64 where held until exchanged on 3/28/65. Reported and was paroled at Augusta, Ga. on 5/3/65. Res. of 290 N. Saratoga St, Baltimore, Md.

**McEVANEY, CHARLES**: Pvt. Enl. on 8/15/61 at Richmond, Va. Pres. on 10/31/61 and 12/61 rolls, then NFR.

**McKENZIE, E. H.**: Pvt. Enl. on 7/1/62 at Charlottesville, Va. In hosp. at Medical College of Va. at Richmond in 11/62. In Chimborazo Hosp. 12/22/62 to 6/16/63 with gunshot wound to foot. Place, date and circumstances of wound not recorded. In C.S.A. Gen. Hosp., Danville, Va. 6/16-7/3/63 with dyspepsia and 7/12-10/13/63 with debility. Pres. on 12/62 and 4/1/64 rolls. Taken POW at Yellow Tavern, Va. on 5/11/64. Sent to Fort Monroe, 5/17/64 and then transferred to Elmira, N.Y. on 8/15/64, paroled there on 2/9/65. Paroled in 5/65, age 42, 5'7", blue eyes, dark hair.

**McLOID, MATTHEW**: Pvt./Corp. Enl. 10/5/61 at Richmond, Va. Pres. on 10/31/61 and 12/61 rolls as pvt. Pres. on 4/1/64 and 8/31/64 rolls as 4th corp. Pres. on 10/31/64 roll as 3rd corp.

**McNULTY, JOHN**: 1st Lt. Enl. on ?. $50 bounty paid on 4/18/62. Commissioned on 7/8/63. Taken POW on 9/13/63 at Culpeper. Sent to Johnson's Island, Ohio. "Sent away surreptitiously Feb 9/64 in the place of Wm. M. Brown." Absent on 4/1/64 roll. Absent, acting aide on General B. T. Johnson's staff on 8/31/64 roll. Paid $200 on 10/16/64 for his horse, which was KIA at Moorefield, W. Va. on 8/7/64. He had requested $2000. Pres. on 10/31/64 roll as jr. 1st lt. Pres. commanding battery on 12/31/64 roll. Paid $100 on 2/8/65. Res. of Prince George's Co., Md.

**MENTZEN (MENTZER), SAMUEL**: Pvt. Enl. on 9/8/62 at New Market, Va. Pres. on 10/31/64 roll. Paroled at Salisbury, N.C. on 5/1/65. He also served in Breathed's Battery, Steuart's Horse Artillery.

**METTEL, CHARLES:** Pvt. Enl. on 8/15/61 at Richmond, Va. Pres. on 10/31/61 and 12/61 rolls. In Gen. Hosp. #21, 7/1-20/62 with diarrhea, then NFR. Perhaps the same as Charles H. Mettee, who later served in the 4th Maryland Artillery. Res. of Baltimore, Md.

**MONAHAN, JAMES J.:** Enl. on 8/15/61 at Richmond, Va. Pres. on 10/31/61 and 12/61 rolls, then NFR. He may have also served in Co. A. Davis' Maryland Cavalry, been from Carroll Co., Md. and been a resident of the MLCSH in old age.

**MORAN, MICHAEL G.:** Pvt. Enl. on 10/25/61 at Richmond, Va. Pres. on 10/31/61 and 12/61 rolls. Absent, sick on 12/62 roll. In Gen. Hosp. Staunton, Va. in 1/63 with rheumatism. Discharged for disability on 3/14/63. Born in Ireland, age 35, 5'10½", dark eyes, black hair, occupation stone cutter.

**MORRISON, JAMES S.:** 3rd Sgt. Enl. on 3/17/62 at Richmond, Va. In Chimborazo Hosp. #4 10/1-25/63. Paid $98.18 for clothing on 1/20/64. Pres. on 4/1/64 as 3rd sgt. Taken POW at Yellow Tavern, Va. on 5/11/64, sent to Fort Monroe 5/17/64, sent to Elmira, N.Y. on 8/178/64. Paroled at Elmira, N.Y. on 10/11/64, exchanged on 10/25/64. Taken POW again in 4/65.

**MORROW, JAMES G.:** Pvt. Enl. on ?. Surrendered at Gainesville, Alabama on 5/10/65. 6'2", blue eyes, brown hair. Res. of Warren Co., Ky.

**MOTH, E.:** Pvt. Enl. on 10/15/61 at Richmond, Va. Pres. on 10/31/61 and 12/61 rolls. Shown as absent, unfit for duty per 12/62 roll, then age 58. Absent sick on 4/1/64 roll. Dropped on 8/31/64 roll. He had been missing for 18 months.

**MUDD, JOHN F.:** Pvt./Blacksmith. Enl. on 7/25/62 at Charlottesville, Va. Detailed as blacksmith from 6/1/63 to 8/31/63. Pres. on 4/1/64, 8/31/64 and 10/31/64 rolls. Paid $53.06 on 8/20/64. $50 bounty also paid. Paroled on 4/22/65.

**MULLEN, CHARLES X.:** Pvt. Enl. on 10/25/61 at Richmond, Va. Pres. on 10/31/61 and 12/61 rolls, then NFR. Later served as pvt., Co. G, 1st S.C. Inf. MLCSH.

**NAYLOR, WILLIAM E.**: Pvt./Blacksmith. Enl. on 9/1/62 at Rappahannock, Va. Absent sick on 12/62 roll. Pres. detailed as a blacksmith for Co. from enlistment per 4/1/64, 8/31/64 and 10/31/64 rolls. Paroled on 4/26/65 age 28, 5'5", light hair, grey eyes. Res. of Frederick Co., Md.

**NEAL (NEIL, NEALE), FRANK (FRANCIS)**: Pvt. Enl. on 9/25/63 at Baskerville, Va. Pres. on 10/31/64 roll. Paroled at Lynchburg, Va. on 4/16/65. Res. of Baltimore, Md. or Port Tobacco, Charles Co., Md.

**NEAL (NEIL) HENRY**: Pvt. Enl. on 9/25/63 at Baskerville, Va. Taken POW at 10/22/63 at Muddy Branch, Md. Pres. on 10/31/64 roll. Paroled at Lynchburg, Va. on 4/16/65. Res. of Baltimore, Md.

**O'GRADY, JAMES**: 2nd Corp. Enl. on 8/15/61 at Richmond, Va. Taken POW at Culpeper C.H., Va. on 9/13/63. Sent to Old Capitol prison. Released on 1/28/64. Several letters were written on his behalf. He was apparently 15 years old when he enlisted. Res. of Carroll Co., Md. (Possibly the same as James O. Grady.)

**OLDSON, WILLIAM H. C.**: Pvt. Enl. on 8/15/61 at Richmond, Va. Pres. on 10/31/61 and 21/61 rolls. In Gen. Hosp. #21, 3/31-4/24/63 with rheumatism, then NFR. May have also served in the 4th Md. Light Artillery and been a res. of Queen Anne Co., Md.

**OWENS, JAMES F.** Pvt. Enl. on 8/15/61 at Richmond, Va. Pres. on 10/31/61 roll, absent sick on 12/61 roll, then NFR until paroled at Appomattox C.H., Va. on 4/10/65. Res. of Baltimore, Md.

**PAINE, WILLIAM**: Pvt. Enl. on 8/15/61 at Richmond, Va. Pres. on 10/31/61 and 12/61 rolls. Taken POW at Culpeper C.H. on 9/13/63 per 4/1/64 and 8/31/64 rolls, but has no Federal record of incarceration. He also served in the Castle Pinkney S.C. Heavy Artillery.

**PEAKE, CHARLES DAVIS**: Pvt. Enl. on 10/25/61 at Richmond, Va. Pres. on 10/31/61 and 12/61 rolls. Taken POW and exchanged in 8/62. Taken POW on 1/2/63 at Sleepy Creek by members of the 15th (West) Virginia. Sent to Wheeling, then aged 21, 6', dark eyes, dark hair, carpenter. Res. of Baltimore, Md. Released on 3/27/63.

**PEMBROKE, GEORGE W.** Pvt./Corporal. Enl. on 8/15/61 at Richmond, Va. Pres. on 10/31/61 and 12/61 rolls as a pvt. Pres. on 4/1/64 and 8/31/64 rolls as 3rd corp. Pres. on 10/31/64 roll as 2nd corp. Res. of Great Mills, St. Mary's Co., Md.

**PEREGOY, CHARLES E.**: Pvt. Enl. on 8/1/63 at Richmond, Va. Pres. on 4/1/64, 8/31/64 and 10/31/64 rolls.

**PIELERT, GEORGE**: Pvt. Enl. on 6/13/62 at Charlottesville, Va. $50 bounty paid. AWOL on 12/62 roll. Also served as armorer, C.S.S. navy Torpedo. Res. of Catonsville, Baltimore Co., Md. MLCSH.

**POEHLMAN, CHRIS**: Pvt./Corp. Enl. on 6/23/62 at Richmond, Va. Pres. on 4/1/64 and 8/31/64 rolls as pvt. In gen. hosp, Charlottesville, Va. in 6/64 with fever. Paid $49.12 on 7/1/64. Absent, on leave as 8th corp. on 10/31/64 roll. Paroled at Lynchburg, Va. on 4/14/65. Res. of Baltimore Co., Md. He also served in Co. G, 12 Va. Cav.

**POINDEXTER, GEORGE**: 2nd Sgt. Enl. on 8/15/61 at Richmond, Va. Pres. as 2nd sgt. On 10/31/61 and 12/61 rolls. Signed forage requisition at Staunton, Va. in 12/62. Absent sick on 12/62 roll. Paid $34 on 1/1/63. Paid $34 on 8/8/63.

**POWERS, JOHN**: 4th Sgt. Enl. on 8/15/61 at Richmond, Va. Pres. on 10/31/61 and 12/61 rolls, then NFR.

**QUAILES, J.C.**: Pvt. Enl. on ?. Paroled at Gordonsville, Va. in 6/65.

**QUINN, WILLIAM S. J.**: Pvt./Corp./Ordnance Sgt. Enl. on 8/15/61 at Richmond, Va. Pres. on 10/31/61 and 12/61 rolls. Appointed Corp. on 11/30/61. Vice Corp. Kirby. Paroled at Winchester, Va. in 7/62. AWOL on 12/62 roll.

**RAYMOND C. C.**: Pvt. Enl. on 10/10/64 at ?. Pres. on 10/31/64 roll. Paroled on 4/21/65 at Winchester, Va., then aged 24, brown hair, hazel eyes. Res. of Rockingham Co., Va. or Carroll Co., Md.

**REILEY (RILEY, REILLEY), JOHN**: Pvt. Enl. on 8/15/61 at Richmond, Va. Pres. on 10/31/61 and 12/61, 4/1/64, 8/31/64 and

10/31/64 rolls. Paid $24 on 4/2/64. Paroled at Lynchburg, Va. on 4/13/65. Res. of Baltimore, Md.

**REIMAN, W. H.:** Pvt. Enl. on 9/1/62 at Frederick, Md. Pres. on 4/1/64, 8/31/64 and 10/31/64 rolls. Paroled on 5/25/65. 5'11", age 21, brown hair, blue eyes.

**REYNOLDS, A. S.:** Pvt. Enl. on 2/6/62 at Richmond, Va. $50 bounty paid. WIA on 9/6/62. He also served in the Wise Legion Virginia Light Artillery.

**RHEIMS (REIMES, RHEIM), WILLIAM G.:** Pvt. Enl. on 6/30/64 in Dallas Co., Alabama. Pres. on 8/31/64 roll. Taken POW at Woodstock, Va. on 10/9/64, sent to Point Lookout, Md. where held until released on oath on 3/20/65, furnished transportation to Baltimore. He also served in Co. C, 17th Va. Inf.

**RHEIMS (RHIEM, RHEIM, RHIEME), JAMES J.:** Pvt. Enl. on 6/30/64 in Dallas Co., Alabama. Pres. on 8/31/64 roll. Taken POW at Woodstock, Va. on 10/9/64, sent to Point Lookout, Md. where held until released on oath on 3/20/65, furnished transportation to Baltimore. He also served in Co. C, 17th Va. Inf.

**RICHARDSON, G. W.:** Pvt. Enl. on 11/1/62 at Winchester, Va. Paid $24 on 4/20/64. Pres. on 4/1/64 and 8/31/64 rolls. Taken POW at Woodstock, Va. on 10/9/64. Sent to Point Lookout, Md. where held until released on oath on 6/17/65, then 5'6", blue eyes, light brown hair. Res. of Baltimore Co., Md.

**RICHARDSON, H. G.:** Pvt. Enl. on 11/1/62 at Winchester , Va. Pres. on 4/1/64 roll. Taken POW on 7/16/64 near Rockville, Md. per 8/31/64 roll, no Federal record of incarceration.

**RICHARDSON, T. J.:** Pvt. Enl. on 11/1/62 at Winchester, Va. Pres. on 4/1/64, 8/31/64 and 10/31/64 rolls.

**RICHARDSON, W. (WALLACE) P.:** Pvt. Enl. on 11/1/62 at Winchester, Va. Paid $24 on 4/20/64. Pres. on 4/1/64, 8/31/64 and 10/31/64 rolls. Took oath on 4/20/65, then age 22, 5'3", brown hair, blue eyes. Res of Whitemarsh, Baltimore, Co., Md.

**ROANE, JAMES:** Pvt. Enl. on 8/15/61 at Richmond, Va. Pres. on 10/31/61 and 12/61 rolls. Taken POW at Culpeper C.H. on 9/13/63.

Sent to Old Capitol Prison where held until released on oath on 12/20/63, then 5'1", brown hair, grey eyes. Res. of Baltimore, Md.

**ROBERTSON, (ROBINSON), GEORGE H.**: Pvt. Enl. on 10/25/61 at Richmond, Va. Pres. on 10/31/61 and 12/61 rolls. In Gen. Hosp. #21 6/30-7/18/62 with diarrhea. Pres. on 4/1/64, 8/31/64 and 10/31/64 rolls. Paroled at Lynchburg, Va. on 4/13/65. Res. of 203 N. Howard St., Baltimore, Md.

**ROBEY, H. A.**: Pvt. Enl. on 8/8/63 at Richmond, Va. Transferred from Co. B., Gilmore's Battalion, Maryland Cav. on 4/21/64. Pres. on 8/31/64 and 10/31/64 rolls. Paroled at Lynchburg, Va. on 4/13/65. Res. of 81 Park St., Baltimore, Md.

**ROBINSON, GEORGE S.**: Pvt. Enl. on 9/1/62 at Frederick, Md. Pres. on 4/1/64, 8/31/64 and 10/31/64 rolls. Took oath on 5/1/65 at Salisbury, N.C. Res of 336 W. Fayette St., Baltimore, Md.

**ROBINSON, WILLIAM WIRT**: Orderly Sgt. Enl. on 4/15/62 at Rappahannock, Va. Absent sick on 12/62 roll. Nurse for brother at C. S. Hosp. at Charlottesville, Va. on 1/5-2/25/63. $50 bounty paid. Paid $42 on 8/8/63. Pres. on 4/1/64, 8/31/64 and 10/31/64 rolls. Paid $85.12 on 8/8/64. Assigned duty as Acting 2nd Lt. on 3/22/65.

**ROGERS, WILLIAM C.**: Pvt. Enl. 5/28/61 in Gloucester Co., Va. Transferred from Co. E, 26th Va. Inf. on 4/15/64. Severely WIA in the head, treated at U. S. Post Hosp. New Creek, WV 8/9-25/64 and taken POW at Moorefield, WV on 8/7/64. Sent to Camp Chase, Ohio on 9/18/64 then age 20, 5'6", grey eyes, light hair, sailor. Transferred to Chicago, Ill. on 3/20/65. Res. of Baltimore, Md.

**RONEY, I. (J.) C.**: Pvt. Enl. on ?. Absent sick on 12/62 roll, then NFR. He also served in Co. A, 2nd Md. Cav.

**ROSS, ANTHONY P.**: Pvt. Enl. on 10/28/61 at Richmond, Va. Pres. on 10/31/61 roll. Absent sick on 12/61 roll. Discharged on 1/12/62. Res. of Talbot Co., Md.

**RUCKER, WILLIAM**: Pvt. Enl. on 8/25/62 at Rappahannock. Pres. detailed as teamster for batter per 12/62, 4/1/64 and 8/31/64 rolls. Absent on 10/31/64 roll.

**SCHAFFER (SHAEFFER), WILLIAM:** Pvt. Enl. on 8/15/61 at Richmond, Va. Pres. on 10/31/61 and 12/61 rolls. AWOL on 12/62 rolls. May have also served in the 4th Maryland Light Artillery.

**SCHAFFER, ADAM F.:** Pvt. Enl. on 4/1/64 at Hanover Junction, Va. $50 bounty paid. Pres. on 4/1/64 in Chimborazo Hosp. #2 6/17-20/64, with leg wound. Taken POW on 7/16/64 near Rockville, Md. per 8/31/64 roll. No Federal record of incarceration.

**SCHENBERGER, JOHN F.:** Pvt./Harness Maker. Enl. on 3/17/62 at Richmond, Va. Absent sick on 12/62 roll. "Disabled" 5/9/63. Detailed to make harness by S.O. #112/25, 5/9/63, then age 24, 5'9", grey eyes, dark hair. Paid $12 on 2/5/64. Absent, detailed in Ordnance Dept., Richmond per 4/1/64 and 8/31/64 rolls. Res. of Baltimore, Md.

**SHARKEY, S.:** Pvt. Enl. on 11/1/63 at Brandy Station, Va. Pres. on 4/1/64, 8/31/64 and 10/31/64 rolls. In Gen. Hosp. #21 4/12-24/62 and 4/27-6/19/62 with rheumatism.

**SHARKEY, WILLIAM:** Pvt. Enl.?. Taken POW at Strausburg, Va. on 6/3/62. Exchanged on 6/26/62. AWOL on 12/62 roll. Taken POW at Charlestown, W. Va. on 11/30/62, discharged at Fort McHenry, Md. on 12/31/62.

**SHAW, J. C.:** Pvt. Enl. on 11/30/61 at Centerville, Va. Pres. on 12/61 roll, then NFR.

**SHAW, PETER:** Pvt. Enl. on 8/15/61 at Richmond, Va. Pres. on 10/31/61, 12/61, 4/1/64, 8/31/64 and 10/31/64 rolls. Paroled on 5/1/65.

**SHIELD, MICHAEL:** Pvt. Enl. on 10/25/61 at Richmond, Va. Pres. on 10/31/61, 12/61 and 4/1/64 rolls. Taken POW at Snicker's Gap, Va. on 7/64 per 8/31/64 roll. Sent to Elmira, N.Y. on 7/25/64, where held until released on 7/11/65. Dark hair, blue eyes, 5'6". Res. of 60 Exeter St., Baltimore, Md.

**SHOCK, W. G.:** Pvt. Enl. on 7/14/63 at Petersburg, Va. Transferred to Second Maryland Artillery by S.O. 18. Paid $24 on 3/21/64. Pres. on 4/1/64 roll. Taken POW in the valley while on sick furlough per 8/31/64 roll. Taken POW on 5/9/64 at Strausburg, Va.

5'10", age 18, blue eyes, light hair, student. Res. of Baltimore, Md. Sent to Camp Chase, Ohio on 5/19/64. Released on 6/16/64.

**SHUE, JACOB J.**: Pvt. Enl. on 9/1/62 at Fredericks, Md. In Chimborazo Hosp. 1-2/64 with diarrhea/dysentery. Pres. on 4/1/64, 8/31/64 and 10/31/64 rolls. Reported and took oath on 8/24/65. Res. of 59 McHenry St., Baltimore, Md.

**SMITH, CARROLL**: Sgt. Enl. on ?. Paroled at Appomattox C.H., Va. on 4/10/65. Res. of Mississippi.

**SMITH, HENRY CLAY**: Pvt. Enl. on 2/26/62 at Richmond, Va. $50 bounty paid. Paid $61 on 10/1/62 and $12 on 11/1/62. WIA per 12/62 roll. Paid $48 on 3/4/63. Pres. on 4/1/64 and 8/31/64 rolls. Paid $53.06 on 8/20/64. Took oath on 4/18/65 in Richmond, Va. Res. of Baltimore, Md.

**SMITH, JAMES HENRY**: QM Sgt. Enl. on 8/15/61 at Richmond, Va. Pres. as Commissary Sgt. on 10/31/61 roll. Pres. as QM Sgt. on 12/61, 4/1/64, 8/31/64 and 10/31/64 rolls. Paroled at Appomattox C.H., Va. on 4/10/65. Took oath on 4/22/65 at age 28, 5'10", brown hair, hazel eyes. Res. of Great Hills, St. Mary's Co., Md.

**SMITH, JOHN E.**: Enl. on 3/13/62 at Richmond, Va. $50 bounty paid. Paid $48 on 3/31/64. Pres. on 4/1/64, 8/31/64 and 10/31/64 rolls. Paroled and took oath on 5/6/65, age 28, 5'11", light hair, blue eyes.

**SMITH, WILLIAM P.**: Pvt./Nurse. Enl. on 10/28/62 at Richmond, Va. Treated at Howard's Grove Hosp. 7/29-9/15/63 for ulcerated wound. At Chimborazo Hosp. #4 9/23-10/26/63 for dysentery. In Farmville C.S.A. Gen. Hosp. 1/20-2/5/64 for ulcer on left leg. Detailed as nurse while not a patient since date of enlistment. Absent, detailed to Chimborazo Hosp. per S.O. 23 per 4/1/64 and 8/31/64 rolls. In C.S.A. Gen. Hosp. Farmville 5/23-9/28/64, 11/14/64-3/20/65 for ulcerated wound. Took oath at Farmville, Va. on 4/13/65. Res. of St. Mary's Co., Md.

**STAMBAUGH, J. E.**: Pvt. Enl. on 5/28/64 at Ashland, Va. $50 bounty paid. Paid $58.90 on 8/22/64. Pres. on 8/31/64 and 10/31/64 rolls. Took oath and was released at Winchester, Va. on 4/19/65, then age 25, 5'4", dark hair, hazel eyes.

## Compiled Service Records Roster 197

**STAYLOR, GEORGE W.**: Pvt. Enl. on 4/13/62 at Richmond, Va. WIA in late June or early July 1862. In Chimborazo Hosp. #5 10/21-12/2/63 with debility. Pres on 4/1/64 and 8/31/64 rolls. Detailed to procure horses for 20 days on 5/1/64. Taken POW at Augusta on 9/21/64, sent to Point Lookout, Md. Exchanged on 3/17/65. Surrendered and took oath at Winchester, Va. on 4/21/65 then age 30, 5'10", dark hair, blue eyes. Res. of 56 Broadway, Baltimore, Md.

**STINSON, ROBERT JAMES**: Pvt. Enl. on 6/1/63 at Woodstock, Va. Pres. on 4/1/64, 8/31/64 and 10/31/64 rolls. Took oath on 5/1/65 at Staunton, Va., then age 23, 5'5", light hair, grey eyes. Res. of Baltimore, Md. MLCSH.

**STOUCH, WILLIAM U.**: Pvt. Enl. on 8/15/61 at Richmond, Va. Pres. on 10/31/61 and 12/61 rolls. Absent on leave per 12/62 roll. Pres. on 4/1/64, 8/31/64 and 10/31/64 rolls. Taken POW on 4/26/65. Res. of Baltimore, Md.

**STUMP, GEORGE**: Pvt. Enl. on 2/6/62 at Richmond, Va. Sick on 12/62 roll. $50 bounty paid. Res. of Baltimore, Md.

**SULLIVAN, J. HENRY**: Pvt. Enl. on 6/23/61 at West Point, Va. Transferred from Co. E, 53rd Va. Inf. By S.O. 93, 4/21/64. Pres. on 8/31/64 and 10/31/64 rolls. Paroled at Lynchburg, Va. on 4/16/65.

**SULLIVAN, JOSEPH D.**: Pvt. Enl. on 8/5/63 at Richmond, Va. Transferred from Co. B, Gilmore's Battn. Md. Cav. By S.O. 93, 4/21/64. Pres. on 8/31/64 roll. Taken POW at Woodstock, Va. on 10/9/64, sent to Point Lookout, Md. on 10/13/64. Exchanged on 3/28/65. Took oath on 4/17/65 at Winchester, Va., then age 26, 5'8", light hair. Res. of Baltimore, Md.

**TALBOT, LEWIS F.**: Corp. Enl. on 4/15/61 at Richmond, Va. Pres. on 10/31/61 and 12/61 rolls as 3rd Corp. In Moore Hosp. Danville, Va. 1/1/62 with debility. Taken POW at Strausburg, Va. on 6/2/62. On Steamer *Katskill* on 8/5/62.

**TARR, WILLIAM J.**: Pvt. Enl. in 1861 at Camp Boone, TN. Taken POW at Strausburg, Va. on 10/9/64, sent to Point Lookout, Md. on 10/13/64 where held until released on oath on 6/21/65. 5'6 1/2", brown hair hazel eyes. Res. of Queen Anne's Co., Md.

**TEXAS, W.**: Musician. Enl. on?. Taken POW at Culpeper, Va. on 9/14/63, sent to Old Capitol Prison, released on oath and sent north on 12/20/63. He also served in Edelin's Maryland Heavy Artillery.

**THOMPSON, THOMAS H.**: Pvt. Enl. on 7/1/62 at Charlottesville, Va. In Gen. Hosp. #212 9/28/62-11/17/62 with diarrhea. In Gen. Hosp. at Camp Winder 12/19/62-1/23/63 with rheumatism. In Gen. Hosp. at Staunton 7/24/63-10/11/63 with syphilis. In Chimborazo Hosp. #2 6/17-7/6/64. Paid $24 on 7/6/64. Pres. on 4/1/64, 8/31/64 and 10/31/64 rolls. Res. of Charles Co., Md. MLCSH.

**WALES, J. C.**: Pvt. Enl. on 8/1/63 at Richmond, Va. Pres. on 4/1/64 and 8/31/64 rolls.

**WALLACE, WILLIAM**: 1st Corp./Sgt. Enl. on 6/3/62 at Charlottesville, Va. In Gen. Hosp. #21 7/3-15/62 with typhoid Fever. Nurse at Culpeper Hosp. discharged 10/24/62. Taken POW at Culpeper C.H., Va. on 9/13/63, sent to Old Capitol Prison 9/14/63 and then to Point Lookout, Md. On 9/26/63, exchanged on 1/17/65. Paroled at Lynchburg, Va. on 4/13/65.

**WALTER, JOHN A.**: Pvt. Enl. on 8/15/61 at Richmond, Va. Pres. on 10/31/61 and 12/61 rolls. AWOL on 4/1/64 roll, actually taken POW while on furlough in Westmoreland Co., Va. in 3/64 per 8/31/64 roll. Taken POW on 3/18/64 at Leonardstown, Md. Sent to Point Lookout, Md., exchanged on 2/13/65. Res. of Baltimore, Md.

**WARD, THOMAS JOSEPH, M.D.**: Pvt. Enl. 9/1/64 at Winchester, Va. Took oath at Lynchburg, Va. on 4/13/65. Res. of Baltimore, Md.

**WARDEN, WILLIAM**: Pvt. Enl. 3/1/63 at Lacy Springs, $50 bounty paid. Pres. on 4/1/64, absent sick on 8/31/64. Pres. on 10/31/64. Surrendered at Appomattox C.H., Va. on 4/10/65. Res. of Rockingham Co., Va.

**WARFIELD, WILLIAM**: Pvt. Enl. on ?. Listed on the 10/31/64 roll. Also served in Co. D, 1st Maryland Cavalry.

**WATKINS, N.C.**: Pvt. Enl. on 9/12/62 at Hagerstown, Md. Pres. on 10/31/64 roll. Paroled on 4/9/65 at Appomattox C.H., Va. Res. of Baltimore, Md.

**WAYS, JAMES C.**: Pvt. Enl. on ?. Took oath at Lynchburg, Va. on 7/27/65. Res. of 181 S. Paca St., Baltimore, Md. He also served in Edelin's Maryland Heavy Artillery. Probably same as J. C. Wales

**WELSH, MARTIN**: Pvt. Enl. on 8/1/63 at Mobile, Alabama. Pres. on 10/31/64 roll. Taken POW on 4/24/65 by the 20th N.Y. Cav. Also served in Co. E, 1st Md. Inf.

**WHALEN, WILLIAM P.**: Pvt. Enl. 4/1/64 at Hanover Junction, Va. $50 bounty paid. Pres. on 4/1/64. Taken POW at Yellow Tavern, Va. on 5/11/64. Sent to Fort Monroe 5/17/64 and then to Elmira, N.Y. 8/15/64 where held until released on 6/18/65. Auburn hair, hazel eyes, 5'11. Res. of Memphis, Tenn.

**WHEELER, ALBERT**: Pvt. Enl. at Richmond. Transferred from Letcher's Va. Artillery by S.O. 93 4/21/64. Taken POW at Snicker's Gap, Va. 7/12/63. Sent to Old Capitol Prison 7/13/64. Transferred to Elmira, N.Y. on 7/25/64 where held until taking the oath on 5/29/65. Black hair, hazel eyes, 5'4". Res. of Wheeling, W. Va. or Baltimore, Md.

**WHITLOCK, CHARLES E.**: Pvt. Enl. on ?. Took oath on 5/5/65. Age 25, shoemaker. Res. of Baltimore, Md. Also served in Lee's Baltimore Light Artillery.

**WILHELM, JAMES T., M.D.**: Orderly Sgt./Lt. Enl. on 8/15/61 at Richmond, Va. Pres. on 10/31/61 and 12/61 rolls. Elected 3rd Lt. on 11/30/61. Pres. on 5/11/62 as 3rd Lt. Pres. on 12/62 roll as 2nd Lt. Taken POW at Heathsville on 6/2/63. Sent to Old Capitol Prison. Transferred to Johnson's Island 8/8/63. Sent to Fort Monroe 10/6/64. Exchanged on 10/11/64. Give eight week leave of absence on 10/17/64. Res. of Meharrin Station, Va. Res. of Leonardstown, St. Mary's Co., Md.

**WILSON, THOMAS J.**: Pvt. Enl. on 10/1/62 at Bunker Hill, Va. Pres. on 4/1/64, 8/31/64 and 10/31/64 rolls. Res. of Annapolis, Anne Arundel Co., Md.

**WOOD, W. H.**: Pvt. Enl. on 9/20/62 at Rappahannock Va. Taken POW, paroled on 10/27/62. Pres. on 4/1/64, 8/31/64 and 10/31/64 rolls. Paroled on 4/28/65. Occupation carpenter. Res. of St. Mary's Co., Md.

**WORTHAM, JOHN B., M.D.**: Asst. Surgeon. Commissioned 6/19/62. Paroled on 5/8/65. Age 25, 5'6", dark hair, hazel eyes.

**WYSING (WYSONG), HENRY**: Pvt./Teamster. Enl. on 8/15/61 at Richmond, Va. Pres. on 10/31/61, 12/61, 12/62 and 4/1/64 rolls. Detailed as teamster 11/62. Taken POW at Moorefield, W. Va. on 8/7/64. Sent to Camp Chase, Ohio 10/7/64. Age 30, 5'10", grey eyes, sandy hair, occupation teamster.

# Bibliography

## Public Records

Compiled Service Records of Confederate Soldiers Who Served in Organizations From the State of Maryland. Record Group 109, Microcopy 321, Rolls 9-10, National Archives, Washington, D.C.

Confederate Adjutant and Inspector General's Office, Letters Received, Record Group 109, National Archives, Washington, D.C.

## Manuscripts

The Batchelder Papers. Gettysburg National Military Park.
Hands, Washington. Civil War Notebook. Courtesy of the Maryland Historical Society, Baltimore, Maryland.

## Periodicals

*Confederate Veteran*, Nashville, Tennessee, 1892-1932.
*Southern Historical Society Papers*, Richmond, Virginia.

## Published Sources

Cole, Scott. *34th Battalion Virginia Cavalry*, Lynchburg, Virginia: H. E. Howard, Inc., 1993.

Cooling, Benjamin Franklin. *Jubal Early's Raid on Washington, 1864*. Baltimore, Maryland: The Nautical and Aviation Publishing Company of America. 1989.

Douglas, Henry Kyd. *I Rode with Stonewall*. Chapel Hill: University of North Carolina Press, 1940.

Driver, Robert J. *The 1st and 2nd Rockbridge Artillery*. Lynchburg, Virginia: H. E. Howard, Inc., 1987.

Goldsborough, W. W. *The Maryland Line in the Confederate Army.* Baltimore, Maryland: Guggenheimer, Weil and Co., 1900.

Hartzler, Daniel D. *Marylanders in the Confederacy.* Silver Spring, Maryland: Family Line Publications, 1986.

Hartzler, Daniel D. *A Band of Brothers: Photographic Epilogue to Marylanders in the Confederacy.* Bookcrafters, 1992

Huntsberry, Thomas V. and Joanne M. *Maryland in the Civil War: The South.* Baltimore, Maryland: J. Mart Publishers, 1985.

Kelly, Tom. (ed.) *The Personal Memoirs of Jonathan Thomas Scharf of the First Maryland Artillery.* Baltimore, Maryland: Butternut and Blue. 1992.

Lewis, Thomas A. *The Guns of Cedar Creek.* New York: Dell Publishing Company, 1988.

McDonald, Archie P. ed., *Make Me a Map of the Valley. The Civil War Journal of Jed Hotchkiss.* Dallas, Texas: Southern Methodist University Press, 1973.

Mitchell, Joseph B. *Decisive Battles of the Civil War.* New York: Fawcett Premier, 1955.

Moore, Edward A. *Story of a Cannoneer Under Stonewall Jackson.* New York: Neale Publishing Co., 1907.

Poague, William T. *Gunner with Stonewall.* Jackson, Tennessee: McCowat-Mercer Press, 1957.

Thomas, Dean S. *Cannons: An Introduction to Civil War Artillery.* Gettysburg, Pennsylvania: Thomas Publications, 1985.

U.S. War Department. *The War of the Rebellion: A Compilation of the Official Records of the Union and Confederate Armies.* 128 Volumes, Washington, D.C.: Government Printing Office, 1880-1901.

Weaver, Jeffrey C. *22nd Virginia Cavalry.* Lynchburg, Virginia: H. E. Howard, Inc., 1991.

Wise, Jennings. *The Long Arm of Lee: The Artillery of the Army of Northern Virginia.* Lincoln: University of Nebraska, 1990.

## About the Author

George Leslie Sherwood, Jr. was educated at Rensselaer Polytechnic Institute, Troy, New York, and Northwestern University, Evanston, Illinois. He worked as a nuclear engineer at the United States Department of Energy and predecessor agencies for 28 years until his retirement in January 1997.

Sherwood served in the United States Army Reserve for 29 years until his retirement as a lieutenant colonel in 1994. He has been an Adjunct Professor of Physics at Montgomery College, Rockville, Maryland, since 1969. He also teaches at Frederick Community College, Frederick, Maryland.

He lives in Frederick, Maryland, with his wife Ruby and son Jeff.

Sherwood has previously co-authored three books with Jeff Weaver. This is his second solo effort.

www.ingramcontent.com/pod-product-compliance
Lightning Source LLC
Chambersburg PA
CBHW050146170426
43197CB00011B/1987